T0305249

The Rise to Market Leadership

The Rise to Market Leadership

New Leading Firms from Emerging Countries

Edited by

Franco Malerba

Professor of Applied Economics, Department of Management and Technology and President of ICRIOS, Bocconi University, Milan, Italy

Sunil Mani

Director and Professor, Centre for Development Studies, Trivandrum, Kerala, India

Pamela Adams

Associate Professor of Management, The Stillman School of Business, Seton Hall University, South Orange, NJ, USA

 Edward Elgar
PUBLISHING

Cheltenham, UK • Northampton, MA, USA

Published by
Edward Elgar Publishing Limited
The Lypiatts
15 Lansdown Road
Cheltenham
Glos GL50 2JA
UK

Edward Elgar Publishing, Inc.
William Pratt House
9 Dewey Court
Northampton
Massachusetts 01060
USA

A catalogue record for this book
is available from the British Library

Library of Congress Control Number: 2016962544

This book is available electronically in the **Elgar**online
Economics subject collection
DOI 10.4337/9781783476794

ISBN 978 1 78347 678 7 (cased)
ISBN 978 1 78347 679 4 (eBook)

Typeset by Servis Filmsetting Ltd, Stockport, Cheshire
Printed and bound by CPI Group (UK) Ltd, Croydon, CR0 4YY

Contents

List of figures   vi
List of contributors   vii
Acknowledgments   viii

1   Introduction   1
    Franco Malerba, Sunil Mani and Pamela Adams

2   The rise to market leadership of a Chinese automotive firm: the
    case of Geely   20
    Bin Guo, Qiang Li and Xiaoling Chen

3   The leading Chinese firms in the biopharmaceutical industry   43
    Hong Song and Wensong Bai

4   Leadership in the automobile industry: the case of India's Tata
    Motors   68
    Sunil Mani

5   Market leadership in India's pharmaceutical industry: the case
    of Cipla Limited   99
    Sunil Mani

6   To market leadership: the evolutionary journey of Hindustan
    Computers Limited   124
    Arun Madhavan

7   Market leadership in the Brazilian automotive industry: the case
    of Marcopolo   150
    Luiz Ricardo Cavalcante and Bruno César Araújo

8   Market leadership in Brazil's ICT sector: the cases of Totvs and
    Positivo   176
    Bruno César Araújo and Rodrigo Abdalla Filgueiras de Sousa

9   Conclusions: the rise to market leadership – a dynamic interplay
    between firms and innovation systems   204
    Pamela Adams, Franco Malerba and Sunil Mani

Index   221

Figures

2.1 The conceptual framework for analysing sectoral innovation
    systems (SIS) in the Chinese automotive manufacturing sector   22
4.1 Trends in exports of automotive from India, 2003–04 to
    2009–10   77
4.2 Trends in sales revenue of Tata Motors (USD billions),
    2002–11   82
4.3 Trends in innovation expenditures of TML, 2000–10   87
4.4 Sales of *Nano* cars, 2010–14   89
5.1 Trends in the trade balance of India's pharmaceutical industry 103
5.2 Trends in patents granted to Indian inventors in
    pharmaceutical technologies at the USPTO   104
5.3 Trends in Cipla's R&D intensity   113
5.4 Generosity of tax regimes with respect to R&D   119
7.1 Bus bodywork manufacturer locations in Brazil   159

Contributors

Pamela Adams, Associate Professor of Management, The Stillman School of Business, Seton Hall University, South Orange, NJ, USA

Bruno César Araújo, Researcher, Institute for Applied Economic Research, IPEA, Brasilia, Brazil

Wensong Bai, PhD candidate, Department of Business Studies, Uppsala University, Uppsala, Sweden

Luiz Ricardo Cavalcante, Legislative Advisor in Economics, Brazilian Federal Senate, Brasilia, Brazil

Xiaoling Chen, College of Business and Administration, Zhejiang University of Technology, Hangzhou, People's Republic of China

Bin Guo, Professor of Innovation Management, School of Management, Zhejiang University, Hanzhou, People's Republic of China

Qiang Li, School of Business, Zhejiang University City College, Hangzhou, People's Republic of China

Arun Madhavan, PhD candidate, Centre for Development Studies, Trivandrum, Kerala, India

Franco Malerba, Professor of Applied Economics, Department of Management and Technology, Bocconi University and President of ICRIOS, Bocconi University, Milan, Italy

Sunil Mani, Director and Professor, Centre for Development Studies, Trivandrum, Kerala, India

Hong Song, Assistant Director, Institute of World Economics and Politics, Chinese Academy of Social Sciences (CASS), Beijing, People's Republic of China

Rodrigo Abdalla Filgueiras de Sousa, Legislative Advisor in Information, Communication and Technology, Brazilian Federal Senate, Brasilia, Brazil

Acknowledgments

This book is part of the 'Catch-up Project' coordinated by Richard Nelson of Columbia University, New York, USA. The 'Catch-up Project', supported by the Earth Institute of Columbia University, provided funding for the meetings that were held in preparation for the volume. The meetings took place in Milan, New York and Berkeley, where the ideas were developed and the various drafts of the book were presented and discussed. We wish to thank Richard Nelson for the encouragement, suggestions and feedback he has provided throughout the development of this book.

While the contents of each chapter reflect the views and writing styles of the individual authors, the book shares a common framework and approach that will be discussed in the Introduction (Chapter 1) and summarized in the Conclusions (Chapter 9). The chapters presented in this volume have all benefited from the intense and lively discussions that the group had during meetings and throughout each stage of the manuscript's preparation.

We wish to thank Alix Bax for her excellent work in copyediting and Matt Pittman of Edward Elgar for his advice and support throughout the preparation of this book.

1. Introduction

Franco Malerba, Sunil Mani and Pamela Adams

1.1 MARKET LEADERSHIP IN EMERGING ECONOMIES

The emerging economies are some of the fastest growing countries in the world. A precise definition of an emerging economy does not exist. However, there is fair amount of consensus that the concept refers to developing countries that have been experiencing extremely high rates of growth on a continuous year-on-year basis and that are increasingly integrated with the world economy through the movement of products and services, capital (for example, foreign direct investments), and persons (for example, cross-border migration). China, India and Brazil are among these countries. They are three of the largest economies in the world not only in terms of GDP, but also in terms of population and size of the domestic market. As the importance of these national economies has grown, so too has the role of these countries in international discussions concerning political, economic and social issues across the globe.

Economic growth in these countries has been accompanied by the emergence of several new domestic firms. These firms have become not only leaders in their own markets but also significant participants in the global economy in both medium and high technology sectors. Moreover, these firms have been able to establish positions of leadership in the face of competition from both established multinational corporations from the US and Europe and newer global players from Asia (for example, Korea, Taiwan). Explaining the sources of such leadership is the focus of this book.

The concept of firm leadership is multidimensional. Our focus is on firms whose competitive position is based either on new products, on advanced process technology, or on production and marketing skills. Like the groundbreaking work by Mowery and Nelson (1999) on the rise to 'industrial leadership', we are concerned with the commercial success of technological innovations rather than with the process of innovation itself.

1

Unlike the cases examined by Mowery and Nelson (1999), however, our cases focus on the sources of market leadership for specific firms.

We identify three dimensions that characterize market leadership:

Dimensions of market leadership

- Dominant position in the domestic market
- Global reach
- Innovativeness in products/processes

Firms that are market leaders hold dominant positions in their domestic market in terms of market share. This does not mean that they are necessarily the largest players in the domestic industry, but they should be *among* the largest. Given the size of the domestic market in all of the emerging economies under study here, it is clear that a dominant position at the domestic level offers significant advantages in terms of scale for further growth and competitiveness. But it is important to note that we do not consider large market share (even in such big markets) as sufficient to confer the title of 'market leader' to specific firms. High market share based on the successful imitation and/or commercialization of products developed by other firms does not denote a market leader.

To be considered market leaders, firms must have two additional characteristics. They must have what we term 'global reach'. This means that these firms are active not only in the domestic market, but also in international markets in one form or another. Their global reach may range from getting access to foreign knowledge through licenses, to R&D agreements with foreign firms and research organizations, to international joint-ventures in R&D, production or marketing, to exports, and to foreign direct investments abroad. Global reach therefore means that a market leader is able to open links at the international level and to become a player in the global arena.

Finally, market leaders are innovative. With the term 'innovation', we encompass a wide range of changes in products and processes, from adaptation to the local market, to original improvements and modifications, to incremental innovations, to radical changes in products, production processes and technologies. Thus, innovativeness means that a market leader is dynamic in terms of technologies, products and processes and is not simply involved in the replication or imitation of existing products.

1.2 WHAT THIS BOOK IS ABOUT

How do new firms in emerging countries rise to market leadership? What factors drive their innovation and growth? These are relevant questions for our understanding of the growth of new sectors, the expansion of the industrial base, and the rise to international competitiveness of domestic firms in emerging countries.

The extant literature on economic development focuses on the development of firm-level capabilities and strategies to explain the increasing competitiveness of firms from emerging economies (Lall, 1992; Bell and Pavitt, 1993; Nelson, 2008; Lee, 2013). The studies in this book take the argument further, to propose that the rise to market leadership by domestic firms in emerging economies results from a combination of both firm-level and system-level factors. System-level factors may be of two types: national and sectoral. National innovation systems concern country-level factors that may either favour or hamper learning and capability accumulation among firms (Freeman, 1987; Nelson, 1993; Lundvall, 1992). Sectoral systems, by contrast, are focused on industries and may be regional or cut across national boundaries and may affect both innovation and production activities at the firm level (Malerba, 2002; Malerba and Mani, 2009; Malerba and Adams, 2014).

This book examines the case of ten firms in three leading emerging economies: China, India and Brazil. The studies focus on the successful combination of learning and capability building by domestic firms and of system factors in three industries: auto and body parts, information and communications technology (ICT), and pharmaceuticals. This introductory chapter discusses the main concepts used in the book and outlines the countries, sectors and firms chosen for analysis. In Section 1.1 we define the concept of market leadership used in this book. Section 1.3 presents the broader conceptual framework at the base of this study and the firm-, country- and sectoral-level factors considered in each of the cases. Section 1.4 contains a short introduction to the cases (by country and sector). Finally, Section 1.5 provides an outline of the structure of the book.

1.3 SOURCES OF MARKET LEADERSHIP: A CONCEPTUAL FRAMEWORK

This book draws on the evolutionary theory of economic change and on the concept of innovation systems to provide a framework for the analysis of the sources of market leadership in emerging economies. Evolutionary theory focuses on processes of learning, innovation and economic transformation (Nelson and Winter, 1982). Boundedly rational agents act, learn and search in uncertain and changing environments. Agents know how to do different things and may do them in different ways. Thus, learning, capabilities and behaviour entail agent heterogeneity in experience and organization. Their different capabilities affect their persistently differential performance. A central place in the evolutionary approach is occupied by the processes of variety creation (in technologies, products, firms and organizations), replication including imitation (which affects continuity in the process of economic development), and selection (which reduces variety in the economic system and weeds out the inefficient or ineffective utilization of resources in the long run) (Nelson, 1995; Dosi, 1997; Metcalfe, 1998).

One key aspect of evolutionary theory is a focus on learning and capabilities as the main drivers of innovation and firm growth. Following this framework, empirical research has shown that in the process of economic development, much of the learning of firms in developing countries involves learning about what firms at the frontier are doing. But catching up and the rise to market leadership does not mean imitation. What domestic firms do invariably diverges in significant ways from practices followed by firms in the countries serving as models. This reflects modifications required to tailor practice to local environments. Moreover, the organizational, managerial and institutional aspects of leading productive practices are often difficult to replicate, and need to be adapted to indigenous conditions, norms and values (Nelson, 2011). Therefore, the rise to market leadership involves innovation in the 'Schumpeterian' sense: a break from traditional ways of doing things. In the process of catching up, the practices used are not necessarily new to the world. They are, however, new to the firms, and using them may require considerable risk and long processes of trial and error for learning to be effective (Katz, 1984; Amsden, 1989; Bell and Pavitt, 1993; Hobday, 1995; Kim, 1997; Malerba and Nelson, 2011).

Empirical research suggests that during the process of catching up and achieving market leadership, domestic firms in emerging economies develop different kinds of capabilities. Such capabilities involve more than what engineers generally mean when they talk about technology. While important aspects of these activities are indeed structured or embodied in machinery or other physical artifacts, they also involve modes of organizing, coordinating and managing activities. These latter capabilities often are more difficult to develop than engineering know-how. Yet they may be required in order to adopt, adapt and modify technologies developed elsewhere, or to introduce modifications and incremental innovations, or even to generate completely new products and processes (Malerba and Nelson, 2011).

Evolutionary theory argues that firms do not operate and innovate in isolation. The national or the sectoral context in which agents operate greatly affect their cognition, behaviour and performance and this context may differ significantly from country to country and from sector to sector. More specifically, evolutionary theory proposes that firms must be seen as operating in the context of innovation systems that include other kinds of economic actors that are involved in supporting and orienting economic activity and innovation: primary and secondary educational organizations, universities, public research systems, government programs, suppliers and users, financial systems, and labour markets.

This book proposes that the concepts of both national innovation systems and sectoral innovation systems are useful for identifying the sources of the rise to market leadership. Analyses of sectoral and national innovation systems share a perspective that multiple actors are involved in the innovation process and in the catching up of firms and countries. The national innovation system concept is particularly oriented to broad national characteristics (see Freeman, 1987; Lundvall, 1992; Nelson, 1993). The notion of a sectoral system, by contrast, adds to such analyses the concept that significant differences exist not only across countries, but also across industries in terms of the key actors, industrial structures and institutions that drive innovation (see Malerba, 2002; 2004; Malerba and Mani, 2009; Malerba and Adams, 2014).

In sum, the framework followed in this book argues that, in order to reach market leadership, firms need to be engaged in processes of continuous learning and capability building, and that these processes are highly affected by the innovation systems – national and sectoral – that surround them. For the sake of simplicity, we will consider industrial clusters and regional systems as part of sectoral systems, since clusters and regions are often specialized in specific industries and are, therefore, highly affected by sectoral variables. The analysis developed in this book thus consists of three levels: the firm, the country, and the sector. In the following pages we identify critical factors that may affect the development of market leadership at each level.

1.3.1 Firm-Level Factors

Drawing on the work of Schumpeter and on evolutionary theory, we identify two broad groups of firm-level factors to explore in order to understand the rise to market leadership in emerging economies: entrepreneurship; and learning, capabilities and strategic orientation.

The first factor refers to entrepreneurship as identified by Schumpeter in his pioneering work in 1934 (Schumpeter, 1934). Entrepreneurs start up new firms, take risks, and innovate. New companies thus emerge because an entrepreneur has the ability, courage and vision to launch a new venture in the face of uncertainty. The presence of entrepreneurs is thus a critical firm-level factor for innovation and firm growth.

The second factor relates to learning, capabilities and strategies. In order to be successful, new companies need to trigger processes of continuous learning and capability building. Such processes are cumulative and take time to produce results (Katz, 1984; Bell and Pavitt, 1993). For indigenous firms this implies the development of capabilities to identify, absorb and adapt new technologies, to generate innovations, and to enter new market segments (Bell, 1984; Lall, 1992; 2000; Amsden and Chu, 2003). Moreover, the types of capabilities required for innovation and growth may change as new firms evolve over time. Kim (1997), in fact, identifies different stages of capability development, from duplicative imitation to creative imitation to innovation. Similarly, Lee (2005) describes the passage from the creation of absorptive capabilities to the development of complementary assets for innovation.

In terms of strategies followed by domestic companies in the rise to market leadership, a detailed discussion of all potential strategies is outside the scope of this book. It is possible, however, to identify a few common characteristics of the strategies followed by market leaders during the process of growth and catching up. They include the decision to purchase technology from abroad in order to access foreign knowledge, the opening of joint ventures and production, R&D and marketing agreements in order to gain relevant knowledge and capabilities, the establishment of networks of cooperation at the national or international level, and mergers, acquisitions and joint ventures related to the internationalization process (Amsden and Chu, 2003; Lee, 2013). In terms of production and marketing strategies, firms in emerging economies often follow a strategic path from original equipment manufacturer (OEM) to original design manufacturer (ODM) to original brand manufacturer (OBM) (Mathews, 2002; Lee, 2005), and climb the ladder in global value chains (Gereffi, 2014). Finally, with respect to technology in dynamic environments, three basic strategies may be identified: path-following, stage-skipping, or path-creation strategies (Lee and Lim, 2001).

1.3.2 Country-Level Factors

The process of learning and capability accumulation is influenced by the characteristics of the country in which a firm operates. In broad terms, the level of development and the type of national institutions actively engaged in economic development may affect firm-level processes. At a more specific level regarding innovation, the features of the national innovation system play a key role in such processes. National innovation systems are characterized by different elements. A first element is the actors that provide relevant knowledge, skills and support to the innovation, growth and international performance of domestic firms: the government and public agencies, universities and public research centers, the education system, financial organizations (Nelson, 1993; Edquist, 1997). A second element is the institutional setting, in terms of policies, standards and regulations, that may play a significant role in either stimulating or hampering innovation and technology diffusion (Freeman, 1987; Nelson, 1993). A third element is the formal and informal relationships that exist between the various actors of the system (Lundvall, 1992). Finally, national systems may be characterized by their effectiveness in generating, diffusing and using knowledge within an economy and in balancing the indigenous creation and diffusion of knowledge with the need to access foreign sources of knowledge and technology (Lundvall, 2007). As each of these dimensions may affect innovation across multiple sectors and multiple firms, it is necessary to examine the strength of each element in each national context.

1.3.3 Sector-Level Factors

We propose that in order to understand the sources of market leadership in emerging economies, it is also necessary to understand the specific sectoral contexts in which new leaders operate. In this book we use the sectoral system framework, which considers sectors as systems and the sectoral environment as a collection of elements that interact and feed back to one another (rather than as single elements working independently). This framework focuses on three main building blocks that characterize a sector: (a) the technology and the knowledge required for innovative activities, (b) the actors involved in innovation, production and commercialization and the networks of relationships and knowledge exchange among such actors, and (c) the institutions that characterize a sector in terms of standards, regulations and other policies (Malerba, 2002; Malerba and Adams, 2014).

While early studies on sectoral systems focused on advanced economies (Mowery and Nelson, 1999; Malerba, 2004), more recent analyses have applied the framework to emerging economies (Gu et al., 2009; Malerba and Mani, 2009). This research shows that major differences exist in the features, structure and evolution of sectoral systems and that new and leading firms from emerging countries are affected by the strengths and weaknesses of the sectoral system in which they operate. These studies point to factors such as the characteristics of domestic demand, supplier networks, user–producer interactions, university-level research, specialized human capital, and public policy.

The sectoral system framework has also been used to explain the catching up of firms and countries in specific sectors (Malerba and Nelson, 2011; 2012). Such analyses have also been extended to examine the effects of changes in the specific elements of a sectoral system – technology and the knowledge base, demand, and public policy and institutions – on catching up cycles over the longer term evolution of an industry. This work shows that new leaders from emerging countries that supplant established firms often end up being supplanted themselves by other new leaders as sectoral systems change and evolve over time (Lee and Malerba, 2017).

It is important to note that the relationship between sectoral systems and national systems (national institutions, national policy, and national non-firm organizations such as finance or universities) is not unidirectional, running from the national to the sectoral level. Rather, it is a two-way relationship that evolves over time (Mowery and Nelson, 1999; Malerba and Nelson, 2011). National systems and national institutional frameworks may positively affect the development and growth of sectors with certain characteristics. But the features of some components that prove effective in one sectoral system may also be replicated or diffused in other sectors of a country (Dodgson et al., 2008; Gu et al., 2009).

1.4   THE CASE STUDIES

1.4.1   The Countries: China, India and Brazil

In order to examine the sources of market leadership, we have chosen firms from three of the world's largest emerging economies: China, India and Brazil. Each of these economies has shown considerable economic growth over past decades to become major players in the global economy. While differences across these countries exist in terms of government policies and the characteristics of their national markets, their national systems were all able to support the emergence of domestic market leaders in diverse sectors.

1.4.1.1   China

China was an extremely closed economy until 1979. Being deeply wedded to a socialist system meant that private business enterprises were virtually absent. However, there was a strong focus on both primary and secondary education, particularly in technical fields such as science and engineering. The turning point came in 1979 when the country embraced a form of market socialism. Since then, the national strategy has been more clearly articulated in terms of a country wanting to be an important player in selected manufacturing industries based primarily on high technology such as telecommunications. During the post-1979 phase, the state has also fostered the growth of private entrepreneurship in a variety of ways including the provision of low-interest bank loans. As a consequence, the number of business enterprises experienced phenomenal growth. In fact, Gu and Lundvall (2006) note that, from almost nothing, business enterprises came to occupy almost two-thirds of the R&D performed in the country by the late 1990s. In addition, China adopted a very open attitude towards foreign direct investments. These investments produced relevant effects in terms of the technological knowledge gained by Chinese firms. An example of this effect is present in the telecommunications equipment industry where Chinese enterprises (for example, Huawei and ZTE) gained early access to foreign technology and have since grown to become global market leaders (Yu et al., 2017). After 1979, the Chinese educational system was also reformed. Not only was education extended to a broader section of the population, but significant investments were also made to increase the quality of education. In fact, several Chinese universities jumped to the top in many international rankings (for example, Tsinghua and Beijing Universities). Overall investments in gross expenditures in R&D also increased to almost 2 per cent of GDP. In conclusion, these three characteristics of an emerging Chinese economy – a clearly articulated national strategy, support for private business enterprises at the sectoral level, and improvements in both the quality and quantity of human resources (Gu et al. 2009) – make China an appropriate context to study the rise to market leadership of domestic firms.

1.4.1.2 India

As an emerging economy, India has undergone significant changes in policy over the past decades. Similar to China, India followed a policy of dirigisme between 1947 and 1991. But unlike China, public policies for strategic sectors were not clearly articulated. Rather, they slowly evolved alongside firm strategies. Where Indian firms had clear strategies for becoming important players in a specific industry, the state supported their efforts by removing unnecessary regulations and, in some cases, by providing them with tax incentives and guaranteed markets through public procurement. Only after 2002, in fact, did public policy begin to move away from a 'one size fits all' model towards sector-specific policies. The role that such policy played in supporting Indian firms in high and medium technology industries, however, is much less significant than that played by the Chinese government. In terms of entrepreneurship, on the other hand, the Indian state moved to promote private entrepreneurship with the 'New Industrial Policy Statement' of 1991. An important manifestation of the new support for private entrepreneurship was the removal of the industrial licensing policy, which was the main barrier to entry for private entrepreneurship. This change also enabled existing Indian companies to grow and achieve economies of scale without being restricted by government regulations. Other important policy changes that occurred over these decades concerned the broad banning of the licensing regime and the development of the patenting regime. Patenting laws, in fact, were instrumental in building up internal technological capability in the pharmaceutical and agrochemical industries (Chaudhuri, 2005). Following the policy shift in 1991, moreover, the government also adopted an active policy towards the privatization of state-owned enterprises, mostly through divestitures. Industries that were exclusively reserved for the public sector were deregulated and opened up to investments from the private sector. As a result, in India as in China, business enterprises began to emerge as the core of the production and innovation system: the share of business enterprises in the performance of R&D in India increased from about 10 per cent of gross expenditure on R&D (GERD) in 1970 to about 36 per cent in 2012. Finally, Indian higher education favoured science-based education, and the state encouraged technical education in general and engineering education in particular. Like China, therefore, India offers a rich context in which to study the rise to market leadership of domestic firms.

1.4.1.3 Brazil

Compared to the other two countries considered in this book, Brazil is different in the sense that it adopted an open policy stance with respect to foreign direct investments early on in its development cycle. As a consequence, a number of industries were traditionally dominated by multinational corporations by 1990, when the country liberalized its economy and became integrated into the global economy. A second difference of the Brazilian case is that the country tried, from very early periods in its development, to develop domestic technological capability in a range of high technology industries such as aircraft, computers and telecommunications. Despite such efforts, however, the country has only been successful in aircraft: the Brazilian firm, Embraer, is the current world leader in regional transport aircraft manufacturing (Vertesy, 2017). Brazil has also been less successful than the other two countries in unleashing domestic private entrepreneurship. Although Brazil was one of the first emerging economies to establish a public laboratory devoted to the development of digital switching systems in telecommunications, for example, the last Brazilian firm in the telecom switching industry was taken over by a multinational corporation in the early 1990s and Brazil remains without a domestic telecommunications firm. This absence of private entrepreneurship has reduced the number of enterprises which could have emerged as potential market leaders.[1] Despite these conditions, however, the country has been able to grow a number of world-class companies through state entrepreneurship (for example, Petrobas in the oil and gas industry and Embrapa in agricultural products). As far as the education system is concerned, the Brazilian higher education system has a number of well-known technological universities (for example, the University of Campinas). The National Council for Scientific and Technological Development (CNP) has also created the National Institutes of Science and Technology (INCT) which functions as a national science and technology network. Despite these advances, however, there is still an insufficient number of qualified technical personnel, a limited interest in science and technology among university students, and a relatively low level of engagement between industry and universities. Given these characteristics, Brazil also represents an interesting context in which to study the rise of market leaders.

1.4.2 The Sectors: Auto and Auto Parts, ICT and Pharmaceuticals

The three industries chosen for study in this book are: the automotive industry (consisting of vehicle manufacturers and auto parts), pharmaceuticals, and the information and communications technology (ICT) industry, including both hardware and software suppliers. These three industries have driven growth in several emerging economies over past decades (for example, South Korea and Taiwan). It is important to note, however, that the sectoral systems of these three industries differ in significant ways. We briefly explore some of these differences in the following paragraphs.

1.4.2.1 Auto
In terms of knowledge base, new technologies related to ICT, environmental technologies and new materials have broadened the knowledge base of the automobile industry. In fact traditional mechanical technologies have been complemented by new technologies related to alternative fuels and engines, energy efficiency, safety, electronics and electronic controls, infotainment, and new materials. Engineering knowledge and engineering skills have become increasingly important in this industry, while pure science has become less relevant. In terms of actors and networks, auto firms are usually large in scale, and international in orientation. Scale is critical for both manufacturing and innovation. Extensive vertical links are present in the industry: supplier networks for parts and components, systems developers (such as for front-end cars), small engineering firms

and software suppliers are quite relevant for both production and innovation processes. In fact, the modularization of both manufacturing and R&D has allowed the creation of networks of specialized actors. Finally, car producers have close relationships with machine tool producers. The manufacturing technologies for cars have become very highly automated with increasing use of robots and other autonomous systems not just for painting and welding but also for stamping and assembly operations (Mokyr et al., 2015).

1.4.2.2   ICT – Software and Computers

ICT does not represent a single sectoral system, but a variety of closely related and interconnected sectors in terms of products, technologies, firms and markets. These different systems have undergone a process of convergence over the past twenty years. *Computer hardware* is composed of large producers of personal computers and computer networks. These producers work with the suppliers of semiconductor components that represent critical partners for innovation and production processes: semiconductors, in fact, represent one of the distinguishing components of many hardware products. Government and public policy has not played a significant role in the hardware sectoral system (Bresnahan and Malerba, 1999; Bresnahan, 2007). *Software* represents a different sectoral system. In software, a highly differentiated knowledge base and a variety of applications have driven innovative specialization in different types of products and applications. This industry is characterized by advanced human capital mobility and clusters of small firms. Users – both individuals and organizations – have played a major role in innovation processes, and extensive co-invention characterizes the sector. Finally, although IPR (intellectual property rights) once played an important role in the industry, its relevance has decreased as both the imitation and modification of products has become diffused (Steinmueller, 2004).

1.4.2.3   Pharmaceuticals

The actors in pharmaceuticals include both large and small pharmaceutical companies, new biotechnology firms, universities and research organizations, financial organizations (for example, venture capital), regulatory agencies, the medical profession, and consumers. In terms of the knowledge base and technology, the sector has witnessed a period of constant transformation and growth over the past four decades. Scientific advances in physiology, pharmacology, enzymology and cell biology were followed by discoveries in molecular genetics and recombinant DNA technology and, subsequently, in genomics, gene sequencing, transgenic animal creation, molecular biology and chemistry. These advances were accompanied by the

capability and strategy and system factors (sectoral and national) are examined.

NOTE

1. This situation may change in the future because the Brazilian government has launched several initiatives to support start-ups. Financial support is provided through grants (Programa Primeira Empresa Inovadora, PRIME), venture capital investments (INOVAR), or reduced interest loan programmes (Juro Zero Programme). In addition, the Pro-Innova programme introduced in 2008 encourages entrepreneurship by diffusing information about the legal tools, facilities and mechanisms available to support initiatives.

REFERENCES

Amsden, A. (1989), *Asia's Next Giant*, New York: Oxford University Press.
Amsden, Alice H. and Wan-wen Chu (2003), *Beyond Late Development: Taiwan's Upgrading Policies*, Cambridge, MA: MIT Press.
Bell, M. (1984), '"Learning" and the accumulation of industrial technological capacity in developing countries', in M. Fransman and K. King (eds), *Technological Capability in the Third World*, London: Macmillan, pp. 187–209.
Bell, Martin and K. Pavitt (1993), 'Technological accumulation and industrial growth: contrasts between developed and developing countries', *Industrial and Corporate Change*, 2(1), 157–210.
Bresnahan, Timothy (2007), 'Creative destruction in the PC industry', in Stefano Brusoni and Franco Malerba (eds), *Perspectives on Innovation*, Cambridge, UK: Cambridge University Press, pp. 105–140.
Bresnahan, Timothy and F. Malerba (1999), 'Industrial dynamics and the evolution of firms' and nations' competitive capabilities in the world computer industry', in D. Mowery and R. Nelson (eds), *Sources of Industrial Leadership*, Cambridge, UK: Cambridge University Press, pp. 79–132.
Chaudhuri, Sundip (2005), *The WTO and India's Pharmaceuticals Industry: Patent Protection, TRIPS, and Developing Countries*, Delhi: Oxford University Press.
Dodgson, Mark, John Mathews, Tim Kastelle and Mei-Chih Hu (2008), 'The evolving nature of Taiwan's national innovation system: the case of biotechnology innovation networks', *Research Policy*, 37(3), 430–445.
Dosi, Giovanni (1997), 'Opportunities, incentives and the collective patterns of technological change', *The Economic Journal*, 107(444), 1530–1547.
Edquist, Charles (ed.) (1997), *Systems of Innovation*, London: Frances Pinter.
Freeman, C. (1987), *Technology Policy and Economic Performance: Lessons from Japan*, London: Frances Pinter.
Gambardella, Alfonso (1995), *Science and Innovation*, Cambridge, UK: Cambridge University Press.
Gereffi, Gary (2014), 'A global value chain perspective on industrial policy and development in emerging markets', *Duke Journal of Comparative and International Law*, 24(3), 433–458.

Gu, Shulin and B.-A. Lundvall (2006), 'China's innovation system, harmonious growth and endogenous innovation', *Innovation Management, Policy and Practice*, 8(1/2), 1–26.

Gu, Shulin, B.-Å. Lundvall, J. Liu, F. Malerba and S. Schwaag Serger (2009), 'China's system and vision of innovation: an analysis in relation to the strategic adjustment and the medium- to long-term S&T development plan (2006–2020)', *Industry and Innovation*, special issue: 'Innovation Systems in China', 16(4–5), 369–388.

Henderson, Rebecca, L. Orsenigo and G. Pisano (1999), 'The pharmaceutical industry and the revolution in molecular biology', in D. Mowery and R. Nelson (eds), *Sources of Industrial Leadership*, Cambridge, UK: Cambridge University Press, pp. 267–311.

Hobday, M. (1995), *Innovation in East Asia: The Challenge to Japan*, Cheltenham, UK and Northampton, MA: Edward Elgar.

Katz, Jorge M. (1984), 'Domestic technological innovations and dynamic comparative advantage: further reflections on a comparative case-study program', *Journal of Development Economics*, 16(1), 13–37.

Kim, Linsu (1997), *Imitation to Innovation: The Dynamics of Korea's Technological Learning*, Boston: Harvard Business School Press.

Lall, Sanjaya (1992), 'Technological capabilities and industrialization', *World Development*, 20(2), 165–186.

Lall, S. (2000), 'The technological structure and performance of developing country manufactured exports: 1985–1998', *Oxford Development Studies*, 28(3), 337–369.

Lee, Keun (2005), 'Making a technological catch-up: barriers and opportunities', *Asian Journal of Technology Innovation*, 13(2), 97–131.

Lee, Keun (2013), *Schumpeterian Analysis of Economic Catch-Up: Knowledge, Path-Creation, and the Middle-Income Trap*, London: Cambridge University Press.

Lee, Keun and C. Lim (2001), 'Technological regimes, catching-up and leapfrogging: findings from the Korean industries', *Research Policy*, 30(3), 459–483.

Lee, Keun and F. Malerba (2017), 'Toward a theory of catch-up cycles and changes in industrial leadership: windows of opportunity and responses by firms and countries in the evolution of sectoral systems', *Research Policy*, forthcoming.

Lundvall, Bengt-Åke (1992), *National Systems of Innovation: Toward a Theory of Innovation and Interactive Learning*, London: Frances Pinter.

Lundvall, Bengt-Åke (2007), 'National innovation systems: analytic concept and development tool', *Industry and Innovation*, 14(1), 95–119.

Malerba, Franco (2002), 'Sectoral systems of innovation and production', *Research Policy*, 31(2), 247–264.

Malerba, Franco (2004), *Sectoral Systems of Innovation: Concepts, Issues and Analyses of Six Major Sectors in Europe*, Cambridge, UK: Cambridge University Press.

Malerba, F. and P. Adams (2014), 'Sectoral systems of innovation', in M. Dodgson, D. Gann and N. Phillips (eds), *The Oxford Handbook of Innovation Management*, Oxford: Oxford University Press, pp. 183–203.

Malerba, Franco and Sunil Mani (2009), *Sectoral Systems of Innovation and Production in Developing Countries: Actors, Structure and Evolution*, Cheltenham, UK and Northampton, MA: Edward Elgar.

Malerba, Franco and Richard Nelson (2011), 'Learning and catching up in different sectoral systems: evidence from six industries', *Industrial and Corporate Change*, 20(6), 1645–1675.

Malerba, Franco and Richard R. Nelson (2012), *Economic Development as a Learning Process: Variation across Sectoral Systems*, Cheltenham, UK and Northampton, MA: Edward Elgar.

Mathews, John A. (2002), 'Competitive advantages of the latecomer firm: a resource-based account of industrial catch-up strategies', *Asia Pacific Journal of Management*, 19(4), 467–488.

McKelvey, Maureen, L. Orsenigo and F. Pammolli (2004), 'Pharmaceuticals as a sectoral innovation system', in F. Malerba (ed.), *Sectoral Systems of Innovation*, Cambridge, UK: Cambridge University Press, pp. 73–120.

Metcalfe, S. (1998), *Evolutionary Economics and Creative Destruction*, London: Routledge.

Mokyr, Joel, Chris Vickers and Nicolas L. Ziebarth (2015), 'The history of technological anxiety and the future of economic growth: is this time different?', *Journal of Economic Perspectives*, 29(3), 31–50.

Mowery, David C. and Richard R. Nelson (eds) (1999), *Sources of Industrial Leadership: Studies of Seven Industries*, Cambridge, UK: Cambridge University Press.

Nelson, R. (1993), *National Innovation Systems: A Comparative Analysis*, Oxford: Oxford University Press.

Nelson, R. (1995), 'Recent evolutionary theorizing about economic change', *Journal of Economic Literature*, 33(1), 48–90.

Nelson, Richard R. (2008), 'Economic development from the perspective of evolutionary economic theory', *Oxford Development Studies*, 36(1), 9–21.

Nelson, Richard (2011), 'Economic development as an evolutionary process', *Innovation and Development*, 1, 39–49.

Nelson, Richard and S. Winter (1982), *An Evolutionary Theory of Economic Change*, Cambridge, MA: The Belknap Press of Harvard University Press.

Pisano, Gary (1991), 'The governance of biotechnology: vertical integration and collaborative arrangements in the biotechnology industry', *Research Policy*, 20(2), 237–249.

Schumpeter, Joseph (1934), *The Theory of Economic Development*, Cambridge, MA: Harvard University Press.

Steinmueller, Edward (2004), 'The European software sectoral system of innovation', in F. Malerba (ed.), *Sectoral Systems of Innovation*, Cambridge, UK: Cambridge University Press, pp. 193–242.

Verstesy, Daniel (2017), 'Changing leadership in the regional jet industry', *Research Policy*, forthcoming.

Yu, J., F. Malerba, P. Adams and Y. Zhang (2017), 'Related yet diverging sectoral systems: telecommunications equipment and semiconductors in China', *Industry and Innovation*, 24(2), 190–212.

2. The rise to market leadership of a Chinese automotive firm: the case of Geely

Bin Guo, Qiang Li* and Xiaoling Chen

2.1 INTRODUCTION

The Chinese government decided to develop the automotive industry in 1987. In 2009, China became the world's largest market for automobiles with a sales volume of 13.6 million vehicles. During the development of the automotive manufacturing sector in China, a typical feature was that multinational companies (MNCs) entered China mainly through joint ventures (JVs) with state-owned enterprises (SOEs). So far, almost all of the world's major auto-makers (such as Volkswagen, General Motors, Toyota, Hyundai, Ford, DaimlerChrysler, Nissan, Peugeot, Honda, and BMW) have established JVs in China.

Against this background, a remarkable phenomenon in the Chinese auto industry is the fast development of several independent local automobile-makers relying on their own efforts to produce independently owned car brands.[1] An interesting question and the starting point for this chapter is how those private firms, with much less in the way of financial resources and technological expertise, could survive the severe competition with large SOEs as well as MNC JVs and build up their technological capability in the early years. By selecting Geely, the first privately owned automobile manufacturing firm in China, as the research subject of a longitudinal case study, this chapter employs an analytical framework from the perspective of sectoral innovation systems to examine the rise to market leadership of domestic leading automotive firms in China as a large emerging economy.

The technological capability of a firm is an outcome of interaction between the available research and development (R&D) resources and the amount of R&D efforts, which depend on the probability of success of the R&D effort (Lee and Lim, 2001). However, Chinese automobile private enterprises like Geely not only face severe constraints on R&D

resources, but also are unlikely to succeed in terms of probability of the actual development of target products. Therefore, we argue that the contexts in large emerging economies are playing a significant role in the successful catching-up of these private enterprises. Furthermore, previous studies have shown that large emerging economies (especially the BRICs nations, Brazil, Russia, India, and China) often exist with several typical or even unique context features. These features may include a large potential domestic market (see, for example, Mu and Lee, 2005; Xie and Wu, 2003), the highly segmented market structure (for example, Gadiesh et al., 2007; Liu and White, 2001; Prahalad, 2004) and the complex interactions among multiple actors inside national innovation systems (for example, Dantas and Bell, 2009). As the essential elements of the catching-up context, these features are expected to have strong impacts on the technological learning and capability building in the catching-up process. Therefore, how did such context-specificity in China increase the opportunity for Geely's catch-up and interactively affect the process of technological catching-up? To further explore such a question, we will employ an analytical framework from the perspective of sectoral innovation systems (Malerba, 2002). We will use Geely as the research subject of a longitudinal case study to examine the research framework.

Finally, it is worth noting that the literature often emphasizes the importance of R&D capability building as it relates to technological catching up (for example, Fan, 2006; Kim, 1997; 1998; Liu and White, 1997). Far less research has been done on the accumulation of manufacturing capability in the catching-up process, as well as the interaction between R&D capability building and manufacturing capability building. Nevertheless, R&D capability and manufacturing capability must be integrated for successful innovation of emerging economies (Malerba and Mani, 2009). Therefore, we aim to investigate the characteristics of manufacturing capability in China and the impacts of the context specificity of China as a large emerging economy on domestic automotive firms' manufacturing capability building.

The rest of this chapter is organized as follows. Section 2.2.1 introduces our analytical framework from the perspective of sectoral innovation systems. Section 2.2.2 briefly provides the case profile of Geely. Section 2.2.3 investigates the influence of context specificity in China on Geely's capability building. In Section 2.2.4, we then examine how Geely built its R&D capability and low-cost manufacturing capability through combining externally accessible expertise and its internal knowledge base. Section 2.3 provides a theoretical discussion and policy implications.

2.2   THE RISE OF GEELY AUTO

2.2.1   Analytical Framework

Innovation, capability building and catching up in a sector are considered
to be significantly affected by three groups of factors: knowledge and technologies; actors, relationships, and networks; and institutions (Malerba,
2002; 2007). However, less comprehension exists on the relationship
between three groups of factors in a sectoral system (actors, knowledge,
and institution) and technological capabilities accumulation (Malerba,
2002; Marques and Oliveira, 2009). Therefore, in this section we introduce
an analytical framework (see Figure 2.1) from the perspective of sectoral
innovation systems to examine the technological catching up and capability building of Geely.

  Firms, suppliers, users, universities, public research organizations, and
financial intermediaries are the key actors in a given sectoral innovation
system (Malerba and Nelson, 2011). Different actors may play distinctive roles in knowledge systems and production systems. Considering the

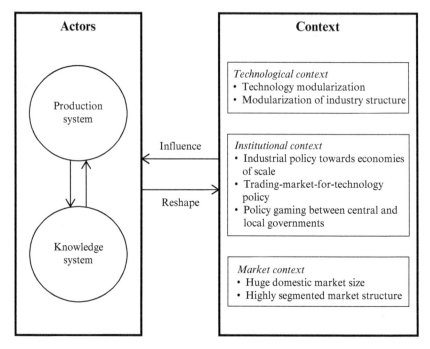

*Figure 2.1   The conceptual framework for analysing sectoral innovation
            systems (SIS) in the Chinese automotive manufacturing sector*

importance of exploring the potential relationship between manufacturing capability building and R&D capability building, we purposively organize these actors into a production system and a knowledge system. In the production system, we focus on the process of Geely's low-cost manufacturing capability building via reverse engineering, hybrid production system, and interaction with its suppliers. In the knowledge system, we mainly illustrate how Geely accumulated its skills and capabilities in product assembly and R&D/design through endogenous R&D efforts and learning from suppliers, JVs, universities, and public research organizations. Furthermore, we include three dimensions of context in this study: (i) technological context; (ii) institutional context; and (iii) market context. Specifically, the technological context of the automotive sector is characterized by its technology modularization (Langlois, 2002; Ulrich 1995), which is accompanied by the modularization of industry structure (Sturgeon and Florida, 2000).

Institutions (including laws, standards, norms, common routines and habits, established practices, and so on) shape the cognition, actions, and interactions of actors in a sectoral system (Malerba and Nelson, 2011). This chapter focuses on those institutions specific to the automobile sector in China. Owing to the importance of the automotive sector in China's national economy, direct and indirect interventions by the central government are made in this sector, such as the industrial policy towards economies of scale (Liu, 2009; Liu and Tylecote, 2009) and the trading-market-for-technology policy (Mu and Lee, 2005; Wang, 2003). We also discuss some policy practices by local governments and the policy gaming between central and local governments (Chu, 2011; Gu and Lundvall, 2006; Montinola et al., 1995).

As to market context, this chapter mainly examines the unique market characteristics in China (large emerging economies), especially the huge domestic market size with its highly segmented market structure (for example, Liu and White, 2001; Mu and Lee, 2005; Xie and Wu, 2003). Considering the large-scale market size in large emerging countries, even a highly segmented market can give latecomer firms a chance to achieve economies of scale. Hence, indigenous firms can sustain their resource accumulation as well as learning and capability building through leveraging the trade-up from low-end markets to up-scale markets in response to domestic demand rather than mainly relying on exports to overseas markets.

Regarding the 'interaction' element in this framework, we put our emphasis on two levels of interaction within sectoral systems of innovation. One is the interaction among actors and the other is the interaction between actors and contexts (technological context, institutional context, and market context). Actors interact with each other through processes of exchange, spillover, cooperation, competition, and command, while their interactions are shaped by institutions (rules and regulations) (Malerba, 2002). Meanwhile, context can influence the behaviors of actors, and in turn, actors can reshape the context.

2.2.2   Case Profile

Li Shufu founded Geely in 1986, initially manufacturing refrigerators, then decoration materials, and motorcycle parts. In 1997, Geely launched its auto manufacturing business and became the first privately owned automobile manufacturing firm in China. Originally, Geely did not have much in the way of financial resources or technology, and even faced industry entry barriers set by the central government. However, within two decades, Geely had developed into one of China's largest privately held auto-makers and even purchased Volvo from the Ford Motor Company for USD 1.8 billion in 2010. Through its considerable efforts in developing technological capability, with the change of its strategy from 'making affordably priced cars' to 'making quality cars that are the safest, most environment friendly and energy efficient,' Geely became the sixth-largest private enterprise in China by the end of 2013. Table 2.1 summarizes the key events in the history of Geely as an auto-maker.

Table 2.1   Key events in the history of Geely as an auto-maker

Year	Key events
1997	Geely launched its auto-manufacturing business and became the first privately owned automobile manufacturing firm in China
1998	Geely successfully launched its first model of car (*Haoqing*) that was based on the imitation and reverse engineering of Xiali
2001	Geely was allowed to produce cars in Linhai of Taizhou with the production licenses of a bankrupt, state-owned automobile factory in Sichuan that had been taken over in 1997
2007	Geely changed its strategy from 'making affordably priced cars' to 'making quality cars that are the safest, most environment friendly and energy efficient'
2009	Geely acquired Australian auto transmission supplier DSI
2010	Geely completed the purchase of Volvo Cars from the Ford Motor Company
2013	Geely finalized the acquisition of Manganese Bronze Holdings
2013	Geely started operations at a European R&D center located in Goteborg, Sweden

2.2.3   Catching-Up Context and Capability Building

The appearance and rapid development of indigenous Chinese auto-makers challenged the long-term rules in the automobile industry, like economy of scale, learning effects, and technical capability accumulation (Luo, 2005). In this section, we will discuss the impact of technological, institutional, and market context in the Chinese automobile sector on the technological capability building of Geely as one of the indigenous auto-makers.

2.2.3.1   Technology context
(1)   Technology modularization and capability building
The automobile industry is characterized by complex mechanical products with a multitude of components and subsystems. A number of components are combined into subsystems (brakes, engines, etc.) and the production process interacts highly with the products themselves (Liu and Tylecote, 2009). In the realm of vehicle design, most auto-makers seek to place a greater number of car models on fewer under-body platforms, allowing for greater commonalization and reusability of parts while retaining the ability to adapt specific vehicle models to local tastes and driving conditions.[2] The general trajectory in the automobile industry is a movement from closed-integral to open-modular architectures (Baldwin and Clark, 1997; Wang and Kimble, 2010).

The trend of modularization in the global automobile industry benefited the technology learning of Chinese indigenous automobile manufacturers by reducing technological complexity in learning and by lowering manufacturing costs. First, modularity can help overcome the difficulty in understanding the nature of the interconnections or interdependencies among the parts, and achieve a managed separation of architectural and component learning (Sanchez and Mahoney, 1996). By decomposition of 'Benz,' 'Hongqi,' 'Anchi,' and other foreign-made vehicles, Geely gradually accumulated the knowledge of automobile structures and acquired first-hand technical information of chassis and component systems. Second, the establishment of JVs in China promoted the specialization of its parts and components industry as world-class automobile suppliers and followed the steps of multinational car assemblers. Since most of the components are standardized and can be produced in volume (Kash and Rycroft, 2000), the economic scale could be achieved by wedging in the local production network of MNC JVs for generic components and modularity, which reduced the costs for independent part design and purchase. Based on its accumulated skills in product assembly, Geely began to emphasize locally purchased components to reduce costs. In its early models, the *Haoqing*

(1998), *Meiri* (2000), and *Youliou* (2001), a majority of the parts and components adopted were exactly the same as those used for mature economic sedans sold in the domestic market.

(2)   Modularization of industry structure and capability building
Modular product systems can lead to modularity in the design of the organizations that produce such products at both the firm level and the industry level (Brusoni and Prencipe, 2001; Henderson and Clark, 1990; Karim, 2006; Langlois, 2002; Sanchez and Mahoney, 1996). Technology modularity is one of the driving forces that enable a greater division of labor and specialization both within and across automobile firms. Although the automobile industry of China can be traced back to the 1950s, the specialization of parts and components in the automobile industry started after the establishment of JVs with foreign companies (Depner and Bathelt, 2005).

Modularization of the automobile industry in China benefited the indigenous auto-makers in many aspects. For instance, entry barriers of the automobile industry fell off because of the specialization of intra-industry, especially for the threshold of resources. When a firm uses contract manufacturing rather than in-house manufacturing, it is using an organizational component that is more independent than building such capabilities in-house (Sanchez and Mahoney, 1996). The firm can switch between contract manufacturers that perform different functions, and the contract manufacturer can similarly work for different firms. In that way, the Chinese local automobile companies may be able to take advantage of the extensive network of component developers' capabilities to reduce the input of resources for their set-up. Further, modular product architectures allow coordination of specialization within and across companies to be achieved with minimum managerial effort (Brusoni and Prencipe, 2001). Consequently, component-level learning processes are carried out concurrently and autonomously by geographically dispersed automobile companies (Schilling and Steensma, 2001). In such circumstances, the indigenous auto-makers gradually accumulate skills in product assembly and build product and engineering knowledge in the key components.

2.2.3.2   Institutional context
(1)   Trading market-for-technology policy
In 1978, China's state-owned industry produced only 15 500 automobiles and the annual production of sedans and sport utility vehicles (SUVs) was less than 5000. The industry was characterized by old-fashioned, low-quality cars that were produced with outdated equipment in labor-intensive processes (Depner and Bathelt, 2005). The strategy of 'trading

market for technology' was first adopted by setting up JVs for funds, technology, and management, with the added benefit of increases in local value-added and job creation (Mu and Lee, 2005; Wang, 2003). In 1984–85, four JVs were approved to establish operations in China, namely Beijing Jeep with Chrysler, Shanghai Automotive Industrial Corporation (SAIC) with Volkswagen, Nanjing Fiat (IVECO) and Guanzhou Peugeot with Peugeot SA. Furthermore, the maintenance of high car-part tariffs encourages the set-up of domestic part supply networks (Wang, 2003). The idea behind these policies was to increase inter-industry linkages with the resulting technology spillover and to stimulate the manufacturing competencies within the region.

(2)   Central–local government policy gaming and capability building
At the initial stage of automobile industry development, strict entry control was set by China's central government to support the access of selected firms to foreign technology and scarce resources. Officially, the purpose was to consolidate the highly fragmented industry, raising the threshold and specialization standards to achieve economy of scale, avoid duplicate construction, and increase industrial clustering (Liu, 2009). Despite the central government's strict entrance limit on automobile projects, the two most noticeable indigenous firms (Chery Automobile Company of Wuhu, Anhui Province, and Geely Automobile Company of Taizhou, Zhejiang Province) were established in 1997.

Although these automobile projects were outside of the central government's plan and even forbidden, they were supported surreptitiously by the local and provincial governments in different ways (Chu, 2011; Luo, 2005). This is closely related to the unique characteristics of relationships between the central and local governments called 'Chinese-style federalism' (Montinola et al., 1995). First, under the market-oriented reforms of the early 1980s, many state-owned enterprises controlled by the central government were delegated to local governments (ibid.). Furthermore, the central government was responsible for formulating industrial policy, but direct implementation usually relied on local governments (Chu, 2011). Since many economic and social development policies were also delegated to the provincial and local governments, they enjoyed a wide range of autonomous authority within the market environment (Gu and Lundvall, 2006; Li, 2009). Finally, local governments had strong self-interests and were eager to safeguard local economic development, job creation, and tax revenue under the GDP-oriented government achievement assessment (Ngo, 2008; Yang and Yu, 2011). The new fiscal system introduced in 1994 induced a strong positive relationship between local revenue and local economic prosperity for all provinces and ensured that governments in each region assumed primary responsibility for economic development (Montinola et al., 1995). Local authorities and local entrepreneurs were able to simultaneously promote their political careers and their own economic interests by stimulating industrial growth in their regions (Gu and Lundvall, 2006). In 2003, 26 out of 31 provinces had facilities making cars. Most of these facilities were under-sized factories with low production volumes.[3]

Under such circumstances, the local governments created growth opportunities by assisting in quietly skirting the automobile industry regulations of the central administration (Liu and Tylecote, 2009; Luo, 2005). For example, national regulations forbade new automobile assembler entries, so the officials of the Anhui and Wuhu governments named such enterprises an 'automobile components company' (Liu and Tylecote, 2009). Geely was allowed to produce cars in Linhai of Taizhou with the production licenses of a bankrupt, state-owned automobile factory in Sichuan that had been taken over in 1997 (Ngo, 2008). Preferential treatment of these enterprises was also given by local authorities[4] (Chu, 2011). With assistance from the local government, land was sold by special tender to Geely for setting up automobile production bases in Linhai, Ningbo, and Hangzhou. Numerous direct subsidies and surpluses were granted by local governments in the name of promoting new and high-tech industrial development (Ngo, 2008). Without these benefits from local governments, it is doubtful whether Geely could have built up R&D and manufacturing capability at the beginning of the production period or competed with the few oligopolies that had been enjoying central government protection (ibid.).

2.2.3.3   Market context
(1)   Domestic market size and capability building
The Chinese economy has one of the largest markets with a population of more than 1.3 billion, and has been enjoying its position as the world's fastest-growing economy, with an average annual growth rate of 10 percent over twenty years. Rising incomes and the explosion of urban middle-class wealth has fueled the demand for sedans (Table 2.2).

The fast growth of China's economy and the skyrocketing domestic automobile market provided those young companies with a good survival environment, within which a firm found it easier to access abundant market resources. Geely sold only about 200 cars in 1998 but reached a very impressive annual sales volume of 326 710 in 2009, with an average annual increase of 96 percent (see Table 2.2). In addition, during periods of high industry growth the competitors have less incentive to aggressively attack each other (Bierly and Daly, 2007). The high growth periods also

Table 2.2 *Annual domestic sales of indigenous Chinese automakers, 1999–2010 (unit: ten thousand)*

	1999	2000	2001	2002	2003	2004	2005	2006	2007	2008	2009	2010
Annual vehicle sale	187	208	237	326	439	507	576	722	879	938	1364	1806
Annual sedan sale	57.1	61.4	72.1	112.6	197.2	231.3	276.8	387.0	479.8	504.7	747.1	949.4
	30.5%	29.5%	30.4%	34.6%	44.9%	45.6%	48.1%	53.6%	54.6%	53.8%	54.8%	52.6%
Indigenous brand	–	–	–	–	–	48.4	72.7	98.3	124.5	130.8	221.7	293.3
Market share of indigenous brand	–	–	–	–	–	20.9%	26.3%	25.4%	26.0%	25.9%	29.7%	30.9%
Annual sales volume of Geely sedans	2000	8000	21000	47800	76274	96693	133041	164495	181517	204025	326710	–

Sources: Annual Report on Automotive Industry in China (2011); China Automotive Industry Yearbook (2011); Annual Report of Geely (2009).

enable firms to create more organizational slack and capital accumulation, and allow firms to direct more resources to R&D (Altenburg et al., 2008; Dess and Beard, 1984), to buy enormous quantities of embodied technology in different forms (such as licenses, machinery, and brands), to hire leading international scientists, and so on. In general, firms will devote more R&D resources when they are confident of the linkage between more R&D input and higher R&D outputs.

(2)   Segmented market structure and capability building
The automobile market in China is not only huge but also segmented. In a study of the telecommunication industry in China, Mu and Lee (2005) characterized it as two kinds of dualism: rural–urban dualism and core–periphery dualism. The literature on marketing also concludes that China is largely a developing country consisting of multiple markets, segmented by two most important dimensions: economic disparity and geographic diversity (Cui and Liu, 2000).

Before the 1990s, the three biggest state-owned auto-makers (all JVs) monopolized the market (Chu, 2011; Liu, 2009), especially on the passenger car side where more than 90 percent of cars were branded by foreign auto-makers (Luo, 2005). For a long period of time in the early stages, the demand for cars came mainly from official usage by government departments,[5] which tended to not be price-sensitive and favored mid-sized cars (Chu, 2011). Only the government, public sectors, companies, and very few rich people could afford sedans. The economical sedan market, especially for the private consumers, was overlooked and underdeveloped (Gao, 2008; Wang, 2008). Following the 1990s, increasing wealth began to foster a market for segment-economical sedans, which mainly consisted of price-sensitive individual consumers (Chu, 2011). Geely has insisted on a low price strategy to fill the low end and private segments since its start-up in 1998. Most of the prices for its car models were around 50 000 yuan, and some were priced even lower than 30 000 yuan.

The market-oriented innovation for the low-end market was one of the key features of Chinese indigenous auto-makers during the process of industrial catch-up.[6] Even though the cars produced by indigenous auto-makers were technologically inferior to those made by foreign firms and JVs, they befittingly took advantage of lower-end or peripheral markets to sell their own cars, especially in minor cities and towns. Moreover, based on the low development and production cost, their cars were provided to Chinese consumers at much lower prices, making them initially popular in the low-end market. For example, the Geely *Haoqing* (similar to the Daihatsu *Charade*) was only priced at about one-third to two-thirds of the *Charades* made by Tianjin Auto Works. By differentiating segmented markets, they successfully avoided direct competition with the JVs, allowing a market space for their initial survival.

Meanwhile, the segmented market structure of China provided a good opportunity for continuous improvement, which was probably a necessary condition for latecomers to narrow the technology gap between themselves and the market leaders (Hobday, 1995). Learning develops in sequences, shifting from simple to complex, from production to investment to innovation capabilities. Through technological accumulation over time, these firms focused their R&D activities on key components of automobiles such as engines and automatic transmissions, eventually introducing their own new models. In the mid 2000s, they gradually moved on to the mid-level market by offering increasingly complex and high quality models.

2.2.4   Capability Building in Catch-Up: Actors and Interactions

Kim (1997) claimed that catching-up firms, particularly those in developing countries, usually reversed the sequence of research, development, and engineering that takes place in advanced countries. From the development history of automobile firms in China, we indeed see that, at first, the catching-up firms like Geely entered the low-end market and sought to develop their own capabilities, first by mastering, and then improving their manufacturing technologies. After duration of engineering capability accumulation, they gradually conducted R&D on products with medium complexity. This section will discuss the process and mechanisms of two-stage capabilities accumulation (manufacturing and R&D capabilities) at Geely.

2.2.4.1   Low-cost manufacturing capability building
(1)   Reverse engineering
Imitation and reverse engineering are typical informal mechanisms of technology transfer and capability accumulation, as can be seen from the catching-up experience of Korea (Kim, 1997). Geely accumulated the basic capabilities in the automobile industry by disassembling the foreign-made vehicles and learning the art of fit, finish, and assembly of the product. Based on the *Charade* model of First Auto Works (FAW) Xiali, Geely developed its first model, the *Haoqing*, with a combination of in-house-produced components and purchased components. Most of the imitation and remodeling were based on the body and chassis (Wang, 2008). Around 60 percent of the *Haoqing* components (including engine and transmission) were the same as the *Charade* and were purchased directly from the *Charade*'s component supplier (ibid.).

At the same time, hard efforts were focused on changes to the design so

as to comply with intellectual property right regulations. As the capability
of mixing-and-matching components increased, Geely developed its own
engines to cope with the soaring purchase costs of Toyota engines, because
of its strong dependence on Toyota.

(2)   Hybrid production systems

As a common phenomenon mentioned by Mu and Lee (2005) and
Zeng and Williamson (2007), Chinese companies often conducted their
assembly operations manually instead of using fully automated production systems, with the aim of saving on capital costs. It is well known
that automated product assembly has the potential benefits of improved
quality and lower costs (Walleigh, 1989). The drawback is also obvious in
that automated assembly initially requires a huge capital investment and
will be costly if lacking economy of scale in production. For the production of ordinary or low complexity parts, numerous Chinese companies
discovered that the manual process, mainly conducted by hand, could be
so productive that automation was no longer justified. Hence, Geely took
advantage of China's cheap labor, and depended on manual work and self-
developed molds for most of its production process. Although product
quality would be sacrificed to some degree, the manual work strongly
supported Geely's low-price strategy in China's low-end segment market
while providing reasonable quality. In addition, Geely imported advanced
production facilities like robot welding (most likely second-hand) for only
the key production processes, to assure the quality of core products and
simultaneously increase the production capacity.

The practice of hybrid production systems has many advantages. In
the short run, substituting manual production of components with low or
medium complexity for automatic production can reduce the initial investment in expensive automatic machines and production facilities. In the
long view, it constructs a firm's low-cost manufacturing capability without
compromising much on the production quality.

(3)   Interaction with local and national supplier networks

The local supplier network, especially the trust-based relationship network
in the early stages, played a significant role in Geely's low-cost strategy
that targeted the low-end segment of the Chinese automobile market.
When starting its car manufacturing activity, Geely did not own any
related technology and the market was highly uncertain. Even so, its previous suppliers in the motorcycle business were quite willing to follow.
However, some of these small suppliers were fragile and risk-averse to
heavy initial investment. Under such circumstances, Geely invested capital
in these companies. It encouraged its small suppliers to follow Geely into

the automobile industry. Since the joint investment represented a firm commitment of long-term cooperation, it strongly promoted the formation of a local supplier system. In contrast to arm's-length relationships, this supplier network was referred to as a Father–Son (Fu–zi in Chinese) supply system, since most supplier firms were run by relatives, friends, schoolmates, or natives of Taizhou (the city in which Geely was founded). Further, Geely requested the suppliers to purchase the assigned manufacturing equipment for production to guarantee the quality of the components. Quality could then be confirmed when a supplier's plant was visited and a trial of samples of components was provided (Wang, 2008). Under such a trust-based supply system, suppliers were extremely loyal and provided components at a price far below the market price, while maintaining a stable and responsive supply network.

Domestic automobile-makers also benefited when the national supplier network originated localized Sino-foreign JVs (that is, made more car parts domestically to replace imports). When the suppliers from the Sino-foreign JVs began to foster supply relationships with domestic automobile-makers, they may have played an intermediary role in the knowledge spillover from Sino-foreign JVs to domestic suppliers. For Geely, the overlap of its procurement network with FAW (First Auto Works), DFM (Dong Feng Motors) and SAIC (Shanghai Automotive Industrial Corporation) brought benefits of technology spillover. That was because the JVs might transfer technology to local suppliers to facilitate building efficient supply chains; or at least the suppliers would try to raise their quality and service standards to meet the JVs' demands. Then, as these suppliers provide products to Geely, the technological capability accumulated from their cooperation with the JVs will spill over. At the outset, half the suppliers to Geely were large suppliers working with the three JV magnates, which had joint ventures with Volkswagen, Toyota, Peugeot SA, Nissan, and General Motors (Wang, 2008). This market-based supply relationship between Geely and its common suppliers, as intermediaries, played a crucial role in the complex technological knowledge learning of Geely.

2.2.4.2 R&D/design capacity building

In the early phase, privately owned firms within the automobile industry focused mainly on learning production and assembly skills of entire automobiles, uncomplicated parts, and improving the automobile part supply system. Based on their accumulated skills in product assembly, firms began to research and develop automobile parts with growing complexity. Simultaneously, Geely expanded its product range from low-end economic cars to middle-range cars.

(1)   Acquiring expertise through the mobility of engineers

An important method of knowledge diffusion between firms is through employee mobility (Franco and Filson, 2006). Spencer (2008) claimed that as knowledge becomes increasingly tacit, recipient firms require more detail about the knowledge itself, as well as a greater understanding of the organizational context in which the technology is embedded. When senior managers left JVs for private automobile firms, even the most tacit knowledge might have been transferred. It brought about extensive technical expertise, organizational practices, and a set of social relationships (Parise et al., 2006). It also benefited recipient firms by enhancing technological capability, reducing costs, and stimulating organization changes (Droege and Hoobler, 2003). For example, when the original general manager of FAW–Daewoo and concurrently the deputy director of the FAW technology center transferred to Geely Ningbo, the annual output increased nearly 200 percent in one year. The previous Chief of Technology Operations of Nanjing Automobile Corporation's (NAC's) NAC–Fiat division took charge of the Geely automobile research institute and quickly built the product development system, technology management system, and product testing system.

(2)   In-house technology development

Geely invested hundreds of millions of dollars to establish the Geely Automobile Research Institute, with its headquarters in Linhai and a branch in Hangzhou. Additionally, an engine research institute and a transmission research institute were built in Ningbo, and an electrical research institute was built in Luqiao. These institutes independently developed the 4G18CVVT engine with a world-leading 57.2kw output per litre, Geely's Z Series AT transmissions, EPS (electronic power steering), BMBS (blowout monitoring and brake systems), alternative energy vehicle technologies, and so on. Today, Geely owns over 1600 patents including more than 110 invention patents and over 20 international patents. The company releases four to six new vehicle designs and part models every year.

(3)   Strong links with university and public research organizations

Effective industry–university links can support the process of technology catching-up, which has predominantly occurred in the application-oriented sciences and engineering. These links are usually oriented towards problem solving and the advancement of technologies of interest to a well-defined user-community (Mazzoleni and Nelson, 2007).

Geely set up the Huapu New Energy Automobile Research Institute to strengthen its R&D cooperation with universities in 2006. The Geely–Tongji Automobile Engineering Research Institute was established in 2007 with a joint investment of 50 000 RMB by the Geely Automobile Research Institute (the subordinate technology center of Geely Holding Ltd) and Tongji University.

(4)   Learning through joint design/development
Since technology intermediaries sit at the intersection of many firms and industries, they can facilitate the exchange of information among firms. The cooperation between local manufacturing firms and these intermediaries can contribute to the innovation of local manufacturing firms by broadening the scope of their external innovation research and reducing their research costs (Zhang and Li, 2010). Beginning in 2002, joint developments were initiated by Geely with foreign technology inter-mediaries such as South Korean Daewoo, Italian Car Project Group, and the German LUC Company. When cooperating with Daewoo, Geely insisted on serving an apprenticeship with technicians of Daewoo. As Jensen et al. (2007) claimed, know-how would typically be learned through apprenticeship relationships where the apprentice observes, studies, and follows the behavior of masters in a community of 'practices.'

(5)   Learning through JVs and serial overseas mergers and acquisitions
Geely began its internationalization in 2007 by setting up overseas factories. Geely soon formed a JV with UK cab firm Manganese Bronze Holdings (MBH). In 2009, Geely acquired the world's second-largest gearbox manu-facturer, Australia's Drivetrain Systems International (DSI), and bought Volvo Car Corporation the following year. Through JVs and mergers and acquisitions, Geely acquired 'different but complementary' resources, and thus accelerated their technological capability building by making use of the local high-tech researchers, infrastructures, and the existing technology patents of acquired firms.

2.3   DISCUSSION AND CONCLUSION

By selecting Geely as the research subject, this chapter employs an analytical framework from the perspective of sectoral innovation systems to examine how the complex interplay among actors and the specificity in the catching-up context would significantly affect the process of learning, capability building, and catching up in China, as a typical large emerging economy.

2.3.1   Market Context Specificity and Technological Catch-Up in a Large Emerging Economy

This chapter has highlighted the impact of market context specificity, in terms of a huge domestic market combined with highly segmented nature, on the learning and capability building during technological catching-up in a large emerging economy. These findings are consistent with the observations in previous literature that illustrated the influence of a large growing market size (Altenburg et al., 2008; Xie and Wu, 2003) and segmented market structures (Mu and Lee, 2005). However, this study moves forward to analyse the combined effect of a huge domestic market size and a highly segmented market structure on the capability building and technological catch-up of latecomers in two ways. First, given the large domestic market size in big emerging economies like China and India, multiple segmented markets from low-end to high-end would be potentially big enough in absolute size for firms to achieve economy of scales. The large low-end markets provide an opportunity for indigenous firms to reduce market entry barriers by avoiding fierce competition from MNCs and reducing the technological prerequisites of market entry. Second, the continuous nature of large fragmented markets also provides the indigenous latecomers a chance to persistently conduct incremental innovation and finally reach the quality levels of MNCs' products. More specifically, such continuous nature is induced by the geographic and economic disparities in the domestic markets of developing countries (Mu and Lee, 2005). Furthermore, the rapid economic development and urbanization in large emerging countries continually breed low-end markets upward into higher-level ones. Thus, a market stepladder is formed for latecomer firms, making it easier to gradually accumulate product and engineering knowledge through learning by doing.

2.3.2   Sectoral Systems Specificities and Technological Catch-Up Opportunities

Malerba and Mani (2009) claimed that understanding the specificities of relevant sectoral systems is fundamental to identification of the sources of innovation and the opportunities for development. This chapter shows that in technology and capital-intensive sectors, emerging market leaders would have more technological catch-up opportunities and move more quickly up the technological ladder under the following conditions. First, the technological knowledge is largely embodied in machinery or other physical artifacts for production processes. The tacit knowledge embodied in capital equipment or machinery makes it inherently easy to be transferred with few existing capabilities or local investments in learning (Radosevic, 1999, pp. 9–14). Second, the industry structure is highly modularized and has evolved into an integrated and mature production system along the industry value chain. In this type of situation, latecomer firms in large emerging countries can enter technology-based competition and move upward on a quality ladder more easily. Although they may not be as skilled in technological innovation, firms can excel by sourcing modules and assembling them, or they can be specialized and achieve economies of scale as they supply their own modules to multiple assemblers (Lu, 2008). Third, the product (or the core part of the product) is technologically modularized at a high level, thereby reducing technological complexity and manufacturing costs through building low-cost manufacturing capability. Fourth, large local markets are characterized by rapid growth and highly price-sensitive segments. The ease of market competition in low-end markets makes it possible for the domestic firms to survive in the initial stages and develop technological capability as they climb gradually up the ladder (Mu and Lee, 2005).

2.3.3   The Role of Policy Gaming between Central and Local Government

Prior literature concludes that governments in latecomer countries usually play an important role in guiding and helping indigenous firms to accumulate their capabilities and catch up with the MNCs (Fan, 2006; Kim, 1997). As to China, several leading Chinese state-owned automobile companies were picked by the central government to be national champions and directly provided with financial, technical, and fiscal resources (Liu and Tylecote, 2009; Mu and Lee, 2005; Yang and Yu, 2011). However, much less attention is given to the role of local governments in supporting the development of private companies. In this chapter, we identify a particularity in China's institutional context, that is, policy gaming between the central government and the local governments. Due to the gradually decentralized structure of governmental hierarchy in the past decade, many officials, especially mayors, have been quietly entrepreneurial to compete between regions (McMillan and Naughton, 1996, p. 179). In the interest of local governments, winner-pickup policies were also adopted, supporting those same successful or technology-intensive private firms, as supported by the central government on the national level. Such policy practices by local governments facilitate the capability building of local private firms in a few ways. First, the local government will help local firms circumvent industrial regulation by the central government, or help local private firms to acquire licenses to enter into regulated markets. Second, local governments often provide local private firms with preferential treatment in terms of lower income taxes, favorable financing terms and priority of access to scarce resources and infrastructures. Hence, it should be pointed out that private firms do not generally receive the same level of support from the central government as state-owned enterprises. However, successful private firms have gained great benefit from the government policy gaming through circumventing the central government's industrial regulations and obtaining access to resources at a rather low cost, with the help from local governments.

2.3.4   Limitations and Future Research Direction

This chapter has some limitations to be considered. As it is based on a single-case study of an exploratory nature, it must be validated further with a more rigorous research method such as a multi-case study and survey-based empirical analysis. Moreover, as the findings are drawn from the longitudinal analysis of the Geely case, one needs to be cautious in generalizing the results to other industries and large emerging economies that face different institutional, technological, and market conditions. Just as Malerba and Nelson (2011) argued, catching up is a process of complex interplay among actors, networks, and contexts that often differ significantly across economic sectors and countries. Further research is necessary to validate and generalize the results to a broader context.

ACKNOWLEDGEMENTS

The authors would like to express their gratitude to Professor Richard R. Nelson and Professor Franco Malerba for their valuable comments to the earlier drafts of this chapter, as well as their funding support for international travel in the Rise to Market Leadership (RIMAL) Research Project.

NOTES

*   Qiang Li is the corresponding author.
1.   Some were developed from old state-owned companies, including Chery (established in 1997) from Anhui province and Great Wall (established in 1976) from Hebei province; others are privately owned companies, such as Geely (established in 1986) from Zhejiang province and BYD Auto (established in 2003) from Guangdong province.
2.   For example, Volkswagen's four major brands, namely VW, Audi, Skoda, and Seat share the same car platforms and components, which include front axles, rear axles, front ends, rear ends, exhaust systems, brake systems, and numerous other elements (Dahmus et al., 2001).
3.   In 2003, 88 companies produced volumes under 50 000 units each; 170 companies produced volumes between 100 and 10 000 (Richet and Ruet, 2008).

4. The local government of Taizhou promised to promote the sale of 10 000 locally made vehicles by means of government purchase and related measures (Ngo, 2008).
5. In 1984, the government allowed private individuals to own vehicles for the first time.
6. Sometimes, the low-end market in China can be the biggest market segment in terms of absolute size. However, to compete in such a segment, low-price and low-cost technologies are often required.

REFERENCES

Altenburg, T., Schmitz, H., and Stamm, A. (2008), 'Breakthrough? China's and India's transition from production to innovation,' *World Development*, Vol. 36, No 2, pp. 325–344.

Baldwin, C.Y. and Clark, K.B. (1997), 'Managing in an age of modularity,' *Harvard Business Review*, Vol. 75, No 5, pp. 84–93.

Bierly, P.E. III and Daly, P.S. (2007), 'Alternative knowledge strategies, competitive environment, and organizational performance in small manufacturing firms,' *Entrepreneurship Theory and Practice*, Vol. 31, No 4, pp. 493–516.

Brusoni, S. and Prencipe, A. (2001), 'Unpacking the black box of modularity: technologies, products and organizations,' *Industrial and Corporate Change*, Vol. 10, No 1, pp. 179–205.

Chu, W.-W. (2011), 'How the Chinese government promoted a global automobile industry,' *Industrial and Corporate Change*, Vol. 20, No 5, pp. 1235–1276.

Cui, G. and Liu, Q.-M. (2000), 'Regional market segments of China: opportunities and barriers in a big emerging market,' *Journal of Consumer Marketing*, Vol. 17, No 1, pp. 55–72.

Dahmus, J.B., Gonzalez-Zugasti, J.P., and Otto, K.N. (2001), 'Modular product architecture,' *Design Studies*, Vol. 22, No 5, pp. 409–424.

Dantas, E. and Bell, M. (2009), 'Latecomer firms and the emergence and development of knowledge networks: the case of Petrobras in Brazil,' *Research Policy*, Vol. 38, No 5, pp. 829–844.

Depner, H. and Bathelt, H. (2005), 'Exporting the German model: the establishment of a new automobile industry cluster in Shanghai,' *Economic Geography*, Vol. 81, No 1, pp. 53–81.

Dess, G.G. and Beard, D.W. (1984), 'Dimensions of organizational task environments,' *Administrative Science Quarterly*, Vol. 29, pp. 52–73.

Droege, S.B. and Hoobler, J.M. (2003), 'Employee turnover and tacit knowledge diffusion: a network perspective,' *Journal of Managerial Issues*, Vol. 15, No 1, pp. 50–64.

Fan, P.-L. (2006), 'Catching up through developing innovation capability: evidence from China's telecom-equipment industry,' *Technovation*, Vol. 26, pp. 359–368.

Franco, A.M. and Filson, D. (2006), 'Spin-outs: knowledge diffusion through employee mobility,' *RAND Journal of Economics*, Vol. 37, No 4, pp. 841–860.

Gadiesh, O., Leung, P., and Vestring, T. (2007), 'The battle for China's good enough market,' *Harvard Business Review*, Vol. 85, No 9, pp. 80–89.

Gao, Y.Q. (2008), 'Institutional change driven by corporate political entrepreneurship in transitional China: a process model,' *International Management Review*, Vol. 4, No 1, pp. 22–34.

Gu, S.L. and Lundvall, B.A. (2006), 'China's innovation system and the move towards harmonious growth and endogenous innovation,' *Innovation: Management, Policy & Practice*, Vol. 8, No 1, pp. 1–26.

Henderson, R.M. and Clark, K.B. (1990), 'Architectural innovation: the reconfiguration of existing product technologies and the failure of established firms,' *Administrative Science Quarterly*, Vol. 35, No 1, pp. 9–30.

Hobday, M. (1995), 'East Asian latecomer firms: learning the technology of electronics,' *World Development*, Vol. 23, No 7, pp. 1171–1193.

Jensen, M.B., Johnson, B., Lorenz, E., and Lundvall, B.A. (2007), 'Forms of knowledge and modes of innovation,' *Research Policy*, Vol. 36, pp. 680–693.

Karim, S. (2006), 'Modularity in organizational structure: the reconfiguration of internally developed and acquired business units,' *Strategic Management Journal*, Vol. 27, No 9, pp. 799–823.

Kash, D.E. and Rycroft, R.W. (2000), 'Patterns of innovating complex technologies: a framework for adaptive network strategies,' *Research Policy*, Vol. 29, No 7/8, pp. 819–831.

Kim, L. (1997), *Imitation to Innovation: The Dynamics of Korea's Technological Learning*, Boston: Harvard Business School Press.

Kim, L. (1998), 'Crisis construction and organisational learning: capability building in catching-up at Hyundai Motor,' *Organization Science*, Vol. 9, No 4, pp. 506–521.

Langlois, R.N. (2002), 'Modularity in technology and organization,' *Journal of Economic Behavior & Organization*, Vol. 49, pp. 19–37.

Lee, K. and Lim, C.-S. (2001), 'Technological regimes, catching-up and leapfrogging: findings from the Korean industries,' *Research Policy*, Vol. 30, No 3, pp. 459–483.

Li, X.-B. (2009), 'China's regional innovation capacity in transition: an empirical approach,' *Research Policy*, Vol. 38, pp. 338–357.

Liu, J.-J. and Tylecote, A. (2009), 'Corporate governance and technological capability development: three case studies in the Chinese auto industry,' *Industry and Innovation*, Vol. 16, No 4, pp. 525–544.

Liu, S.-J. (2009), 'Lessons from China's automobile industry,' *China Economist*, available at: http://ssrn.com/abstract=1516302.

Liu, X.-L. and White, S. (1997), 'The relative contributions of foreign technology and domestic inputs to innovation in Chinese manufacturing industries,' *Technovation*, Vol. 17, No 3, pp. 119–125.

Liu, X.-L. and White, S. (2001), 'Comparing innovation systems: a framework and application to China's transitional context,' *Research Policy*, Vol. 30, No 7, pp. 1091–1114.

Lu, X.-L. (2008), 'China's development model: an alternative strategy for technological catch-up,' Working Paper, SLPTMD (Department of International Development, University of Oxford).

Luo J.-X. (2005), 'The growth of independent Chinese automotive companies,' available at: http://global-production.com/scoreboard/resources/luo_2005_independent-chinese-automotive-companies.pdf.

Malerba, F. (2002), 'Sectoral systems of innovation and production,' *Research Policy*, Vol. 31, No 2, pp. 247–264.

Malerba, F. (ed.) (2007), *Sectoral Systems of Innovation: Concepts, Issues and Analyses of Six Major Sectors in Europe*, Cambridge, UK: Cambridge University Press.

Malerba, F. and Mani, S. (eds) (2009), *Sectoral Systems of Innovation and Production in Developing Countries: Actors, Structure and Evolution*, Cheltenham, UK and Northampton, MA: Edward Elgar.

Malerba, F. and Nelson, R. (2011), 'Learning and catching up in different sectoral systems: evidence from six industries,' *Industrial and Corporate Change*, Vol. 20, No 6, pp. 1645–1675.

Marques, R.A. and de Oliveira, L.G. (2009), 'Sectoral system of innovation in Brazil: reflections about the accumulation of technological capabilities in the aeronautic sector (1990–2002),' in Malerba, F. and Mani, S. (eds), *Sectoral Systems of Innovation and Production in Developing Countries: Actors, Structure and Evolution*, Cheltenham, UK and Northampton, MA: Edward Elgar, pp. 156–206.

Mazzoleni, R. and Nelson, R.R. (2007), 'Public research institutions and economic catch-up,' *Research Policy*, Vol. 36, No 10, pp. 1512–1528.

McMillan, J. and Naughton, B. (1996), *Reforming Asian Socialism: The Growth of Market Institutions*, Ann Arbor, MI: University of Michigan Press.

Montinola, G., Qian, Y.-Y., and Weingast, B.R. (1995), 'Federalism, Chinese style: the political basis for economic success in China,' *World Politics*, Vol. 48, No 1, pp. 50–81.

Mu, Q. and Lee, K. (2005), 'Knowledge diffusion, market segmentation and technological catch-up: the case of the telecommunication industry in China,' *Research Policy*, Vol. 34, No 6, pp. 759–783.

Ngo, T.W. (2008), 'Rent-seeking and economic governance in the structural nexus of corruption in China,' *Crime Law Social Change*, Vol. 49, pp. 27–44.

Parise, S., Cross, R., and Davenport, T. (2006), 'Strategies for preventing a knowledge-loss crisis,' *MIT Sloan Management Review*, Vol. 47, No 4, pp. 31–38.

Prahalad, C.K. (2004), *The Fortune at the Bottom of the Pyramid: Eradicating Poverty through Profits*, New York: Pearson Professional Education.

Radosevic, S. (1999), *International Technology Transfer and 'Catch-Up' in Economic Development*, Cheltenham, UK and Northampton, MA: Edward Elgar.

Richet, X. and Ruet, J. (2008), 'The Chinese and Indian automobile industry in perspective: technology appropriation, catching-up and development,' *Transition Studies Review*, Vol. 15, No 3, pp. 447–465.

Sanchez, R. and Mahoney, J.T. (1996), 'Modularity, flexibility, and knowledge management in product and organization design,' *Strategic Management Journal*, Vol. 17, pp. 63–76.

Schilling, M.A. and Steensma, H.K. (2001), 'The use of modular organizational forms: an industry-level analysis,' *Academy of Management Journal*, Vol. 44, No 6, pp. 1149–1168.

Spencer, J.W. (2008), 'The impact of multinational enterprise strategy on indigenous enterprises: horizontal spillovers and crowding out in developing countries,' *Academy of Management Review*, Vol. 33, No 2, pp. 341–361.

Sturgeon, T. and Florida, R. (2000), 'Globalization and jobs in the automotive industry,' a study by Carnegie Mellon University and the Massachusetts Institute of Technology, Final Report to the Alfred P. Sloan Foundation.

Ulrich, K. (1995), 'The role of product architecture in the manufacturing firm,' *Research Policy*, Vol. 24, 419–440.

Walleigh, R. (1989), 'Product design for low-cost manufacturing,' *Journal of Business Strategy*, Vol. 10, No 4, pp. 37–41.

Wang, H. (2003), 'Policy reforms and foreign direct investment: the case of the

Chinese automobile industry,' *Journal of Economics and Business*, Vol. 1, pp. 287–314.

Wang, H. (2008), 'Innovation in product architecture: a study of the Chinese automobile industry,' *Asia Pacific Journal of Management*, Vol. 25, pp. 509–535.

Wang, H. and Kimble, C. (2010), 'Low-cost strategy through product architecture: lessons from China,' *Journal of Business Strategy*, Vol. 31, No 3, pp. 12–20.

Xie, W. and Wu, G. (2003), 'Differences between learning processes in small tigers and large dragons: learning processes of two color TV (CTV) firms within China,' *Research Policy*, Vol. 32, pp. 1463–1479.

Yang, M. and Yu, H. (2011), 'China as the world's largest automobile market,' in Yang, M. and Yu, H. (eds), *China's Industrial Development in the 21st Century*, Hackensack, NJ: World Scientific, pp. 17–36, doi: http://dx.doi.org/10.1142/97 89814324755_0002.

Zeng, M. and Williamson, P.J. (2007), *Dragons at your Door: How Chinese Cost Innovation is Disrupting the Rules of Global Competition*, Boston, MA: Harvard Business School Press.

Zhang, Y. and Li, H. (2010), 'Innovation search of new ventures in a technology cluster: the role of ties with service intermediaries,' *Strategic Management Journal*,Vol. 31, No 1, pp. 88–109.

3. The leading Chinese firms in the biopharmaceutical industry

Hong Song and Wensong Bai

3.1 INTRODUCTION

The pharmaceutical industry, especially the biopharmaceutical industry, is a burgeoning industry for developing countries. The modern pharmaceutical industry originates from western industrial countries and is controlled by multinational companies (MNCs) from those countries. Take 2011 as an example. The top fifteen pharmaceutical companies in the world all came from industrial countries, dominated by United States (US) firms in terms of number and sales (IMS, 2012). At the same time, the industry in developing countries appeared negligible and the markets in these countries were not the focus of leading MNCs. Therefore, special needs and diseases in developing countries were and often continue to be ignored by the R&D activities of these companies.

Along the global value chain, we observe the international division of labor between developing countries and industrial countries. The industrial countries mainly control the whole global value chain, especially patent drug development and sales, as well as the brands and whole market networks. Developing countries, as the marginal markets, get involved in the market sales stage. Additionally, they take advantage of backwardness to produce and market generic drugs for domestic markets. Some of these countries, such as Israel, India, and China, even export some types of generic drugs to industrial markets.

The 1990s witnessed a dramatic change in the pharmaceutical industry. Prior to that, the dominant strategy for leading firms in this industry was to internalize the whole value chain. But in the 1990s, firms started to fragment the traditionally integrated value chains. They subcontracted portions of upstream activities such as the discovery of new drugs to firms in low-cost countries such as China, India, and so on. Since then, along with the shift of some R&D activities from developed countries to developing countries, have appeared fast-growing firms like the contract research organizations (CROs) in developing countries. A new cooperative and complementary division of labor between those two types of countries has emerged. CROs exploit the significant number of well-trained human resources that are the result of developing countries' huge investment in higher education and thus are able to conduct basic research with much lower costs than those of MNCs in developed countries. Consequently, MNCs now tend to subcontract portions of their R&D activities that were previously internally integrated to CROs in developing countries and concentrate on their core business.

Given this background, to analyse the development of the biopharmaceutical industry in developing countries, one needs to pay attention not only to sectoral innovation systems in those countries, but also to the international background of such systems together with the impacts of the same industry in developed countries under local conditions. For example, MNCs from industrial countries get involved in the development of industry in developing countries. The entry of those firms will change the local market structure and the nature of competition. MNCs also take advantage of local factor conditions to develop their network, and so on. Therefore in this chapter, when the sectoral innovation system framework (Malerba, 2002; 2004; Malerba and Mani, 2009) is used, the global industrial background in terms of the global value-chain changes. The entry and impacts of MNCs from developed countries is also properly taken into account. Perhaps this framework could be called the two-tiered sectoral innovation system. Furthermore, in firm-level case studies, the environment and condition of the whole industry, especially the development of other rival firms, are also integrated. The reasons behind this are to guarantee proper selection of the representative case firms and to eliminate the chance elements from the success of these firms.

Section 3.2 describes the development of the Chinese biopharmaceutical industry and its principal sectoral background. In Section 3.3, the growth path of three Chinese firms is explored. Section 3.4 includes more in-depth analysis related to how successful these firms are when compared with the leading MNCs. Finally, Section 3.5 provides the conclusions of this study.

3.2   THE CHINESE BIOPHARMACEUTICAL INDUSTRY

The biopharmaceutical industry in China is an emerging industry. The total production value, profit, and sales within this industry in 2011 were USD 24.83, 3.47, and 23.62 billion respectively, which is equivalent to that of a multinational biopharmaceutical company.[1] In 2014 for example, the total revenue of Amgen was USD 20.1 billion, product sales were USD

19.3 billion and R&D expense was approximately USD 4.1 billion.[2] The share of China's pharmaceutical industry within Chinese industrial sales was 1.72 percent, and its biopharmaceutical industry share was only 0.18 percent, which is far lower than that of industrial countries.[3]

Though it is regarded as a high-tech industry, the biopharmaceutical industry's R&D intensity in China is quite low compared to that of industrial countries and it may even be regarded as a low-tech industry when compared to the benchmark of industrial countries. For example, the ratio of R&D to sales in the biopharmaceutical industry in 2011 was 1.92 percent, while the whole industrial ratio was only 0.71 percent. Thus far, there are 13 categories, 25 types, and 382 bioengineered drugs and vaccines produced by the biopharmaceutical industry in China. Of these, only 6 categories, 9 types, and 21 drugs and vaccines are new and developed by Chinese firms, with the generics comprising the remaining categories, types, drugs, and vaccines. Therefore, the share of original or new drugs developed by Chinese firms is only 5.5 percent, over 70 percent are generic drugs, and the remaining 20 percent are off-patent drugs.[4] There were 731 firms in China's biopharmaceutical industry in 2011. Of these, only four firms can be classified as large firms. Approximately 100 are medium firms and the rest are small firms. What they produce are ordinary vaccines, early biopharmaceutical generics such as human blood protein, recombinant interferon, erythropoietin (EPO), and so on.

There are a total of 257 R&D institutions that can be further classified into 3 categories. The first category comprises the indigenous R&D centers that target local diseases and demand. Very few firms have this type of R&D institution. The second category is CROs, which constitute the majority of the 257 R&D centers. There are three subtypes of R&D centers within the CROs, including: (a) the R&D centers of big MNCs in China; (b) new biopharmaceutical firms established by Chinese scholars after returning to China from overseas; and (c) local private firms. The third category consists of globalized R&D centers that were set up by globalized, independent R&D-oriented firms. This would include the widely known BGI of Shenzhen.

From the perspective of sectoral innovation, the firm-level innovation capability of China's biopharmaceutical industry is limited. However, China has rather strong research bases in non-firm organizations such as governmental institutes and universities. For example, China has established nationwide centers for disease control and prevention (CDCs) as well as six well-known pharmaceutical institutes since the 1950s. In recent years, especially thanks to the International Human Genome Project (HUGO), of which Chinese scientists were responsible for 1 percent in 1999, a number of national human genome engineering laboratories have been established throughout China. Based on these infrastructures, Chinese scientists have accomplished several world-class achievements. For example, the rice genome sequencing completed by BGI scientists is regarded by *Science* as third in the 2002 Global Top 10 Accomplishments. And the detailed map of the rice genome ranks number one in the Chinese Top Ten Scientific and Technological Advances. In addition, China has a very strong education system within the biology and chemistry specialties. Most of China's more than 1000 colleges and universities include chemistry and biology departments that produce 0.8 million graduates annually. Furthermore, a large number of Chinese students study chemistry and biology around the world.

The development of biotechnology and related industries are a priority of government policy. The Chinese government has supported this industry since the 1980s. Benefits from China's 1999 participation in HUGO included support such as the construction of new laboratory buildings, recruitment of new leading scientist teams, and so on. In China's twelfth five-year plan (2010–15) as well as its thirteenth five-year plan (2015–20), this industry was identified as one of the seven strategic emerging sectors in China. Over the next few years, more sectoral innovation platforms such as genome databanks, regional laboratories, test centers, and training centers will be set up or strengthened.

China's biopharmaceutical industry is also characterized by high-level globalization as foreign firms hold large shares in terms of investment, sales, profit, and production. Take investment as an example. Among the investments in the industry in 2011, the share of foreign firms (including foreign capital as well as capital from Hong Kong, Macao, and Taiwan) was 26.49 percent. Since the year 2000, the average investment share of foreign firms has accounted for approximately one-third of the industry, which is very high when compared to China's other high-tech industries. More specifically, foreign firms have become deeply involved in three key fields including local sales, generic drug production through joint ventures, and subcontracting of upstream R&D activities to local firms or their subsidiaries.

As far as institutions and regulations are concerned, there are two major defects in China. First, management of drug production needs to be improved. For example, the application process for obtaining drug production licenses was less strict and professional in the past. Consequently, there are too many firms producing the same drug today, which results in fierce competition and poor quality. Second, regional protectionism fragments the nationwide market such that few firms can grow up to become internationally competitive. Without internationally competitive firms, China's biopharmaceutical industry can't be integrated into global markets, nor can it compete with industrialized countries.

In summary, there are two tiers within China's biopharmaceutical industry. First, at the international sectoral level, competition and cooperation prevail between foreign firms and local firms. Within this tier, entry of foreign companies into local markets changes and even dominates development of China's biopharmaceutical industry. Second, at the indigenous sectoral level, different factors and actors together with local institutions and regulations have an impact on local firms as well as foreign firms.

3.3 CASE STUDIES OF LEADING FIRMS

We conduct a multiple case study in order to demonstrate the innovation system of the biopharmaceutical sector in China within its real-life context. Based on the rich data that portrays the development process of these cases in the context of China, we try to identify key elements of this sectoral system of innovation. The chosen cases are three leading Chinese biopharmaceutical and technological firms that are representative within their respective categories.

Sinovac, founded in 1999, is one of the leading Chinese firms specializing in vaccine research and production. This company represents the firms doing indigenous R&D and targeting local diseases and demand. Sinovac developed the world's first vaccine for H1N1 and China's first self-owned vaccine for hepatitis A. Currently, it holds a 37 percent market share of vaccines for hepatitis A in China.

WuXiPharmaTech ('PharmaTech') was founded in December 2000 as a global, leading CRO. Since most Chinese biopharmaceutical firms with their own R&D centres are CROs, PharmaTech, one of most successful CROs, is a typical firm representing this category. It is well equipped, with a fully integrated service and technology platform. With over 7000 researchers, it is the world's second-largest CRO and the largest in China.

The last case is BGI, which is an exemplar representing globalized, independent R&D-oriented firms. Firms within this category are newly emerging forces competing on the global stage. With the world's largest-scale production capacity in the area of DNA sequencing, it holds over 70 percent of the DNA sequencing market share in China. An overview of the three case firms is provided in Table 3.1.

3.3.1 Sinovac

3.3.1.1 The vaccine for hepatitis A: learn by doing and learn by imitation
The key asset of Sinovac since it was set up in Beijing is the vaccine for hepatitis A, *Healive*. It should be emphasized that this vaccine is only

Table 3.1   Overview of the cases

	Sinovac	WuXiPharmaTech	BGI
Founding circumstances	Founded 1999 by a former CDC researcher	Founded 2000 by returnee entrepreneur from the USA	Founded 1999 by former scientists in the China Academy of Science
Firm profile	A leading vaccine developer and producer; 614 employees; 50.77 million RMB revenue in 2012	Global leading CRO; over 7000 employees; 407.2 million RMB revenue in 2012	Globally competitive DNA sequencing provider; 3680 employees; 200 million RMB revenue in 2012
Technological profile	Vaccine R&D, targeting the demand of the Chinese market, such as hepatitis A, B, the H5N1 influenza virus, the influenza A H1N1, and the SARS virus	A fully integrated services and technology platform, biggest scale of human resources	The largest scale of production capability in the world, member of HUGO project
Initial funding source	Government project, venture capital, and loan	Venture capital and government investment	Venture capital and government project
Market profile	37% of market share of vaccine for hepatitis A in China, focusing on the Chinese market	The top two in the world and the top one in China, targeting customers around the world	70% of market share of DNA sequencing in China, 30% of revenue from international sales

a successful, new vaccine in China, rather than in the world. The same vaccine had already been developed decades ago by MNCs. Market immaturity provided the opportunity for Chinese firms to develop a cheap and localized vaccine. More specifically, foreign firms did not set up sufficient distribution networks targeting the promising but underdeveloped market in developing countries. Therefore the price of the MNCs' vaccine has been too high to be affordable by local Chinese customers. Meanwhile, due to protection by the government, local Chinese markets are not completely open to foreign goods. Consequently, local Chinese firms have a very strong incentive to pursue the so-called import-substitution strategy and develop the same goods that already exist in developed countries.

China is one of the countries severely exposed to hepatitis A and hepatitis B. Mr Yin WeiDong, the founder of Sinovac, graduated from a nursing school and was sent to his home town to work in the Tangshan CDC in 1983. At that time, the epidemic of the hepatitis A virus in Tangshan was severe. Deeply touched by the suffering of the patients, he promised to do something to change this situation. In 1985, through his arduous efforts, Mr Yin managed to separate the virus of hepatitis A, TZ84, which is still in use today. In order to conduct this research, Mr Yin referred to an enormous number of books and then imitated what other people had done. Meanwhile, the infrastructure and researchers at the Tangshan CDC provided him with a lot of aid. It was a great achievement at that time in China, since only two other state-owned institutes had finished a similar separation of the virus.

After the successful separation of the virus, Mr Yin received financial support (80 000 RMB) from the science and technology committee of Hebei Province to develop a diagnostic reagent for hepatitis A. He successfully accomplished this task in 1988.

At that time, an epidemic of hepatitis A broke out in Shanghai, China. Over 310 000 people were infected and 47 people died. While facing this severe situation however, there were only two different types of vaccine provided to the public. One was from GlaxoSmithKline and cost around USD 100. The other was from China's biopharmaceutical institutes, which was not an inactivated vaccine and thus those vaccinated retained some infection risk. Mr Yin was deeply alarmed by this situation and was determined to produce a high-class vaccine that the Chinese could afford. Obviously, this event urged Mr Yin to move forward again and resulted in the development of China's self-owned hepatitis A vaccine.

To complete the work of developing a diagnostic reagent for hepatitis A, in 1992 Mr Yin borrowed 50 000 RMB and set up his first company in Tangshan. During that year, his company cooperated with the National Bio-manufacturing Institute, and successfully applied for national funding of 300 000 RMB to develop the hepatitis A vaccine. However, the R&D for vaccines is hugely expensive and the company's income could not cover its expenses.

The lack of funding forced Mr Yin to enter into a joint venture arrangement in 1993 with a Singaporean businessman who brought an investment of USD 200 000. Nevertheless, expenses caused the company to quickly run through this investment as well. In 1998 Mr Yin borrowed another 5 million RMB to develop the vaccine. Finally, in December 1999, the vaccine was developed successfully and licensed by the Chinese government. This inactivated vaccine for hepatitis A is the first Chinese, independently developed vaccine.

However, the company still had no money to build a factory and produce the vaccine. After tough negotiations, a new company, Sinovac, was established in 1999. Located in Beijing, the company had registered capital of 133.6 million RMB and 30 employees.

In some ways, the successful development of the vaccine for hepatitis A by Mr Yin was carried out under extremely difficult conditions. Inspired, and with a very strong sense of his mission, Mr Yin succeeded, based mainly on imitation and learning by doing.

3.3.1.2 A vaccine for severe acute respiratory syndrome (SARS): an effort of original research and development

SARS broke out in Beijing shortly after the Chinese Spring Festival in 2003 and quickly spread to other neighboring cities. As one of the Chinese government's response actions, two R&D teams were set up in Beijing to develop a vaccine for SARS. While one team consisted of experts and researchers from Sinovac, the National Institute for Viral Disease Control and Prevention and the Laboratory Animal Science of the Chinese Academy of Medical Sciences (CAMS), the other team consisted of scholars and researchers from the Academy of Military Medical Science together with the National Vaccine and Serum Institute. Obviously, to be chosen as a member of this group was recognition of Sinovac's excellent reputation. It also provided an opportunity for the firm to move forward. Sinovac set up an internal team led by Mr Yin to do this study.

For previous research projects other than the SARS project, Sinovac had always been able to find existing references developed by researchers in other countries. This allowed Sinovac to easily imitate and repeat international experiences in China. By contrast, the SARS virus was so new that nobody had encountered and investigated it before. In other words, there was no previous knowledge about the form of the virus, its proteomics, or its genome sequencing, etc., that Sinovac could draw on. The SARS project was Sinovac's first research project that was started from scratch. To participate in this project was highly demanding in terms of innovation. Sinovac organized scientists from various fields such as virologists, zoologists, and biological and molecular experts to work together.

After nearly two years of hard work, Sinovac finally developed the vaccine for SARS. The firm successfully finished clinical test I in December 2004. This was the world's first inactivated vaccine for SARS that had completed a clinical test. After being injected with this vaccine, each of the 24 volunteers had produced antibodies to SARS. Though the SARS project was a failure in terms of a business investment, it was an invaluable project in terms of capacity building. The project's success gave Sinovac the strong confidence to develop new vaccines for any new viruses and diseases. This successful experience was priceless.

3.3.1.3 Influenza viruses: imitation and innovation

After the SARS project, Mr Yin started pursuing a new strategy: imitation and innovation. On the one hand, Sinovac continued to develop and produce its traditional vaccines for hepatitis A and influenza; on the other hand, the firm worked on vaccines for new viruses that did not exist before. The vaccine project for human bird flu (H5N1) is a very good example of this strategy, though it is still not successful in terms of business.

H1N1 provided another chance for Sinovac to build its capacity and even to manipulate its whole value chain and make a profit. Sinovac's excellent performance in the development of vaccines for SARS and H5N1 resulted in the firm receiving attention from the International Federation of Pharmaceutical Manufacturers & Associations (IFPMA). As a result, Sinovac was accepted as the only member of the Influenza Vaccine Supply International Task Force (IVSITF) from a developing country. This membership allowed Sinovac to enjoy the advantage of receiving more information about H1N1 cases, cooperation with international communities, and so on, when developing this new vaccine. In close cooperation with scientists from other countries, especially those from the US, Sinovac developed the vaccine for H1N1. The firm finished all its testing procedures and registration on September 3, 2009, only 87 days after obtaining the virus from the US. This was the world's first vaccine for H1N1 and was approved by the Chinese government.

These research projects assisted with Sinovac's growth and development. As a result, the firm gradually established its own routine for developing new vaccines.

3.3.2 WuXiPharmaTech

PharmaTech is the second enterprise which its president, Dr LiGe, established. In 1993, Dr LiGe graduated from Columbia University in New York City with a PhD in Chemistry. Based on his patented technology, 'marked combinatorial chemistry technique,' and together with his supervisors, he received venture capital investments and founded a biopharmaceutical firm, Pharmacopeia Inc. This firm, which mainly develops drugs, was successfully listed on the NASDAQ in 1995. Through this process, Dr LiGe obtained first-hand experience in terms of the skills required for the development of new drugs through R&D as well as marketing drugs in the US.

In 1999, Dr LiGe was invited to return to China for a visit. At that time, the Chinese domestic pharmaceutical R&D market was still in its initial stages, in that global outsourcing of pharmaceutical R&D was not well known in China. There were many accusations related to intellectual property issues from abroad. However, with the acuteness derived from his rich R&D and business experiences Dr LiGe felt that there would be great advantage in terms of human resources if outsourcing of pharmaceutical R&D could be operated in China. In 2000, and through collaboration with investors from Jiangsu Province, Dr LiGe established a new firm, WuXiPharmaTech in Wuxi; a firm in which he invested his intellectual property rights, derived from the field of biology.

During its establishment, Dr LiGe determined that the business model of PharmaTech was a CRO. With the CRO model, PharmaTech provides an open R&D platform, driven by the diverse demands of different customers. The firm mainly provides laboratory R&D and Active Pharmaceutical Ingredient R&D services. However, the value of CRO services does not seem to be recognized and is less accepted by domestic customers. Large pharmaceutical firms have their own R&D departments while the small and medium firms could not afford the cost of outsourcing their R&D. The one thing PharmaTech could do was to locate itself in China while orienting its business to the international markets. Thanks to the extensive network that Dr LiGe had built globally, especially in the US, PharmaTech's major market was outside China.

PharmaTech's first client was Dr LiGe's American firm, Pharmacopeia Inc. When the first budget year finished in 2002, PharmaTech's income was 25 million RMB. In 2004, the firm's income exceeded 170 million RMB and had increased to more than 500 million RMB by 2006. Today, PharmaTech has over 80 global clients, many of which are among the top pharmaceutical firms in the world.

Meanwhile, in order to boost its scale, the firm's R&D personnel have increased year by year. In August 2007, PharmaTech was listed on the New York Stock Exchange and raised USD 180 million. With those funds, PharmaTech expanded its new R&D bases in Tianjin, Shanghai, and Suzhou. By early 2008, the domestic R&D team consisted of 2700 employees. When including the approximately 700 researchers in the firm's US branch, PharmaTech's R&D capability has been ahead of many global pharmaceutical firms, according to Dr LiGe. Benefiting from its large-scale R&D personnel, PharmaTech is able to run hundreds of projects at the same time. These projects range from small ones such as synthesizing new compounds to production of tons of Active Pharmaceutical Ingredients (APIs). R&D timeframes range from one month to one or two years. Figuratively, as a result of having more employees, where the R&D

process used to take one year with one person, it now takes just a half-year with two persons.

The direct competitors of PharmaTech include R&D centers set up by MNCs, Chinese subsidiaries of global CROs, and some indigenous CROs. While the strategy of the subsidiaries of MNCs and global CROs is 'in China for China,' PharmaTech's strategy is 'in China for the World.' PharmaTech appears as a bridge between China and the world and takes advantage of low cost, highly qualified Chinese researchers. With 7000 employees, PharmaTech has the largest scale of R&D researchers among pharmaceutical firms globally. And when compared with the local indigenous CROs, PharmaTech's advantage lies in 'the same thing but doing it better,' which is demonstrated in the firm's first-mover advantage, strict management, and large-scale human resources. Of course, the strong cooperation among the leading global biopharmaceutical firm networks, as well as the overseas educational background of the firm's founders are unique and beyond the reach of most local indigenous CROs.

PharmaTech's target goal is to set up an integrated R&D platform and shorten the duration of R&D processes. Therefore, PharmaTech focused on the acquisition of other firms while developing internal R&D ability. In January 2008, PharmaTech paid USD 160 million to acquire AppTech, a US firm that provides drug testing, contractual research, and R&D services for the biopharmaceutical and medical apparatus industries. With this acquisition, PharmaTech further enhanced its integrated services with analytical and bioanalytical services. Additionally, PharmaTech recently built its capacity to provide clinical research and regulatory services. The firm's broad and integrated R&D capacity is enough to make PharmaTech proud, for there is no other company like PharmaTech in the world.

3.3.3   BGI

3.3.3.1   To be a member of the Human Genome Project (HUGO)
The inception of BGI, to a large degree, may be attributed to HUGO. During the first five years of the 1990s, while HUGO was focused on the development of a sequencing method, Dr Yang and Dr Wang, the two co-founders of BGI, were trained at US research institutes along with several other BGI scientists. Notably, Yang and Wang worked at the University of Washington Genome Center in Seattle, an important site for HUGO research. The experience of being on the staff at the Genome Center in the US allowed them access to the latest progression of the HUGO project, while also impressing them a lot. Yang and Wang recognized that genomic research and the huge accompanying benefits derived from its commercial development had strategic implications for national

competitiveness in the twenty-first century. And they believed that as a country with a huge population and diverse species of animals, plants, etc., China needed to participate in the international project for genomic research and thus promote its own research capability in the genome field. Otherwise, China would lose another opportunity to catch up with technological advancements.

Yang and Wang returned to China in 1998 determined to initiate a new epoch in the country's biotech industry. To accomplish this goal, they started working at the Genetics Center of the Chinese Academy of Sciences (CAS). They later established a human genome research center, specifically to join the HUGO project, and proceeded to undertake 1 percent of the project. The HUGO project had been implemented almost ten years previously and was supposed to be completed in 2005. Yang, Wang, and their colleagues contended that China's participation in the HUGO project would be a critical chance for learning. The knowledge and technological progress that could be derived from participating in the HUGO project might further boost China's own sequencing capability. However, the subject raised considerable controversy when the plan was submitted to the Chinese government. Through fierce debate, the government decided not to join the HUGO project. Therefore, in 1999, Yang, Wang and other colleagues decided to break through the institutional constraints in their own way. They drew the starting capital of 5 million RMB from their own savings and other social capitalization and set up another genome center, BGI, in the form of a joint stock, non-profit organization. BGI is independent from the genome center of the CAS.

As the HUGO project had already been in place for around ten years, it was not easy for BGI to be accepted as a new member. It was difficult for the firm to become involved in the international collaboration project, particularly when it was from a developing country with less technological capability to make contributions. However, BGI managed to persuade the global consortium by lobbying through personal relationships and joined the HUGO project in 1999.

3.3.3.2 To go into business

After being accepted as a member of HUGO, BGI bore the 1 percent project participation along with two other Chinese national genome centres, with financial support from the Chinese government. Yet new problems arose as the HUGO project was coming to an end. BGI was a private, non-profit research organization without a stable and sustainable source of funding following the HUGO project. As a result, BGI had to seek new funding for its future development when the financial support for the HUGO project ceased. Throughout its participation in the HUGO project, BGI had been growing in size and in sequencing capability. At that time, the firm had more than 200 employees and around 50 machines for sequencing. Thus, it had to find a way to support its existing sequencing capability as well as its sustainable development.

The top management pushed BGI forward with the idea of competing for large-scale projects and funding from both domestic sources and through international cooperation. Hence, BGI devoted its efforts to launching as many sequencing projects as possible with both domestic and international partners. In order to persuade the government to increase investment in the sequencing area, BGI proposed an ambitious plan, called the National Biological Resource Genomes Project. The aim of the project was to sequence the genomes of most Chinese species of animals, plants, etc., that were economically or scientifically significant. In the wake of the HUGO project, BGI started two such sequencing projects in 2000; one cooperated with the CAS for sequencing indica rice and the other in cooperation with the Danish Pig Genome Consortium for sequencing the pig. BGI had received USD 2.5 million from the CAS as a downpayment for continuing to enhance its sequencing capability and for initiating these projects.

Besides the aforementioned two projects, BGI had participated in other international projects that attracted much academic attention. These projects included the Silkworm genome-sequencing project with the CAS in 2003, the Chick genome sequencing with the United Kingdom (UK) in 2004 and the international HapMap project with laboratories from five other countries. For these projects, BGI played an active role in providing a sequencing service.

3.3.3.3   To be a globalized R&D center

With the belief that BGI could build and strengthen its own capability through collaboration with domestic and international partners, the company established a network connecting global collaborators through which ideas and knowledge are generated and transferred. International expansion includes a strategy of spreading the network abroad. The overseas sales representatives of BGI act as tentacles that enlarge the scale of the network and look for novel information. In addition, the company attends and participates in conferences and seminars in Europe and America.

During the networking process, international orientation obviously is the most important strategy for BGI. Since the first day of BGI's founding, the company has aimed at the latest technological developments worldwide. BGI has maintained close cooperation with international research institutes via the founders' social network in order to acquire knowledge from partners. BGI's goals include building the world's top institute for DNA sequencing and bioinformatics. Thus far, BGI has established strategic cooperation relationships with the world's top ten pharmaceutical firms as well as with first-class research institutes and universities worldwide.

3.3.4 Why Did These Firms Become Leaders in the Chinese Market?

As leaders in the biopharmaceutical sector in a developing country, the growth of these case firms required some necessary sectoral conditions. Drawing on Malerba's (2002; 2004) sectoral innovation framework and taking into account the influence of international players in the Chinese market, we can identify the basic elements that impact the development of the biopharmaceutical sector as well as the growth of Chinese firms in this sector. Some basic but key elements are summarized in the following table (Table 3.2).

In the case of Sinovac, three sectoral factors are critical for its development. Externally, the market demand for vaccines is great, which provides an opportunity for Sinovac. Due to the continual outbreaks of influenza in China, there is a large demand by the Chinese public for vaccines. However, MNCs do not develop localized vaccines specifically for the Chinese market and few indigenous firms can provide qualified products. Consequently, the imbalance between supply and demand for vaccines in China provides business opportunities for those firms that are determined and able to develop effective and affordable vaccines for hepatitis A and B, fulfilling the considerable needs of the Chinese public.

To grasp the opportunity, Sinovac conducted its internal learning process, namely the imitation and innovation strategy, thus facilitating the company's knowledge-base building. Although Sinovac lacked a knowledge base about related issues at the time, it managed to accomplish the development of a vaccine for hepatitis A through learning by doing. On the one hand, Sinovac researched related reference materials and then imitated what others had done. Through its learning-by-doing strategy, Sinovac accumulated experience and successfully transformed external knowledge into its own knowledge base. On the other hand, Sinovac closely cooperated with governmental research institutions, which provided it the opportunity to utilize the facilities and researchers of public institutions as well as access the latest information. This cooperation was due in great part to the Sinovac founder's close relationships with China's central and local governments. After the primary stages of knowledge learning and accumulation, Sinovac possessed certain innovation capabilities and has thus been able to conduct original, innovative projects such as developing vaccines for SARS and H1N1. At this stage, Sinovac worked in

Table 3.2   *Summary of key sectoral elements for case firms*

	Sinovac	WuXi PharmaTech	BGI
Firm-level factors	*Entrepreneurial founder; internal capacity building, project by project, and step by step*; knowledge learning through international cooperation, strategy of focusing on domestic market	*Entrepreneurial founder; knowledge base derived from founder's research capacity in USA; acquired foreign company*; learning by doing, developing an integrated services and technological platform project by project	*Learning by doing; knowledge base derived from participating in the HUGO project*
Country-level factors	*Government funding: loan*	*Government financial support; favorable governmental policy*; multinational firms as competitors; strong education systems providing human resources	*Government funding: loan; favorable governmental policy*; strong education systems providing human resources
Sector-level factors	*Strong regulation for particular niche market; national research institutes and universities*	Large scale of human resources; *shift of global value chain, particularly the global shift of R&D activities from industrial countries to developing countries*; weak protection for intellectual property rights	The shift of global value chain; *cooperation with national research institutes and universities; intensive cooperation with scientists around world; strict regulation in some business areas; large scale of human resources*

Note: We italicize the elements that are the key factors for each respective case firm.

cooperation with American scientists with the aim of further enhancing its innovation capabilities.

Institutionalization is another external factor critically facilitating Sinovac's growth. Strong regulation by China's government led to the formation of a specialized market environment for Sinovac and its main product, vaccines. Vaccines and the diseases they treat are not only the concerns of the CDC (in certain situations), but also a top priority of the China's central government for the country as a whole. A typical example was the situation that occurred in early 2003 when a SARS epidemic broke out in Beijing. Thus, in China vaccines are a government monopoly. In other words, the Chinese government strictly manages the research, development, and sale of vaccines in China. Any firm that intends to do business related to vaccines must meet the eligibility requirements and get licenses from government. After production, all vaccines will be purchased by the Chinese government and then supplied to the public free, or at a very low price.

Therefore, the firms in this field must have a strong sense of social responsibility, as well as a close and good quality relationship with the CDC, or with the central government. The stronger the sense of responsibility and the deeper and more diverse a firm's relationship is with the CDC or central government, the more beneficial it is for the firms. Sinovac exactly meets these requirements. First, the main actor and founder of Sinovac, Mr Yin, has a strong sense of mission. It is this mission that drives Mr Yin always to get deeply involved in new vaccine development projects, thus building an excellent reputation. Second, Sinovac and Mr Yin have good relationships with the government. They have worked for the government and in return, they have received government support. For example, different governments provided almost all the funding for the hepatitis A vaccine project. It is the same case for other major vaccine projects such as SARS and H5N1.

In comparison to Sinovac, PharmaTech's growth path demonstrates the transformation resulting from international sectoral systems. Externally, the shift of global value chains, particularly the shift of R&D activities from industrial countries to developing countries, brings about significant business opportunities to developing countries and leads to the rise of CROs in these countries. The business model of PharmaTech is that of a typical CRO model. CROs are the result of outsourcing R&D activities by pharmaceutical MNCs with the aim of upgrading technology and capability in a cost-efficient way. Since technology, especially biotechnology, advances so quickly, it is difficult for the traditional, chemistry-based pharmaceutical firms to catch up with those changes. Outsourcing is one of the best options for those firms to deal with technology challenges. Meanwhile, the cost of new drug development is very high due to strict clinical tests, application procedures, and the high failure rate of new drugs. CROs, especially those from low-cost countries with high-quality expertise in many fields, can provide badly needed professional services to pharmaceutical firms and help them reduce the cost and risk of developing new drugs. CROs from China and other developing countries, like PharmaTech, derive significant advantages from their ability to employ as many cheaper yet qualified researchers as possible. With modern biotechnology, new drug development often leads to the discovery of new chemical compounds, which, in turn, can significantly increase the chances of successfully developing new drugs while reducing risk at the same time. However, the discovery of new compounds requires a lot of high-quality researchers and experts, which are very expensive and scarce in industrial countries. Take Dr Chen Hongwei, the vice-president of PharmaTech, as an example. Dr Chen has had over 200 publications in international chemistry journals and holds a large number of patents in the US. But he had only 20 assistants working with him at ImClone Systems in the US. Since returning to China and joining PharmaTech, his team has expanded to more than 200 researchers. This is due to the fact that the cost of hiring one researcher in China is only a tenth of that in the US. With PharmaTech's well-equipped laboratory and other facilities, more new chemical compounds have been discovered and produced by his team. Obviously, this dramatically increases the possibility of successful new drug development and correspondingly reduces the risk of failure.

Internally, the international standardized knowledge base PharmaTech possessed contributed to its establishment of a leading position among CROs in China. The founder, as a returnee entrepreneur, brought back advanced technological knowledge and business skills that constituted PharmaTech's competitive knowledge base. Furthermore, PharmaTech utilized its founder's overseas social capital to extend its cooperation network around the world, particularly in the US. This global network transfers unending knowledge to PharmaTech, which the firm uses to absorb and innovate, project by project. It is a virtuous cycle in that the increasing number of researchers and the larger scale of CROs result in more cost benefits that CROs from developing countries may enjoy. Furthermore, with enhanced R&D capabilities, a CRO becomes more competitive and is more capable of taking business risk. In this way, PharmaTech has successfully become a global CRO with fully integrated services and technology platforms after more than ten years of development.

Similar to PharmaTech's CRO business model, BGI is taking advantage of the large scale of cheap human resources in China to conduct

R&D projects for its customers around the world for financial returns. However, the difference is that BGI is an independent firm and develops its own new products and patents. With its initial knowledge base derived from participating in the HUGO project, BGI intensively implements international and domestic projects in cooperation with national research institutes and universities while developing its own capacity externally and internally. Externally, BGI has been strengthening its capability in several aspects. First, BGI's manpower, particularly its technicians, possesses a rich experience built through cooperation with world-class fellows, meaning they are standing on the shoulders of giants to reach the latest developments in the field of bioinformatics research. Interacting and learning from these partners, BGI can develop intellectual property rights with its partners and then employ this new knowledge in China as well as other markets. Furthermore, this collaboration helps BGI augment its knowledge structure, filling in its knowledge gaps.

Second, in order to establish its own scientific reputation in the international community and attract new network partners, BGI also focuses on building its internal capability. For example, the indica rice genome project was one of BGI's seminal research achievements, independently accomplished, which made a name for BGI. At that time, there were several research groups around the world endeavoring to sequence the rice genome. BGI and Syngenta were in the leading positions to achieve completion. BGI focused on the indica rice that grows throughout China and in most of the rest of the rice-eating Asian countries, while the Syngenta team focused on the Japonica variety. Even though the focus on rice varieties was different, the two teams – particularly BGI with its goal of demonstrating sequencing capability and winning honor for China – were eager to be the first to publish draft sequencing of the rice genome. BGI split its sequencing team into two twelve-hour shifts to keep the machines running 24 hours a day. In the end, BGI made it: the firm was the first institute to release the sequencing results. BGI then published a paper in *Science* (Yu et al., 2002). The cover story in that issue, which captured much attention, profiled BGI.

Although PharmaTech and BGI paid more attention to international resources and sectoral influences, the effects of close government relationships and favorable institutional support were just as important to these two firms as they were to Sinovac.

The Chinese government recognized innovation as the engine of future economic development and recently started advocating for transformation of China's economic development structure. As a result, the biotech industry and its relevant companies have received much attention from the Chinese government, from the central government to municipal governments. For example, the Chinese central government invested over USD 6 billion in state subsidies for new drug development between 2012 and 2015. Meanwhile, the state-owned China Development Bank provided around USD 17 billion in special funding to support development of the biotech industry. Under these circumstances, leading biotech firms have received lots of attention and support from the central and local governments. Take BGI, for example: leaders of the Chinese central government visited BGI several times and spoke highly of BGI's work. Furthermore, BGI cooperated with several municipal governments and established branches in other areas of China. As a case in point, BGI's strong reputation derived from its participation in the HUGO project helped the firm convince Hangzhou municipal officials to provide a rent-free building together with a grant of around USD 10 million. With this support, the BGI Hangzhou Genome Institute, affiliated with Zhejiang University, was established. Towards the end of 2006, in exchange for USD 1.5 million in start-up fees and USD 3.5 million in annual grants, as well as free rental buildings provided by the Shenzhen municipal government, BGI headquarters relocated to a former shoe factory in Shenzhen.

To sum up, the evolution of international sectoral systems has had profound impacts on the growth and rise of Chinese market leadership as demonstrated with these three cases. The global shift of the pharmaceutical industry's R&D activities to developing countries has led to the emergence of new demands, which in turn has stimulated the growth of indigenous firms. When serving the demand of foreign and local customers, the Chinese firms comprehensively compete as well as cooperate with global giants through networks. The Chinese firms benefit from the network structure of organized innovation activities such that their knowledge base continues to be updated and gradually approaches the international competitive level. Actors within the network, including universities, research institutions, and national health systems, play an important role in the firms' innovative processes. Externally, demand and institutions (such as regulations, national health systems, and favorable institutional environments) greatly affect the firms' growth. Internally, the learning strategy of firms, characterized by imitation, absorption, and re-innovation, is of considerable importance to upgrade knowledge as the firms become internationally competitive.

3.4 DISCUSSION

Based on the analysis and case studies described above, there are several key requirements for a country to build a global biopharmaceutical

industry in general and leading enterprises in particular. The key requirements are as follows:

1. A close link between biopharmaceutical companies and R&D insti-
    tutions or universities must be established. As a high-tech industry,
    the biopharmaceutical industry endures fast changes that are driven
    forward by large-scale, basic findings that result from research done in
    universities and public R&D institutes. Therefore, close contact with
    universities and public institutions is one of the prerequisites for the
    industry or an enterprise to develop and survive.
2. Substantial financial support must be injected into this industry and
    its firms from outside sources including other industries, other firms,
    capital markets, or venture capital. In order to obtain more capital,
    many biopharmaceutical enterprises were listed on stock exchanges
    and some of them even received injections of large amounts of capital
    from outside investors. The preferred sources for this financial support
    include the involvement of, or investments from, traditional pharma-
    ceutical enterprises.
3. The government and firms must constantly concentrate on the
    biopharmaceutical industry and gradually accumulate their capacities.

The biopharmaceutical industry and firms from developing countries
must also meet some additional conditions. Four of these conditions are
as follows:

1. Entrepreneurial founders that lead firms to pursue innovative
    knowledge play a critical role in the capability building and develop-
    ment of those firms. As shown in the three cases presented herein,
    the founders are proactive in seeking new knowledge either through
    learning by doing or through learning by linkage and imitation. As a
    result of benefits derived from the founders and their influence, firms
    build and develop preliminary yet essential innovative capabilities,
    which provide competitive advantages for firm growth in knowledge-
    intensive industries such as the biopharmaceutical industry.
2. The government must be determined to cultivate and support the
    leading local firms. One of the key benchmarks for the global,
    competitive biopharmaceutical industry is whether or not there are
    leading indigenous firms with global reach. It is relatively easy for a
    government to successfully support a single firm on a one-time basis.
    However, it is rather difficult for a government to provide support
    for that firm several times over. The leading indigenous firms that
    comprise the global, competitive biopharmaceutical industry need

focused, long-term support. Many of these types of cases can be found by studying the experiences of Japan and South Korea after the Second World War. The cases in our study show the importance of government support. Clearly, these cases demonstrate a considerable need for proper protection and strong support from the government. Even with such protection and support, it will take quite a long time for these case firms to achieve this growth.

3. The local markets must be big enough to support a global, competitive industry and a group of firms. Therefore, only when a country reaches certain levels of per capita income and/or has a very large population will it generate the conditions and environment for a global, competitive biopharmaceutical industry to emerge. It is impossible for such an industry to emerge from a low-price market or in an environment where intellectual property rights are only loosely protected.

4. The evolution of global value chains and the global shift of the pharmaceutical industry's R&D activities to developing countries are important factors. These changes bring about opportunities, such as international markets and knowledge learning. They also bring about challenges such as fierce competition with global pharmaceutical giants. As shown in these cases, managing to grasp the opportunities and handle the challenges is one key to becoming a future, leading global firm.

Could China's biopharmaceutical industry and its firms become global competitors in the near future? As far as the Chinese cases are concerned and according to the above discussions, it seems that there is a long way to go. First, the local biopharmaceutical market isn't mature enough to support a global competitive firm. Truly, very few people in China can afford the high price of new or patented drugs at this moment. Second, there is limited opportunity remaining for the Chinese government to institutionally support indigenous firms. And actually, other governments have already criticized China for its mercantile policies. How the Chinese government can move forward remains a question. And third, based on the case studies of leading Chinese firms in this chapter, it is obvious that there is a big gap between them and the leading global one.

Regarding Sinovac, its success mainly depends upon two factors. The first factor is the regular disease prevention and control system in China. The foundation of this firm in terms of technology and R&D comes from the entrepreneur's work and research experience at the CDC in Tangshan, Hebei Province. The huge network of CDCs spreads across the whole country, extending down to the county level. It connects the national system of disease surveillance and prevention, the national R&D

capabilities, and the vaccine market. It thus provides Sinovac with convenience and a competitive advantage. The second factor is the Chinese government's attention to disease surveillance and prevention. The monitoring and control of major diseases is of high importance to the government as it relates to the security and stability of society in China, even worldwide. In these fields, the Chinese government has constructed a complete set of networks. Sinovac tempered itself and established a good reputation through its R&D and production experiences with the vaccines for SARS and the H5N1 avian influenza. Close cooperation with the government not only gives Sinovac unique opportunities to obtain financial support for conducting R&D, but also to engage in R&D collaboration with leading research institutions and universities in China. During the development of Sinovac, most of its R&D funding came from the government, and most of the cooperation was with universities or public institutions.

However, when compared with large multinational pharmaceutical enterprises, Sinovac is very tiny. So, the key questions involve determining whether or not Sinovac can develop and grow as big as any of the international giants, and how Sinovac would achieve that growth.

The special nature of the vaccine markets limits the size, locally, of the firms in this specialized field. For example, in China the total demand and supply for vaccines is equivalent to no more than 10 billion RMB. Can Sinovac break through this limitation? To some extent, Sinovac remains a professional company with very limited businesses and products. Up until now, Sinovac has only sold four to five vaccines. Could Sinovac gradually expand its businesses and product lines and transform itself into a core pharmaceutical company, able to withstand the global market competition? Could the firm become a multinational enterprise in the future? It may be possible in the long run, but would be very difficult to achieve in the near future. Given Sinovac's capabilities of R&D and the firm's cash flow, it cannot currently afford the cost of engaging in large-scale innovation of new drugs and diversification.

The success of PharmaTech combines several advantages, including: (a) the strong educational background of Dr LiGe and the extensive overseas networks he established; (b) the abundant supply of high-quality but cheap biopharmaceutical and chemistry researchers and experts in China; and (c) the firm's strong support by the Chinese government. Most importantly, the business model of CRO firms in general and PharmaTech specifically is integrated with globalization of the world biopharmaceutical industry, which, in particular, features the fragmentation and offshore migration of pharmaceutical R&D in industrial countries.

Two of the most critical problems PharmaTech faces impact its potential for growth. First, it cannot engage in its own development of new drugs.

This is a common dilemma that CROs face. If they engaged in self-product development, MNCs would not outsource their R&D to these CROs. This is because the purpose of R&D is to discover and screen chemical formulas. However, CROs can follow the research trends of their MNC customers, even the molecular structure of new drugs. But if these companies do not engage in self-product development and simply rely on contract business, they will always be in a dependent state, and cannot therefore grow to be true pharmaceutical MNCs. Second, a CRO cannot expect to get more contract business from local firms since the local companies can take advantage of local R&D personnel themselves.

Regarding BGI, on the one hand its development depends upon close collaboration with international partners in order to tap into advanced research capabilities and technological knowledge. On the other hand, its development is dependent on public projects and governments that provide funding. With its internationally sourced knowledge and public funding support, BGI has become the largest genomic sequencing center in the world. The firm has accumulated a huge amount of genomic knowledge, derived from sequencing various species. However, BGI hasn't developed a business model that is able to exploit its knowledge base and convert it into commercialization. In other words, BGI remains dependent on its genomic sequencing services, providing data to other companies who then generate profits. While the growth of this market demand is tending towards stability, increasingly fierce competition has started diminishing BGI's advantage relative to new market entrants. If BGI cannot establish a business model that goes beyond its current sequencing service business, then BGI will be even more negatively impacted by the constraint of its financial resources. Consequently, the firm would not have the ability to use its own funds to focus on what it deems as important or to develop its pool of patents with the goal of long-term expansion.

Sinovac, PharmaTech, and BGI remain founder-owned enterprises, or entrepreneur-owned enterprises. The development of these firms is strongly influenced by their founders' character, preferences, visions, and so on. As the founders approach retirement, the future development of these companies will be accompanied by a lot of uncertainty.

In summary, in comparison to the leading global companies, the leading Chinese biopharmaceutical firms are still in the early stages of their development. They each have a long way to go to catch up with the global leaders. Considering the base of indigenous firms, the whole biopharmaceutical industry in China is scattered with small, specialized firms and an integrated industry is still under development.

3.5   CONCLUSIONS

Based on the case studies, several conclusions can be reached. Such conclusions are described below.

1. After developing four to five vaccines one after another, Sinovac gradually grew up to become one of the leading, specialized vaccine firms in China. However, it is still a small company in terms of sales and revenue, when compared with the leading global biopharmaceutical firms.
2. Thanks to the global shift of pharmaceutical R&D activities to low-cost countries, PharmaTech, by taking advantage of China's low-cost but highly qualified biological and chemistry students, quickly became one of the leading CROs in China. However, the business model of this firm has its limitations.
3. Based on the experience accumulated during participation in the Global Human Genome Project, BGI was founded, and it expanded quickly. After integrating unique Chinese chemists and biologists with overseas training, this firm transformed into a leading global independent R&D firm. However, without self-owned core manufacturing capacities and adequate institutional support, it will be difficult for BGI to achieve further growth.
4. All the firms studied in this chapter were established around the turn of this century. Therefore, these firms are just over ten years old: still very young. Each of the firms has a long way to go before becoming a global leader in the biopharmaceutical industry.
5. Overall, China not only lacks a large enough market, but it does not have a favorable market environment with good institutions and the regulations necessary to support a global biopharmaceutical industry. The Chinese biopharmaceutical industry is scattered with small, specialized firms and the integration of this industry is still under development.

NOTES

1. The sources of data about China's pharmaceutical industry in general and the biopharmaceutical industry in particular are from China's high-tech industry statistics yearbook, 2012, tables 20–55 and 20–56, and the databank at www.cyk.cei.gov.cn.
2. See http://www.amgen.com/pdfs/misc/Fact_Sheet_Amgen.pdf (accessed March 31, 2015).
3. Usually, the share in developed countries is 10 percent of GDP.
4. Interview with Ms Tao JianHong, a researcher from the Southern pharmaceutical economic institute.

REFERENCES

IMS (2012), *Health World Review Analyst*, London: IMS Health.

Malerba, F. (2002), 'Sectoral systems of innovation and production,' *Research Policy*, 31(2), 247–264.

Malerba, F. (2004), *Sectoral Systems of Innovation: Concepts, Issues and Analyses of Six Major Sectors in Europe*, Cambridge, UK: Cambridge University Press.

Malerba, F. and Sunil Mani (2009), *Sectoral Systems of Innovation and Production in Developing Countries: Actors, Structure and Evolution*, Cheltenham, UK and Northampton, MA: Edward Elgar.

Yu, J., S. Hu, J. Wang, G.K.S. Wong, S. Li, B. Liu, and M. Cao (2002), 'A draft sequence of the rice genome (Oryza sativa L. ssp. indica),' *Science*, 296(5565), 79–92.

FURTHER READING

IMAP (2011), *Pharma & Biotech Industry Global Report*, Istanbul: IMAP.

Mowery, David C. and Richard R. Nelson (1999), *The Sources of Industrial Leadership: Studies of Seven Industries*, Cambridge, UK: Cambridge University Press.

Odagiri, H., A. Goto, A. Sunami, and R. Nelson (eds) (2010), *Intellectual Property Rights and Catch-up: An International Comparative Study*, Oxford: Oxford University Press.

OECD (2006), *Innovation in Pharmaceutical Biotechnology: Comparing National Innovation Systems at the Sectoral Level*, Paris: OECD.

4. Leadership in the automobile industry: the case of India's Tata Motors

Sunil Mani

4.1 INTRODUCTION

Tata Motors Limited (TML) is India's largest automobile company, with consolidated revenues of USD 38.9 billion in 2013–14. It is the leader in commercial vehicles in each segment and among the top three companies in passenger vehicles with products in the compact, midsize car, and utility vehicle segments. The company is the world's fourth-largest truck manufacturer, and the world's second-largest bus manufacturer. Established in 1945, TML's presence indeed cuts across the length and breadth of India. Over 6 million Tata vehicles travel on Indian roads since the first one rolled out in 1954. The firm has six manufacturing plants spread throughout India. Following a strategic alliance with Fiat in 2005, TML set up an industrial joint venture with Fiat Group Automobiles at Ranjangaon (Maharashtra) to produce both Fiat and Tata cars and Fiat power trains. However, this joint venture came to an end in 2013. TML's dealership, sales, services, and spare parts network comprises over 3500 locations or touch points across the country. In fact, TML is one of India's leading brands in the automotive industry, especially when it comes to trucks and buses. Its recent forays into car production and particularly its attempt at designing an extremely cheap compact car have garnered fair amounts of national and international acclaim. An interesting aspect of the company is that it is extremely integrated, vertically speaking, having close access to raw materials and equipment (such as steel and machine tools) from its wholly owned subsidiaries or other member firms in its larger business group. These favorable factors have added to TML's leadership position in India's fast-growing automotive industry. This chapter is primarily focused on the origins of the leadership position achieved by TML.

Beginning with the Introduction here in Section 4.1, this chapter is structured to present the findings of our case study. Section 4.2 discusses the emergence of a number of leading firms in India, including TML. Section 4.3 provides some detailed information about the recent resurgence of India's automotive industry. Section 4.4 discusses our rationale for considering TML a market leader. Section 4.5 delves into the origins of the leadership position achieved by TML in terms of firm-, sector-, and country-level factors. Finally, Section 4.6 summarizes the main findings of our case study.

4.2   INDIA'S RECENT GROWTH PERFORMANCE AND THE EMERGENCE OF LEADING FIRMS

Since 1991, India's growth performance has spawned a fair amount of interest in both academic and policy circles. It is interesting to note that, unlike China, much of India's growth performance in recent years is attributed to the services sector. This sector consists of an assortment of subsectors ranging from the celebrated information and communications technology (ICT) sector to the more mundane public administration and defense. But history has shown us that most countries in the developed world, and even in the developing world (for example, Korea, China, and the group of countries usually referred to as the Asian tigers), have all had sustained economic growth by increased focus on manufacturing. It is in the manufacturing sector that output is more tangible and most of the innovations are first generated. The recent global financial crisis has shown us that the growth performance of the services sector in general, and the financial services sector in particular, can be a statistical factor. Indeed, at least some of the innovations in the financial sector especially are highly suspect and subject to varying interpretations. In fact, there are very few countries in the world that have demonstrated sustained economic growth of respectable magnitudes by focusing only on the services sector. Furthermore, employment growth can only be increased if the country has a robust manufacturing sector. Thus, multiplier effects cause increases in employment not only in the manufacturing sector, but also in other sectors that are linked to it. For instance, growth of the automobile industry increases the demand for the auto components industry and the growth of the mobile handsets industry may jump-start the local manufacturing of a whole host of semiconductor devices, electronic components, and so on.

The fact that India's manufacturing sector is very small can be gauged from two statistics: in 2014, the size of India's manufacturing sector (in terms of constant manufacturing value added) is only about 13 percent of that of China, and further, the share of the sector in India's GDP has been stagnating at around 15 percent even when the sector has been growing at about 10 percent in real terms, especially since the late 2000s. Also, India is not known for exporting manufactured goods and is therefore, externally speaking, not competitive for a number of manufactured goods. All these factors have forced the government to consider various ways and means of rejuvenating its manufacturing sector, thus enabling India to become more innovative. It is projected that India will significantly raise manufacturing's share of GDP to about a quarter of the country's entire GDP by 2022. This thinking process started with the set-up of a new institutional establishment, the National Manufacturing Competitiveness Council (NMCC) in 2004. The Council is, in its own words, 'an interdisciplinary and autonomous body at the highest level to serve as a policy forum for credible and coherent policy initiatives.' After much deliberation, in 2006 the Council came up with the 'National Strategy for Manufacturing.' The strategy paper identified a set of twelve challenges facing the sector. These challenges included general framework conditions such as ensuring macroeconomic stability, strengthening education and skill, infrastructure development of specific policies that deal with promoting investments in technology and innovations to increase the usage of ICT, and improving firm-level and specific industry-level competitiveness. The strategy paper made a number of general as well as specific recommendations to deal with the challenges[1] (see National Manufacturing Competitiveness Council, 2006, pp. 59–78). Following the publication of this paper, the Indian government also announced a number of sector-specific policies, for example those relating to the automotive and telecommunications industries, just to name two. Further, a number of general framework conditions were created through successive union budgets. A case in point is the raising of the research and development (R&D) subsidy scheme to 200 percent of the volume of R&D conducted and extending it to all industries through recent union budgets. Furthermore, The Ministry of Commerce published a strategy paper for doubling exports during the three-year period from 2011–12 through 2013–14. This export strategy also covered a number of manufactured goods in sectors such as engineering, pharmaceutical, textiles, synthetic fibers, polymers, etc.

Since the turn of the twenty-first century, many Indian companies have become important market leaders in their specific (and narrow) areas of operation. These range from low-technology-based laminated tube manufacturing, to medium-technology-based compact cars and auto parts, to high-technology-based pharmaceuticals. Table 4.1 presents a list of Indian firms that have become important market leaders in their respective industries. While the list of these niche areas is diverse, there are some concentrations in two specific areas of manufacturing: the automotive and pharmaceutical industries.

Table 4.1   Indian firms that are considered to be market leaders

Company	Industry
Arcelor Mittal	Steel
Infosys	Information and technology
Bharat Forge	Automotive components
Essel Propack	Manufacturer of laminated and plastic tubes, medical devices
Hindalco	Aluminum manufacturer
Mahindra & Mahindra	Tractor manufacturer
Hidesign	Leather products
Marico	Consumer packaged goods (coconut-based hair oils, hair creams, and gels)
Godrej	Consumer product and engineering company
VIP	Luggage manufacturer
Suzlon	Wind energy
TML	Engineering (automobile)
Tata Steel	Materials
Tata Consultancy Services	Information technology
Tata Tea	Consumer products (tea)
Tata Chemicals	Chemicals
Taj Hotels	Hotels

Source: Adapted from Kumar et al. (2009).

Although India is not considered to be a manufacturing powerhouse, since the turn of the twenty-first century two manufacturing industries have come to occupy an important place in the country's manufacturing establishment. These are the automotive and pharmaceutical industries. Although the technologies involved are different, given that one is mechanical engineering based and other is chemistry based, these industries have been two of the fastest-growing manufacturing industries in India. These industries are increasingly globalized and also, relatively speaking, innovative. Table 4.2 maps out the relative size of the two industries in terms of sales, exports, and export intensity.

The pharmaceutical industry is much more export-intensive than the automotive industry, which basically caters to the domestic market. However, even during the short period under consideration, the export intensity of the automotive industry has shown some appreciable increases.

India is slowly becoming an important player in the field of automotives, especially markets for small trucks, compact cars, tractors, and motorcycles. At the same time, the country has established itself as a highly

Table 4.2   The Indian automobile industry vs its pharmaceutical industry

Year	Automobiles		Pharmaceutical	
	Sales (USD millions)	Exports (number of vehicles)	Sales (USD millions)	Exports (USD millions)
2005–06	–	806 222 (0.83)	13 512.04	4 685.81 (34.68)
2006–07	30 476	1 011 529 (9.12)	17 179.10	6 207.24 (36.13)
2007–08	36 612	1 238 333 (11.41)	18 457.69	6 747.29 (36.56)
2008–09	33 250	1 530 594 (13.70)	19 682.92	8 226.65 (41.80)
2009–10	43 296	1 804 426 (12.84)	22 855.82	9 284.83 (40.62)
2010–11	58 583	2 319 956 (12.97)	–	10 188.27
2011–12	–	2 910 055 (14.29)	–	–

Note: Figures in parentheses represent export intensity. Export intensity of automobiles are calculated by export/production*100.

Source: Department of Pharmaceuticals, Society of Indian Automobile Manufacturers.

credible supplier of generic drugs across the globe to both developed and developing countries.

As far as the automotive sector is concerned, by 2010 India had become the largest tractor manufacturer, the second-largest two-wheeler manufacturer, the fifth-largest commercial vehicle manufacturer, and the eleventh-largest car manufacturer in the world. Although there are a large number of multinational corporations (MNCs) operating in India's industrial sector, in terms of sales revenue shares, the market is evenly divided between domestic and foreign firms.

Since the mid 1980s, Indian pharmaceutical firms have accumulated considerable technological capability in manufacturing generic versions of off-patented drugs. Currently (c. 2014), it accounts for approximately 10 percent of the global pharmaceutical industry in volume and 1.4 percent in value terms. India's growing leadership position in this industry is also evident from a number of indicators such as significant increases in the number of Abbreviated New Drug Applications (ANDAs) granted to Indian pharmaceutical firms in the USA, significant increases in exports R&D intensity, and also in the number of patents granted to pharmaceutical inventors from India at the United States Patent and Trademark Office (USPTO).

In this context, the purpose of this chapter is to identify and discuss an Indian firm in the country's automotive industry that has achieved a leadership position not only among its peers in India, but also among its counterparts elsewhere in the world. The specific focus herein is to identify the sources of achievement that contributed to leadership positions held by these enterprises from an emerging economy. Sources identified in the relevant literature as the contributing factors include the role of the key entrepreneur behind the enterprise in question, the technological capability building and learning strategies employed by these firms, and the enabling system-specific factors from the sectoral system as well as the national system in which the sector is situated.

4.3   INDIA'S AUTOMOTIVE INDUSTRY

In this section, we consider the growth of India's automotive industry. And we go on to discuss the leadership position achieved by one of the domestic enterprises, namely TML.

Our choice of the automotive industry is based on the following facts: (i) the industry has a growing share in outward foreign direct investment (OFDI) from India, in fact the primary reason for some acquisitions in other input industries may ultimately be traced to the automotive industry; (ii) with a compound average annual growth rate of about 15 percent since the late 2000s, the automotive sector is justifiably described as the next sunrise sector of the Indian economy;[2] (iii) the value added contribution of the automotive sector to India's GDP has doubled from 2.77 percent in 1992–93 to about 6 percent in 2010–11 and the industry provides direct and indirect employment to about 13.1 million people; (iv) in 2010–11, the total turnover of the industry stood at USD 73 billion and its contribution to manufacturing GDP and excise duty collection was 22 percent and 21 percent, respectively; and (v) in 2010–11, India became the sixth-largest vehicle manufacturer in the world. This recent growth of the industry may be explained to a certain extent by its inorganic growth in terms of acquisitions abroad. Automotive and pharmaceuticals are two manufacturing industries that account for a significant share of manufacturing OFDI from India and there are indications that these investments are showing an increasing trend. All these factors make the automotive industry a good candidate for in-depth industrial leadership analysis.

4.3.1   Development and Structure of the Automotive Industry

The automotive industry consists of two separate industries: (i) the automobile industry and (ii) the automobile components or parts industry. The automobile industry in turn has three subsectors: (i) two-wheelers, (ii) three-wheelers, and (iii) four-wheelers (passenger vehicles and commercial vehicles).

Table 4.3   Three phases in the evolution of India's automotive industry

Phases	Main features
Phase 1: 1947–83	● Closed market ● Growth of market limited by domestic supply ● Very few innovations, outdated model, fuel inefficient ● Number of firms: 5
Phase 2: 1983–93	● Joint venture between government of India and Suzuki to form Maruti Udyog ● Number of firms: 6
Phase 3: 1993–	● Industry delicensed in 1993 ● Major MNC original equipment manufacturers (OEMS) commenced assembly in India ● Implementation of the value added tax (VAT) ● Imports allowed from April 2001 ● Number of firms: >35

Source: India Brand Equity Foundation (2010).

Researchers have found it expedient to map out the history of the Indian automotive industry from 1947 until now, dividing it into three phases. See Table 4.3 for a summary of these three phases.

4.3.2   Trends in Domestic Production

Production of automobiles (in numbers) has doubled during the period under consideration, as shown in Table 4.4. While the growth rate of output had plummeted, due essentially to the financial crisis in 2008–09, it picked up in all categories the following year and indications are that this high growth rate was maintained during 2010–11 as well.

This leads to two important findings. First, two-wheelers account for the lion's share of production (in numbers), followed by passenger vehicles (cars). Thus, the driving force behind the spectacular growth of this industry is the output of two-wheelers (motorcycles and scooters) and cars. The second finding is that, over time, India has become a base for exports of automobiles. Once again, cars account for the majority of the exports. In fact, India has become a base for the manufacture of compact cars.

Table 4.4 Trends in production of India's automobile industry (in numbers)

	Passenger vehicles	Growth rate (%)	Commercial vehicles	Growth rate (%)	Three-wheelers	Growth rate (%)	Two-wheelers	Growth rate (%)	Grand Total	Growth rate (%)
2003–04	989560	–	275040	–	356223	–	5622741	–	7243564	–
2004–05	1209876	22.26	353703	28.60	374445	5.12	6529829	16.13	8467853	16.90
2005–06	1309300	8.22	391083	10.57	434423	16.02	7608697	16.52	9743503	15.06
2006–07	1545223	18.02	519982	32.96	556126	28.01	8466666	11.28	11087997	13.80
2007–08	1777583	15.04	549006	5.58	500660	–9.97	8026681	–5.20	10853930	–2.11
2007–09	1838593	3.43	416870	–24.07	497020	–0.73	8419792	4.90	11172275	2.93
2007–10	2351240	27.88	566608	35.92	619930	24.56	10512889	24.86	14049830	25.76

Source: Compiled from the website of the Society of Indian Automobile Manufacturers, http://www.siamindia.com/.

4.3.3   Trends in Exports

Exports have also registered some appreciable increases, as shown in Figure 4.1. Overall, about 11 percent of the total output is exported, although the export intensity varies across the various categories, ranging from as high as 24 percent in the case of three-wheelers to as low as 9 percent in the case of commercial vehicles. Much of the exports, in quantitative terms, are accounted for by cars and motorcycles, reflecting their proportionate share in domestic production. What is interesting is that India has now become *a* base for the manufacture and export of compact cars.

Here, we focus primarily on the vehicle-producing sector. This sector consists of domestic firms as well as affiliates of a large number of MNCs. The industry was largely domestic for a long period of time. MNCs' entry to the industry started with the joint venture Maruti Suzuki and their plans to build small compact cars. Gradually, a number of MNCs have established their manufacturing activities in India. Maruti itself has diluted its domestic equity held by the union government in favor of a larger shareholding by its parent firm. Over time and especially since 1991, there has been entry to the industry by a large number of MNCs. MNCs are focusing much more on passenger cars and motorcycles, while the domestic firms have their presence across the entire spectrum of vehicles. In terms of total sales, the industry is roughly divided between the two segments, although on an average, since the mid 2000s, the domestic firms have held a slightly higher share. This is largely due to the fact that the two largest commercial vehicle firms are in the domestic sector. The comparison is shown in Table 4.5.

On the export front, the foreign firms not only have a higher share of sales, but also higher export intensity as well, on average two times that of the domestic firms. This demonstrates that the MNCs are actually using India as a base for their exports.

4.3.4   Innovations in the Automotive Industry

There have been many instances of new product development in the Indian automotive industry. Some examples are as follows:

- The development of the *Nano*, the innovative USD 2250 car, has demonstrated India's ability to design and innovate;
- *Reva*, India's first electric car, is also an example of design and innovation;
- Companies like M&M and the Hero Group are planning to develop electric vehicles;

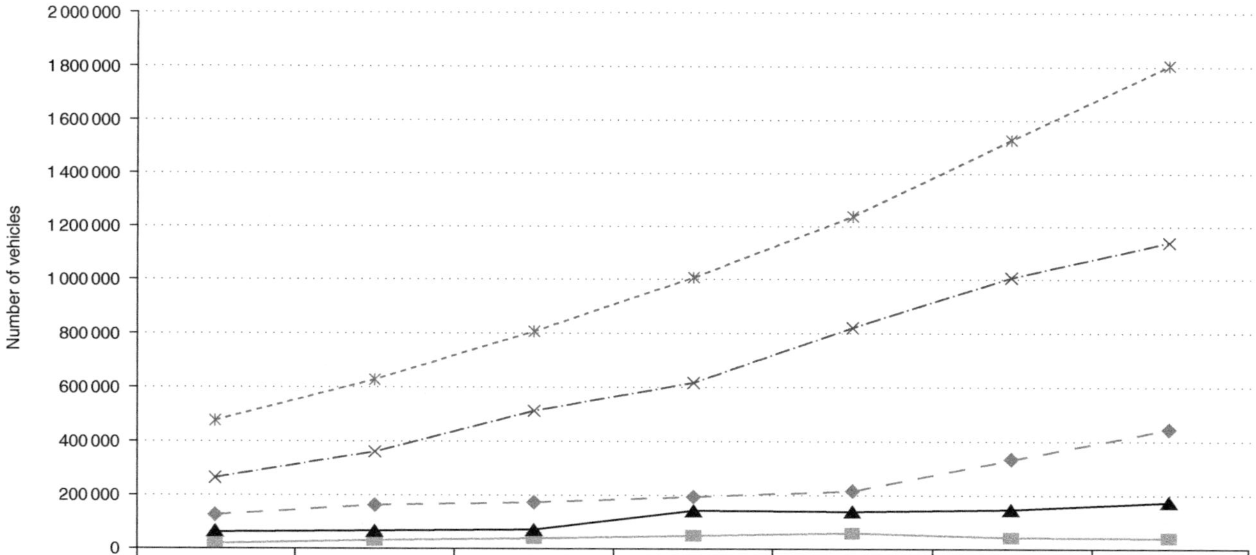

	2003–04	2004–05	2005–06	2006–07	2007–08	2008–09	2009–10
Passenger vehicles	129 291	166 402	175 572	198 452	218 401	335 729	446 146
Commercial vehicles	17 432	29 940	40 600	49 537	58 994	42 625	45 007
Three-wheelers	68 144	66 795	76 881	143 896	141 225	148 066	173 282
Two-wheelers	265 052	366 407	513 169	619 644	819 713	1 004 174	1 140 184
Grand total	479 919	629 544	806 222	1 011 529	1 238 333	1 530 594	1 804 619

Number of vehicles

Source: Society of Indian Automobile Manufacturers, http://www.siamindia.com/.

Figure 4.1   Trends in exports of automotive from India, 2003–04 to 2009–10

77

Table 4.5 *Sales and exports of automobiles: domestic vs MNCs (Rs in Crores)*

Year	Exports of goods (Rs Crores)		Sales (Rs Crores)		Exports of goods to sales (%)		Ratio of domestic to MNC	
	Domestic	MNC	Domestic	MNC	Domestic	MNC	Exports	Sales
2000	1077.46	2433.72	22298.37	19519.52	4.83	12.47	0.44	1.14
2001	1197.82	2501.76	21883.20	20993.81	5.47	11.92	0.48	1.04
2002	1001.55	2157.87	22122.72	19789.59	4.53	10.90	0.46	1.12
2003	1001.57	3229.19	26227.74	21440.01	3.82	15.06	0.31	1.22
2004	1699.89	2428.32	34330.25	30308.19	4.95	8.01	0.70	1.13
2005	2535.77	3512.2	40455.42	39256.1	6.27	8.95	0.72	1.03
2006	3483.47	3726.4	47276.37	44637.8	7.37	8.35	0.93	1.06
2007	4540.04	4192.76	61429.95	53514.79	7.39	7.83	1.08	1.15
2008	7426.48	4891.48	75810.47	55992.37	9.80	8.74	1.52	1.35
2009	7593.78	27610.06	70464.44	63379.07	10.78	43.56	0.28	1.11
2010	7389.76	17246.04	89928.63	55402.27	8.22	31.13	0.43	1.62
Average	–	–	–	–	6.67	15.17	0.67	1.18

Source: Compiled from CMIE Prowess Dataset.

- In the commercial vehicles space, Tata Daewoo, a subsidiary of TML, has recently developed an LPG-based medium-sized commercial vehicle (4.5 ton), the *Novus*, which conforms to the Euro V emission norm;
- Ashok Leyland has developed India's first six-cylinder compressed natural gas (CNG) engine for buses that uses the multipoint fuel injection system and conforms to Euro IV emission standards; and
- Two-wheeler manufacturers Bajaj Auto, Hero Honda and Mahindra are in discussions with Energtek, a provider of absorbed natural gas products, for technology that will enable two-wheelers to run on natural gas instead of gasoline.

The automotive industry is one of the largest R&D spenders within India's industrial establishment, closely following the leader in this sphere, namely the pharmaceutical industry. See Table 4.6.

Although the automotive industry consists of domestic companies and MNCs, most new product development has come from the domestic companies. In order to examine this further, we analysed the two major costs of developing new technologies: in-house R&D expenditures and the cost of purchasing technology from abroad. The source of data for this exercise is the *CMIE Prowess Dataset*.

Two indicators are developed: (i) the R&D-to-sales ratio, signifying the research intensity of the sector as shown in Table 4.7; and (ii) the ratio of

Table 4.6   *Relative share of India's automotive industry in total private sector in-house R&D expenditures (Rs in Crores)*

	In-house R&D expenditure	Rate of growth (%)	R&D intensity	Total private sector industry	Auto industry as a share of private sector industry
1998–99	420.62		0.87	2177	19.32
1999–00	431.37	2.56	0.73	2178	19.80
2000–01	451.96	4.77	0.77	2411	18.74
2001–02	528.61	16.96	0.81	2787	18.96
2002–03	434.27	−17.85	0.77	2785	15.60
2003–04	546.50	25.84	0.80	3643	15.00
2004–05	862.80	57.88	0.99	5076	17.00
2005–06	1047.20	21.37	1.07	6268	16.71

Note: Rs 1 core = Rs 10 million.

Source: Department of Science and Technology (2009).

Table 4.7 *Research intensity: domestic vs foreign firms (values are in Rs Crores)*

Year	R&D expense (Rs Crores)		Sales (Rs Crores)		R&D to Sales (%)		Ratio of domestic to MNC	
	Domestic	MNC	Domestic	MNC	Domestic	MNC	R&D	Sales
2000	146.83	164.56	22 298.37	19 519.52	0.66	0.84	0.89	1.14
2001	159.31	77.45	21 883.20	20 993.81	0.73	0.37	2.06	1.04
2002	292.18	62.84	22 122.72	19 789.59	1.32	0.32	4.65	1.12
2003	364.79	51.47	26 227.74	21 440.01	1.39	0.24	7.09	1.22
2004	439.92	102.96	34 330.25	30 308.19	1.28	0.34	4.27	1.13
2005	751.54	123.24	40 455.42	39 256.1	1.86	0.31	6.10	1.03
2006	900.35	106	47 276.37	44 637.8	1.90	0.24	8.49	1.06
2007	1 301.71	103.39	61 429.95	53 514.79	2.12	0.19	12.59	1.15
2008	1 939.72	120.6	75 810.47	55 992.37	2.56	0.22	16.08	1.35
2009	2 663.34	154.6	70 464.44	63 379.07	3.78	0.24	17.23	1.11
2010	2 401.38	210.87	89 928.63	55 402.27	2.67	0.38	11.39	1.62
Average	–	–	–	–	*1.84*	*0.34*	*8.26*	*1.18*

Source: Compiled from the Prowess Database.

Table 4.8   Average propensity to adapt: foreign vs domestic firms

Year	R&D expenses (Rs Crores)		Forex spending royalty/ technical knowhow (Rs Crores)		Average propensity to adapt, R&D to tech knowhow (%)	
	Domestic	MNC	Domestic	MNC	Domestic	MNC
2000	146.83	164.56	53.95	164.7	2.72	1.00
2001	159.31	77.45	51.66	208.11	3.08	0.37
2002	292.18	62.84	63.25	224.68	4.62	0.28
2003	364.79	51.47	51.26	330.29	7.12	0.16
2004	439.92	102.96	44.69	377.08	9.84	0.27
2005	751.54	123.24	114.34	657.86	6.57	0.19
2006	900.35	106	111.77	879.73	8.06	0.12
2007	1 301.71	103.39	227.03	1 134.65	5.73	0.09
2008	1 939.72	120.6	247.89	1 258.95	7.82	0.10
2009	2 663.34	154.6	313.61	1 554.52	8.49	0.10
2010	2 401.38	210.87	278.75	1 488.66	8.61	0.14
Average	–	–	–	–	*6.61*	*0.26*

Source: Compiled from the Prowess Database.

R&D expenditures to the cost of purchasing technology from abroad, signifying the relative importance of domestic technology-generating efforts as shown in Table 4.8. These ratios are presented separately for domestic companies and MNCs.

Although R&D expenditures for both sets of firms have increased, it is the domestic firms that have registered not only faster growth rates in the absolute levels of intramural R&D investments, but also in their intensity. By contrast, the R&D intensity of MNCs has hardly shown an increase, but rather just inter-year fluctuations.

Consequently, the main source of technology for the foreign firms is the technical knowhow they import from their respective parent firms, and as such, their ratio of in-house R&D to technology purchases from abroad (referred to as the average propensity to adapt) is significantly less than unity in all the years. This implies that that the amount spent on in-house R&D is significantly less than the amount spent on importing technology from abroad, and is also significantly less than that for domestic firms. See Table 4.8.

4.4   WHY DO WE CONSIDER TML AS A MARKET LEADER?

As mapped out in Chapter 1, our definition of a market leader implies fulfilling three conditions: (i) the firm in question must occupy a substantial portion of the market for its main product; (ii) it must have significant global reach; and (iii) it must be innovative. In the following, we argue that TML fulfills all three conditions admirably well.

4.4.1   Market Share

TML has a very high market share in the truck and bus categories. In this segment, its share in terms of value is about 60 percent, primarily due to its dominance in the truck category. Although it has a wide range of cars, from the cheapest *Nano* to the most luxurious Jaguar and Land Rover, its rank in terms of market share in the passenger car segments is only third. The main distinguishing aspect of TML from every other company in the industry is that it has the widest range of vehicles, both passenger and commercial, and its vehicles range from ordinary to luxury models. Another interesting aspect of TML is the growth in its revenue from just under USD 2 billion in 2002 to about USD 39 billion in 2014. Figure 4.2 shows the trends in total revenue up to 2011. Therefore, in terms of market share and sales revenue, TML is clearly a market leader.

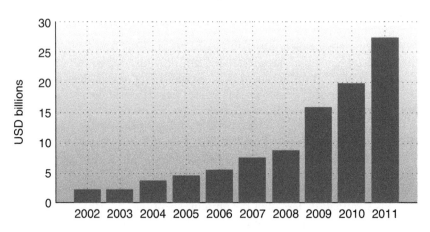

Source: http://www.investmentu.com/article/detail/27806/tata-motors-air-powered-cars#. VNRGSFWUc_N (accessed February 6, 2014).

Figure 4.2   Trends in sales revenue of Tata Motors (USD billions), 2002–11

4.4.2 Global Reach

Global reach exists in terms of exports and acquisitions abroad. TML has an extensive global reach on both these counts, as the following subsections explain in detail.

4.4.2.1 Exports

TML has also been expanding its global reach through exports since 1961. Its commercial and passenger vehicles are already being marketed in several countries throughout Europe, Africa, the Middle East, South East Asia, South Asia, and South America. It has franchise/joint venture assembly operations in Kenya, Bangladesh, Ukraine, Russia, Senegal, and South Africa. Over one decade (namely the years 2000–10), and despite serious international competition, the company managed to maintain an average export intensity of 8 percent per annum.

4.4.2.2 Acquisitions abroad

TML, the first company from India's engineering sector to be listed on the New York Stock Exchange (September 2004), has also emerged as an international automobile company. Through subsidiaries and associate companies, TML has established operations in the UK, South Korea, Thailand, and Spain. Among these operations is Jaguar Land Rover, a business comprising two iconic British brands that was acquired in 2008. In 2004 TML acquired the Daewoo Commercial Vehicles Company, South Korea's second largest truck-maker. The rechristened Tata Daewoo Commercial Vehicles Company has launched several new products in the Korean market, while also exporting these products to several international markets. Today, two-thirds of heavy commercial vehicle exports out of South Korea are from Tata Daewoo. In 2005 TML acquired a 21 percent stake in Hispano Carrocera, a reputable Spanish bus and coach manufacturer, and acquired the remaining 79 percent stake in 2009. Hispano's presence is being expanded into other markets. In 2006, TML formed a joint venture with Brazil-based Marcopolo, a market leader in bodywork manufacturing for buses and coaches (the case of this firm is discussed in Chapter 7), to manufacture fully built buses and coaches for India and other select international markets. In 2006 TML entered into a joint venture with the Thonburi Automotive Assembly Plant Company of Thailand to manufacture and market the company's pick-up vehicles in Thailand. TML's new plant in Thailand produces the Xenon pick-up truck, which was launched in Thailand in 2008. TML is thus one of the leading MNCs from India.

4.4.3   Generator of Innovations

TML has always relied on its strong in-house R&D center. R&D expenditures both in absolute terms and research intensity have been increasing over the years. A number of new products have been launched, in both cars and small trucks. By introducing a compact and most inexpensive car, TML pioneered the concept of frugal engineering in vehicle production and this is one of the primary reasons it has become an important leader in the world automotive industry itself. Additionally, TML has many 'firsts' to its credit, including the *Indica* (India's first indigenously manufactured car), the *Sumo* (India's first sports utility vehicle), the *Ace* (India's first indigenously manufactured mini-truck), the *Nano* (the world's most affordable car), and its latest effort, the *Indica EV* (an electric version of the best-selling small car for European markets).

In short we consider TML to be a market leader in India's automotive industry because:

- it accounts for a substantial portion of the market for automotive vehicles in India;
- it is a highly globalized company with strong exports, manufacturing and R&D presence in a large number of countries including Western European countries; and
- it is highly innovative, primarily in commercial vehicles but also in passenger cars.

4.5   ORIGINS OF LEADERSHIP POSITION

How did TML, an Indian firm that had a rather long history of being protected by the state from either domestic or foreign competition, manage to become a leader of sorts in its narrow specific areas of operation? Three such factors can be identified. The first regards entrepreneurship. TML is an important constituent of one of India's leading business houses that are professionally managed, while at the same time the firm has access to guidance given by a 'family' of key entrepreneurs whose actions have been important not just for firms in the Tata household, but also for the growth and performance of India's industrialization as a whole. Second is the internal strategy employed by the enterprise. And third are the benefits that it derives from its sectoral system of innovation. Regarding the internal factors, two aspects stand out: (i) continuous investments in in-house R&D; and (ii) strategic acquisition of knowledge assets abroad and effecting the transfer of knowledge to the patent company from these acquired

assets. These two approaches are not mutually exclusive but rather complementary to each other. We discuss these factors in some detail below.

4.5.1 Firm-Level Factors

4.5.1.1 Vibrant entrepreneurship

TML is one of the constituents of one of India's largest conglomerate
business groups, the house of Tatas. The Tatas have always played a very
important role in the industrialization of the country and were instrumental in the establishment of several prestigious science and technology
institutions, such as the famous Indian Institute of Science at Bangalore.
TML also benefited from the strong and professional leadership provided
by a set of western-educated CEOs belonging to the Tata family. The Tata
house is highly diversified with manufacturing units producing a variety of
goods from mineral water to steel to aerospace products as well as service
providers in computer and information services. There is also a fair amount
of synergy between the units. For example, certain recent acquisitions have
resulted in the group having control over the raw materials required for the
production of automotive vehicles. The expertise of Corus in making the
various grades of steel used for automobiles and in aerospace has proved
useful to TML. The company is also highly vertically integrated with its
own production of machine tools. TAL Manufacturing Solutions Ltd,
a wholly owned subsidiary of TML, has the technological capability to
design and build machine tools, material handling systems, test rigs, painting systems, assembly and process lines, robotic welding solutions, fixtures
and tooling, fluid power solutions, etc. Each of these aspects has made
TML extremely competitive.

4.5.1.2 Learning, capabilities, and strategies

The foundation of TML's growth over the last 50 years is a deep understanding of economic stimuli along with customer needs and the ability
to translate such needs into customer-desired offerings through cutting-
edge R&D. With over 3000 engineers and scientists, TML's Engineering
Research Centre, established in 1966, has enabled the development of pioneering technologies and products. Today TML has R&D centers in India
(Pune, Jamshedpur, Lucknow, Dharwad), South Korea, Spain, and the
UK. Its in-house R&D expenditures have shown sharp increases both in
absolute terms and in terms of their intensity. Throughout the decade that
began in 2000, on average TML spent about 2 percent of its sales revenue
on in-house R&D, the highest among Indian automotive firms. Given the
highly professional nature of TML, learning and capability building have
become institutionalized rather than person-dependent. Its growth as an

industrial leader rests upon two major strategies that TML put in place right at the beginning and that have continued since the mid 1990s. These two strategies, which complement each other, are: (i) considerable expansion of R&D activity not only in terms of its depth but also in terms of its spatial expansion; and (ii) many strategic acquisitions abroad that have resulted in TML's possession of a range of technologies and capabilities that it did not have previously. We discuss these two strategies in more detail below.

4.5.1.3   Strong in-house R&D

In-house R&D at TML has three clear approaches (Mishra, 2012). They are:

1. *New product development* This approach includes understanding the requirements of a product, listening to the needs of the customer, creating an engineering concept followed by detailed engineering, testing, and validation processes to prove that the concept can be executed, then releasing the production tooling, finding the parts, and finalizing the manufacturing process to build the product;
2. *Acquiring new technologies* This approach includes acquisitions of technologies, particularly those TML does not have but are available in the rest of the world. For instance, a new generation of suspension for cars. While this approach is about acquiring new technologies and working with universities and vendors, it does not include development of breakthrough technologies. The two approaches are therefore complementary to each other. Acquiring new technologies from abroad and developing new technologies through working with local universities and vendors are complementary to each other. In other words, the firm first acquires new technologies from abroad and then works with local universities and vendors to adapt those acquired technologies to local usage conditions.
3. *Developing new technologies* This approach includes true R&D and is also the one that carries maximum risk. It involves research in anything from materials to electronics and alternative fuels. Ideas generated at this stage may not always come to fruition. The R&D is implemented by creating small groups that are then given a focused project. This could be done by way of linkages, and over time a group may emerge as a center of excellence in a particular field.

In fact TML's total innovation expenditure intensity, proxied by the sum of in-house R&D investments, imports of disembodied and embodied technology, and then expressed as a percentage of its sales turnover, has

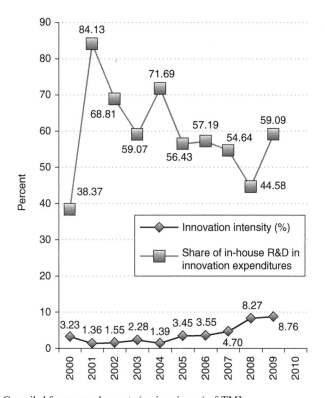

Source: Compiled from annual reports (various issues) of TML.

Figure 4.3 Trends in innovation expenditures of TML, 2000–10

tripled during the period. Among the three components of innovation expenditures, in-house R&D still accounts for a majority of the share, as shown in Figure 4.3. The increases in innovation expenditures have been accompanied by the market introduction of a number of new vehicles, ranging from small cars to large trucks.

Tata also has an R&D service company called Tata Technologies (TT). TT was founded in 1989 and is a global leader in engineering services outsourcing and product-development IT services to the global manufacturing industry. The company is a strategic partner for developing complete vehicles (VPD group), engineering subsystems and components (E&D), managing the NPI process and collaborative engineering (PLM), and tying together information created and used throughout the extended manufacturing enterprise (ESG). Tata Technologies is headquartered in Singapore with regional headquarters offices in the United States (Novi, Michigan),

India (Pune), and the UK (Coventry). TT has an office in Thailand as well. This is yet another example of an outward investment venture through which considerable knowledge transfers do take place, although the knowledge generation is actually through consulting agreements with clients located in these countries.

4.5.1.4 Illustrations of new product development

It was TML that developed the *Light Commercial Vehicle*, India's first indigenously developed sports utility vehicle, and, in 1998, the *Tata Indica*, India's first fully indigenously developed passenger car. Within two years of its launch, the *Tata Indica* became India's largest selling car in its segment. In 2005, TML created a new segment by launching the *Tata Ace*, India's first indigenously developed mini-truck. As of February 2015, the firm had sold 100 000 *Tata Ace Zip*s.

In January 2008, TML unveiled its 'People's Car,' the *Tata Nano*, which India and the world had been looking forward to. The *Tata Nano* was subsequently launched in India, as planned, in March 2009. In a development that was a first for the global automobile industry, the *Nano* brought the comfort and safety of a car within the reach of thousands of families. The standard version was been priced at Rs 100 000 (excluding VAT and transportation cost). However, as Figure 4.3 shows, the sales of *Nano* cars after reaching maximum sales of 9000 cars in July 2010 had plummeted to just 500 or so cars by November 2010. Several reasons have been advanced for the lackluster performance of the *Nano*, lack of proper advertising being one such factor. Of late, Tata have started a serious advertising campaign to regain lost numbers but unfortunately that does not seem to have reversed the sagging sales figures of the *Nano*.

In May 2009, TML ushered in a new era in the Indian automobile industry, in-keeping with its pioneering tradition, by unveiling its new range of world standard trucks called *Prima*. With the *Prima*'s power, speed, carrying capacity, operating economy, and trims, they established new benchmarks in India and matched the best in the world for performance at a lower life-cycle cost. TML is equally focused on environment-friendly technologies for emissions and alternative fuels. It has developed electric and hybrid vehicles for both personal and public transportation. It has also been implementing several environment-friendly technologies in manufacturing processes, significantly enhancing resource conservation.

An interesting aspect of the firm's innovative position was its introduction of the compact *Tata Nano* car. But the sales of these cars have shown some cyclicality, as shown in Figure 4.4.

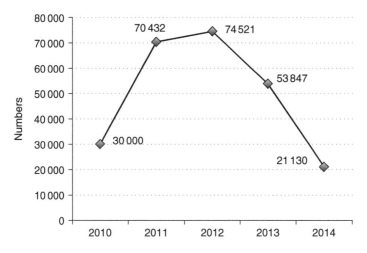

Source: Compiled from annual reports of TML.

Figure 4.4 Sales of Nano *cars, 2010–14*

4.5.1.5 Foreign acquisitions and knowledge transfer as an important strategy

TML had ambitions of, over time, becoming a global player in the automotive industry. However, the company lacked certain types of technologies in large trucks, luxury cars, and off-road vehicles. As part of TML's strategy, in 2004 the company acquired the truck division of Daewoo Commercial Vehicle Company for about USD 102 million and rechristened it as Tata Daewoo Commercial Vehicles (TDWCV). The Tata Group's acquisition presents an uncommon example of how an Indian firm acquired a firm in South Korea while overcoming a series of cultural and other barriers. Three specific motives can be attributed to this acquisition: (i) access to the R&D capabilities of Daewoo and knowledge transfer from South Korea to India and, in some cases, from India to South Korea; (ii) access to new markets in the Asian region especially, to support Tata Motors' globalization drive; and (iii) the ability to develop a complementary product range to ensure faster time-to-market.

In the following, we further discuss the Tata–Daewoo investment in terms of the deal becoming a conduit for knowledge transfer between the acquirer (TML, TM) and the target (Daewoo Commercial Vehicles Company, DWCV). In order to appreciate this, we start by presenting some basic facts about DWCV. The Daewoo Group established DWCV in 1982 and it became the second-largest truck manufacturer in South Korea.

Table 4.9   Comparison between TM and DWCV

	DWCV	Tata
Major market	South Korea	India
Export intensity (%)	5	10
Product range (gross vehicle weight)	Heavy trucks (15 to 45 tons)	Light and medium trucks (20 to 40 tons)
Engine types	210 to 420 hp	50 to 210 hp
Engine source	Cummins	In-house, joint venture with Cummins
Major drive train components	Sourced externally	Internal manufacture

Source: Kadle (2007).

However, the bankruptcy of the Daewoo Group led to the bankruptcy of Daewoo Motors in 2000. The car business of Daewoo Motors was sold to General Motors (GM) in 2002. DWCV had an installed capacity of 20 000 vehicles from a very modern plant built in 1995. The firm produced more than 90 truck models in the heavy commercial vehicle range (210–400 HP engines). Table 4.9 compares DWCV and Tata in terms of a number of parameters.

TM's acquisition of DWCV has led to knowledge transfer between the two companies. For instance, TM could obtain the technology to design and manufacture heavier trucks, of 300 HP and above. This partnership led to the introduction of the *Novus* brand of trucks into the Indian market. These trucks can be used for heavy-duty applications and can therefore be used in mines and on construction sites. A significant advantage of the *Novus* is the non-computerized engine which can be easily serviced almost anywhere. Meanwhile, knowledge transfer from TM to TDWCV resulted in TDWCV launching a new range of medium trucks in 2006. This was TDWCV's first major product launch since 2000. TDWCV was also able to increase its exports significantly following 2004–05. Furthermore, the company was able to increase its domestic market share from 25 percent to 28 percent in the case of heavy commercial vehicles and achieved a domestic market share of 13.5 percent in the case of medium commercial vehicles. Moreover, both firms were able to pool their competences and jointly develop a 'World Truck.' For some time, TM had been keen on launching a large truck for global markets. The Daewoo purchase gave TM an opportunity to leverage Daewoo's skills and technology in the heavy commercial vehicles segment and fast-forward its dreams of introducing a top-end product. Furthermore, two more truck technologies developed by TDWCV were transferred to TM, the 'Prima' and 'Ultra' series of trucks.

4.5.2   Sector-Level Factors

In order to discuss the Sectoral System of Innovation (SSI) of the sector, we invoke the version of the framework that is due to Malerba (2005). The SSI of the sector consists of three major building blocks: (i) mastering the sectoral knowledge base; (ii) the presence of capable actors and links with advanced networks; and (iii) effective sectoral institutions.

4.5.2.1   Mastering the knowledge base

According to Sagar and Chandra (2004), the Indian automobile industry has seen rapid technological changes since the mid 1990s in terms of product characteristics as well as manufacturing processes. Furthermore, according to them, these deepening technological changes were not confined to vehicle manufacturers, but also had spillovers to the auto parts manufacturers as well. The main technological changes in the automotive industry were mainstreaming of contemporary technology, improvements in manufacturing practices, higher levels of indigenization and increased local sourcing of parts, deepening of technological capabilities, and improvements in service and maintenance practices. The extent to which each of these technological changes happened is discussed in detail by Sagar and Chandra (ibid.).

4.5.2.2   Effective sectoral institutions

We begin with a discussion on structure of the industry that will aid us in developing some informed opinions about the lead firms and institutions in the industry. India's automotive industry consists of both domestic and foreign enterprises. Up until 1991 the industry was a closed one, with very little competition either domestically or from international sources, and then, in that year, the industry was opened to foreign competition. With the lowering of barriers to entry, several new foreign firms entered India's automotive industry, particularly in the passenger vehicle segment. This increased competition from new foreign competitors seems to have forced the domestic incumbents to pull up their socks and climb the technological ladder. In fact, one can see a number of new innovations defined both in terms of a new breed of vehicles (for example, the Tata *Nano* and Mahindra *Scorpio*), emanating from the industry subsequent to the entry of MNCs and the competition that ensued between the MNCs and the domestic incumbents. An interesting aspect of TML is that it has resorted to a variety of strategies to acquire technologies from abroad. However, given the rigidities in the market for especially disembodied technologies, the firms have had to employ a variety of rather unusual strategies. This included the employment of foreign consultants and, in some cases, taking over foreign firms that had the necessary technologies that domestic firms were interested in possessing. This external integration of the firms with the rest of the world is an important characteristic of the SSI of the Indian automotive industry. A further distinguishing aspect of the industry is the virtual absence of a government research institute (GRI). In fact, the automotive industry is one of the few industries in India where there is no dedicated GRI.[3] Many of the technological needs are met by the industry itself through either its own in-house R&D efforts or by various technology purchase deals including, as noted before, through acquisition of firms abroad. The most critical intervention of India's government thus far in the automotive sector has come in the form of an ambitious project on setting up world-class automotive testing and R&D infrastructure in the country, named the National Automotive Testing and R&D Infrastructure Project (NATRIP).[4] NATRIP envisaged the setting-up of world-class automotive testing and homologation facilities in India with a total investment of Rs 17 billion by 2011. The principal facilities have come up in the three automotive hubs of India, specifically the south, north, and west. Although the government had not been involved in charting the course of this industry in any precise manner, it began to do so from 2002 onward when an explicit auto policy was announced and was followed by an auto mission plan in 2006. The plan had certain specific targets to be achieved by 2016: (i) to continue as the largest tractor and three-wheeler manufacturer in the world; (ii) to continue as the second-largest two-wheeler manufacturer in the world; (iii) to emerge as the fifth-largest car producer (as compared to the seventh-largest at that time); (iv) to double the contribution of the automotive sector to GDP from around 5 percent in 2006 to 10 percent in 2016; (v) to provide direct and indirect employment to about 35 million persons; and (vi) to export USD 35 billion in automotive products by 2016. The main agencies for putting this strategy into operation were the lead domestic firms. It is against this strategy that one has to analyse the external strategies of leading firms such as TML. In this context, it is very interesting to note that industrial policy in India is rapidly changing from being general to becoming very specific, and from being reactive to becoming proactive. These changes are based on the realization that 'one size does not fit all' and that one needs to have specific targets and incentive systems for specific industries and, also, that policies must strengthen the hands of the private sector after it has demonstrated some actual successes.[4]

4.5.2.3 Sectoral-level government policies

India never had specific industrial policies for a long time. What it did have were general industrial policies not targeted at any specific industry with the notable exception of the pharmaceutical and electronics industries where there was always a sectoral-level policy in place. However, a major break with the past occurred in 2002 with the announcement of an automotive policy. The policy had the most proximate objective of establishing a globally competitive automotive industry in India and also of doubling its contribution to India's GDP by 2010 or so. In order to achieve these objectives, the policy suggested the following measures: (i) encourage FDI to the industry up to 100 percent through the automatic route; (ii) adjust import tariffs in a manner so as to facilitate development of manufacturing capabilities as opposed to mere assembly without giving undue protection; (iii) ensure a balanced transition to open trade; (iv) promote increased competition in the market and increase purchase options to the Indian customer; (v) rationalize the excise duty structure in such a way that it encourages chassis manufacturers to build complete trucks and buses; (vi) improve road infrastructures which will increase the demand for automotive vehicles and thereby, through increased size of the domestic market, will put pressure on domestic manufacturers to innovate; (vii) encourage investment in domestic R&D by essentially offering tax incentives to the manufacturers committing additional resources to in-house R&D; and (viii) develop environmental policies in terms of having more fuel-efficient and less polluting engines.

Many of the initiatives contained in the policy have been implemented through successive union budgets. For instance, the following measures have already been implemented:

- Encourage the automotive industry through a five-year extension of the 200 percent weighted deduction of R&D expenditures under the Income Tax Act and introduce the weighted deduction of 150 percent for expenditure on skills development. These measures will help the industry improve its products and performance.
- The increase in customs duty on cars and multi-utility vehicles (Mugs) valued above USD 40000 from 60 percent to 75 percent seems to be a step to encourage local manufacturing, value added, and employment.
- The concessional import duty on specified parts of hybrid vehicles has been extended to lithium ion batteries and other parts of hybrid vehicles. This will help the industry to achieve better cost efficiency.

The Indian government plans to push the supply of vehicles powered by electricity over the next eight years. It is expected that there will be a demand of 5 to 7 million electric vehicles by 2020. The government also plans to introduce fuel-efficiency ratings for automobiles to encourage the sale of cars that consume less petrol or diesel.

The rapid improvements in infrastructure, huge domestic market, increasing purchasing power, established financial market, and stable corporate governance framework have made India a favorable destination for investment by major players in the global auto industry, as per the Automotive Mission Plan (AMP) (2006–16). The AMP aims at doubling the contribution of the automotive sector in GDP by taking the turnover to USD 145 billion in 2016 with special emphasis on the export of small cars, Mugs, two- and three-wheelers, and auto components.

4.5.2.4　The role of increasing domestic demand for vehicles

No discussion of the contribution of the sectoral system is complete without drawing out the link between local demand and innovation. Increased local demand is best proxied by the increase in per capita income. This has led to the emergence of increasing purchasing power by a growing middle class, who are also known to be quite discerning. In real terms, based on 2004–05 prices, this demand has been growing at a rate of over 6 percent per annum since the mid 2000s (Central Statistical Organization, 2013). Further, the number of new vehicles registered has also been growing at an average annual rate of 10 percent per annum (Ministry of Road Transport and Highways, 2012). All these indicators point to a growing demand for automotive vehicles in the country. This growing market for new vehicles on an unprecedented scale from domestic and international sources has resulted in firms like TML increasing their market share.

Thus, given the changing structure of the industry in terms of increased competition between firms, co-evolution of proactive government policies favoring innovations, and strong growth in demand, there has been significant generation of innovations in the automotive industry, defined in terms of the development of a new breed of vehicles that are more energy-efficient and with lower emission levels. There have also been significant improvements in manufacturing processes in terms of using new automated production methods.

4.5.3　Country-Level Factors

The country-level factors identified in Section 4.2 as facilitating the emergence of industrial leaders are the following: (i) active public policies in support of specific industries; (ii) policies to unleash private entrepreneurship; (iii) changes in the education system; and (iv) untapped local markets. We discuss each of these seriatim.

4.5.3.1   Active public policies to support specific industries

As discussed earlier, a major break with the nature and type of industrial policies occurred in the country after 1991 and gathered momentum in the period following 2000. There has been a clear moving away from the rhetoric of 'one size fits all' policies to 'one size does *not* fit all' types of policies. Currently, India has a number of sector-specific policies with clear objectives to be achieved for each of those specific sectors. Instruments and institutional structures that are relevant for a specific sector suggested that the objectives set out in the applicable policy are to be achieved within a definite period of time. A number of policy documents that range from those relating to specific industries such as automobiles, biotechnology, chemicals, electronics, electrical equipment, information technology, and telecommunications, to a more general policy on manufacturing and science, technology and innovation policy, etc., were announced at a rather a feverish pitch. It is almost as if the underlying belief is that having *some* policy statements is better than no policy at all. Nonetheless, these policy exercises have had the positive effect of bringing in some strategic thinking with respect to very specific sectors. Strategic thinking is quite necessary for an important area like innovation. In this type of situation, where fast-changing technologies that require updating strategies successfully unfold in many countries, especially in Asia, it is essential for an emerging country like India to have a clearly articulated set of policy instruments and insti-tutions which can enable the country to achieve the kind of technological leadership that she is aspiring to have. This present exercise has been pre-ceded by a number of statements and quasi policy documents on innov-ation. Two examples of these so-called quasi policy statements could be mentioned. First is the aborted attempt at passing a National Innovation Act. Second is the rather long conversation that took place both inside and outside parliament to pass legislation to incentivize publicly funded R&D programmes (Protection and Utilisation of Public Funded Intellectual Property Bill, 2008). The recent 'Make in India' program takes the sector-specific approach to a more tractable regime, enabling specific sectors to emerge as important leaders.

4.5.3.2   Policies to unleash private entrepreneurship

Until the announcement of the new industrial policy statement of 1991, entry into Indian manufacturing was regulated through a variety of controls and especially the licensing policy. This erected a sort of barrier to entry and a consequence of this regulation was the lack of domestic competition between firms that led to the firms becoming very lethargic and not having any inclination or commitment to innovative activity. In fact it also encouraged the firms to look inward as the profits to be made in a sheltered and protected market would be significantly higher if they exported. All this has changed since the virtual abandoning of industrial licensing in 1991. This lowered the barriers to entry and facilitated large-scale entry not only by domestic firms, but also by MNCs. The entry of MNCs in India's automotive industry facilitated technology spillovers to domestic manufacturers through channels of competition and labor turn-over. Beginning in 2000, the state also actively encouraged Indian firms to go abroad and acquire knowledge assets, which could immediately improve their ownership of intangibles such as knowhow, trademarks, etc. In fact this proactive policy of removing the fetters to the evolution and growth of private-sector firms was an important facilitating factor for firms such as TML, allowing them to seize the opportunity and grow faster.

4.5.3.3   Changes in the education sector

The change in the Indian higher education sector from favoring science education to engineering education was helpful to manufacturing indus-tries as it resulted in access to a veritable supply of engineers. However, doubts are often expressed about the employability of these engineers in view of their low-quality training. Most firms, of course, made up for this through having large and comprehensive in-company training programs, post recruitment. In fact the in-house training outfits of some of the Indian companies compare quite well to some western university types of training. For those Indian companies who wanted to grow, improved engineering education facilitated that growth by providing easy access, relatively speaking, to cheap engineers.

4.5.3.4   Untapped local markets

A fast-growing economy with a young working-age population ensured that per capita incomes were on the increase, improving the purchasing power of the average Indian consumer. Additionally, improvements in the financial sector, with banks providing cheap vehicle loans, also encouraged and improved the size of this untapped market. Physical improvements in road infrastructures were another important contributing factor.

4.6   CONCLUSIONS

In this chapter, we have demonstrated that TML is a market leader in India's fast-growing automotive industry. TML fulfills the three market-leadership conditions of market share, global reach, and innovation, exceptionally well. The origins of this leadership were described through a series of firm-, sector-, and country-level factors. However, maintaining leadership on a continuous basis for a reasonably long time may not be taken for granted. Leadership positions can easily be challenged in a globalized market. Potential new leaders may emerge that could challenge what is currently presumed to be TML's unassailable leadership position. For this reason, a leader must continue to be eternally vigilant from the innovation point of view. Fortunately, for TML continued innovation seems to be the accepted corporate strategy.

NOTES

1. Sunrise industries are those with high actual rates of growth over a long period of time. The information technology services industry is one such industry.
2. For a long time – until the 1990s – the automotive industry was not considered to be a priority industry as the government gave more importance to mass transportation technologies such as the railways. The Council of Scientific and Industrial Research (CSIR), which operates a network of 39 laboratories throughout the length and breadth of the country, does have one laboratory (by the name of the Central Mechanical Engineering Research Institute) that comes close to performing research on automotive technologies. This laboratory focuses almost entirely on machinery in general, although it does have capabilities and interest in farm machinery like tractors and in post-harvest technology. Its development of 20 hp Swaraj tractors is now famous. There is of course a cooperative research institute in the field of automotive technologies by the name of the Automotive Research Association of India (ARAI). However, recently the government has established a public R&D project, NATRIP, to strengthen the testing, validation, and R&D capabilities of domestic companies.
3. The source of information on the NATRIP project is based on Department of Heavy Industry (2012).
4. The earlier case of success in IT services clearly demonstrates this way of thinking that policies should be reactive and this alone can lead to optimal results. Firms must demonstrate some successes through their own strategies and government should come forward to support these successes to the next level by putting in place a reactive policy.

REFERENCES

Central Statistical Organization (2013), *Statistical Abstract India*, Delhi: Ministry of Programme Implementation.
Department of Heavy Industry (2012), *Annual Report 2011–12*, Delhi: Government of India.
Department of Science and Technology (2009), *R&D Statistics*, Delhi: Government of India.
India Brand Equity Foundation (2010), *India's Automobile Industry*, Delhi: India Brand Equity Foundation.
Kadle, Praveen P. (2007), 'Challenges in mergers and acquisitions, Tata Motors case study,' Presentation slides, Dun and Bradstreet India, available at: http://www.dnb.co.in/FESConfTool/Uploads/Presentations/85/Mr.P.P.Kadle.pdf.

Kumar, Nirmalya, Pradipta K. Mohapatra, and Suj Chandrasekhar (2009), *India's Global Powerhouses: How They are Taking on the World*, Boston: Harvard Business Press.

Malerba, Franco (2005), 'Sectoral systems of innovation: a framework for linking innovation to the knowledge base, structure and dynamics of sectors,' *Economics of Innovation and New Technology*, Vol. 14, No 1–2, pp. 63–82.

Ministry of Road Transport and Highways (2012), *Road Transport Year Book*, Delhi: Ministry of Road Transport and Highways, Government of India.

Mishra, Asish K. (2012), 'Tata Motors' R&D Focus', Forbes India, available at: http://www.forbesindia.com/printcontent/32332.

National Manufacturing Competitiveness Council (2006), *National Manufacturing Strategy*, Delhi: Government of India.

Sagar, Ambui and Pankai Chandra (2004), 'Technological change in the Indian passenger car industry,' Discussion Paper 2004-05, Energy Technology Innovation Policy, John F. Kennedy School of Government, Harvard University, available at: http://live.belfercenter.org/files/2004_Sagar_Chandra.pdf (accessed May 20, 2015).

5. Market leadership in India's pharmaceutical industry: the case of Cipla Limited

Sunil Mani

5.1 INTRODUCTION

Since the 1980s, Indian pharmaceutical firms have accumulated considerable technological capability in manufacturing generic versions of off-patented drugs (Chaudhuri, 2005). In 2014, these firms accounted for about 10 percent of the global pharmaceutical industry in volume and 1.4 percent in value terms. The growing leadership position of the industry is also evident from a number of indicators such as significant increases in the number of Abbreviated New Drug Applications (ANDAs)[1] granted to Indian pharmaceutical firms in the United States (US), significant increases in exports, research and development (R&D) intensity, and the number of patents granted to pharmaceutical inventors from India at the United States Patent and Trademark Office (USPTO). The industry consists of about 5000 Indian and foreign firms, although the industry is largely dominated by domestic enterprises.

The Indian pharmaceutical industry has some distinctive characteristics:

1. It is dominated by formulations, the process of combining different chemical substances to produce a drug, and employs over 400 active chemicals for use in drug manufacturing, known as Active Pharmaceutical Ingredients (APIs).
2. It is very active in the global market for generic pharmaceuticals, even supplying developed countries.
3. It enables India to be self sufficient in most pharmaceutical drugs, as indicated by a growing positive trade balance.
4. It is one of the most innovative industries in India in terms of R&D and the number of patents granted, both in India and abroad.
5. As a corollary of the above, it is one of the industries where a clearly identifiable sectoral system of innovation exists, in terms of

the three building blocks: knowledge domain, key institutions, and demand.

6. It is an industry in which the state has intervened rather heavily by designing its sectoral system of innovation. The single most instrumental government intervention was the Indian Patents Act of 1970, which did not recognize product patents in pharmaceuticals, agro chemical, and food products. Research has shown that this enabled Indian pharmaceutical companies to develop considerable technological capability for inventing new molecules, manufacturing and then marketing new drugs based on these molecules both in India and abroad at a fraction of their original price. The prevailing patent regime enabled the firms to acquire this important capability through reverse engineering. The Indian government did not recognize product patents in pharmaceuticals, but it did recognize process patents in them. This enabled Indian pharmaceutical companies to invent very cost-effective processes to design and manufacture known drugs at a fraction of their original price.

7. The larger firms in the Indian pharmaceutical industry have invested heavily in their in-house R&D. The R&D capability has given the firms the ability to acquire a strong technological learning capability as well. Furthermore, the larger firms have good corporate strategies for becoming important players in their respective segments of the industry.

8. The larger firms also resorted to a serious Mergers and Acquisition (M&A) strategy by which they acquired a large number especially of generics drug manufacturers abroad, primarily in the United States of America to serve markets there.

Thus, within India's rather small manufacturing base, the pharmaceutical industry occupies an important place. In fact, based on indicators such as value added, exports, trade balance, R&D, and patents, it is one of India's leading manufacturing industries. In short, India's pharmaceutical industry can justifiably qualify itself to be a market leader.

This case study is about the market leadership of Cipla Limited, a domestic pharmaceutical firm. The firm was established almost eight decades ago by a knowledge-intensive entrepreneur, is the largest company among the Indian pharmaceutical firms, and has made a name for itself as a producer of inexpensive generic drugs. Cipla is also one of the most innovative firms in the Indian industrial establishment, having a large number of US patents to its credit.

The chapter is structured as follows. Section 5.2 will survey the main features of India's pharmaceutical industry to show that the industry itself is a leader within India's small manufacturing sector. Section 5.3 will discuss why we have chosen Cipla as our candidate to represent the market leader from several contending domestic pharmaceutical firms. Section 5.4 will discuss the origins of Cipla's leadership position in terms of firm-level, sector-level, and country-level factors, most of which the pharmaceutical industry shares with the automotive industry. Section 5.5 concludes this case study.

5.2   INDIA'S PHARMACEUTICAL INDUSTRY

India's pharmaceutical industry has three characteristics that are worth noting:

1. India is an important player in the production and supply of generic drugs;
2. India is virtually self-sufficient as it pertains to most pharmaceutical drugs; and
3. the pharmaceutical industry is very innovative.

In the following subsections we discuss each of these three features in more detail.

5.2.1   An Important Global Generic Drug Manufacturer

India's pharmaceutical production can be broken down into three broad categories: (i) 72 percent consists of generic drugs; 19 percent is over-the-counter (OTC) medicines; and 9 percent is patented drugs. Generic drugs represent the largest segment of the global pharmaceutical market and, in terms of volume, India alone accounts for 20 percent of the global market for generic drugs. This makes India the largest supplier of generic medicines in the world, earning it the sobriquet 'pharmacy of the developing world.' India manufactures and sells over 60 000 generic brands across 60 therapeutic categories. The number of ANDAs approved by the United States Food and Drug Administration (USFDA) may be seen as an indicator of the innovation capability of generic drugs manufacturers. Over 40 percent of the ANDA patents issued by the USFDA in 2012 and 2013 have been awarded to Indian pharmaceutical firms. This has been the case historically, as shown in Table 5.1 (Mani and Nelson, 2013). India has more than 100 manufacturing facilities approved by the USFDA. Only drugs manufactured in USFDA-approved manufacturing facilities can be exported to the US. Official figures published by the

*Table 5.1   Number of ANDAs granted to Indian pharmaceutical firms in
             the USA*

	Number of ANDAs approved	Share of the world (%)
2004	26	6.8
2005	49	14.2
2006	72	19.5
2007	98	24.6
2008	126	29.1
2009	126	31.3
2010	130	30.9
2011	154	34.8
2012	201	40.3
2013	158	42.7

Source: Based on USFDA data cited in CRISIL (2014, p. 7).

USFDA indicate that 6300 active Drug Master Files (DMFs) have been filed with the regulatory body, of which 26 percent or 1700 are from Indian companies.

5.2.2   India is Self-Sufficient in Drugs

India is self-sufficient in most drugs, other than a small number of patented, lifesaving drugs. Pharmaceutical exports have been continuously rising and stood at USD 11.56 billion in 2014. As result of increasing exports, the trade balance has also been rising and has remained positive through the years 1996 to 2014. Pharmaceuticals are one of the few manufactured products where the trade balance has been consistently favorable and has risen over time, as demonstrated in Figure 5.1. The increase in pharmaceutical exports is the result of India's considerable technological capability in the design, manufacture, and sale of generic drugs which are essentially off-patent. Chaudhuri (2005) has shown that this capability is, to a large extent, explained by the Indian Patents Act of 1970 which enabled domestic firms to do reverse engineering – the practice of taking apart an object to see how it works in order to duplicate or enhance the object. The role of the state in enabling domestic firms to acquire this important capability hardly needs to be emphasized.

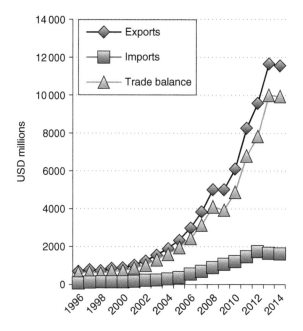

Source: Computed from UN Comtrade.

Figure 5.1   Trends in the trade balance of India's pharmaceutical industry

5.2.3   The Pharmaceutical Industry is Very Innovative

The pharmaceutical industry is one of the leading innovative industries in India. In fact, the industry dominates in terms of conventional innovation measures such as R&D expenditures incurred as well as in patents granted. In fact, the industry alone accounts for over 20 percent of business enterprise R&D (Mani, 2015). The number of patents granted to the industry, even after the implementation of Trade-Related Aspects of Intellectual Property Rights (TRIPS) compliance, has increased significantly, as shown in Figure 5.2. The main features of the industry are summarized in Box 5.1.
    In short, the industry satisfies all the criteria of market leadership:

1. It has a dominant position in India's manufacturing industry in terms of both manufacturing value added and employment.
2. It is a highly globalized industry with exports accounting for over 50 percent of the total sales of the industry.
3. It is one of the most innovative industries in India's manufacturing sector.

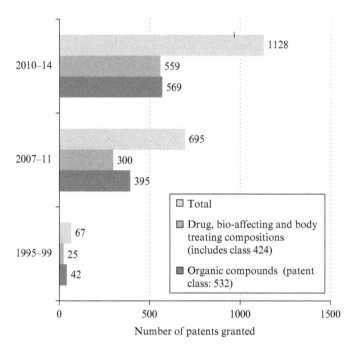

Source: Author's compilation based on USPTO data.

Figure 5.2   Trends in patents granted to Indian inventors in pharmaceutical technologies at the USPTO

BOX 5.1   MAIN FEATURES OF INDIA'S PHARMACEUTICAL INDUSTRY IN 2014

Share of global sales (2014): 1.4 percent in value terms and 10 percent in volume terms
World market shares in generics: 20 percent
Global ranking: 4th in volume, 13th in value
Exports (2014): USD 11.56 billion
Imports (2014): USD 1.62 billion
Direct employment: 0.8 million (20 percent of which is in R&D)
Production costs: Among the lowest in the world, estimated to be 70 percent less than the west

Source: Adapted from Green (2007), India Brand Equity Foundation (2015), and UN Comtrade.

5.2.4 Structure of the Industry

The industry consists of approximately 5000 enterprises of various sizes, business house affiliations, and history (Mani, 2009). However, the four-firm concentration ratio in 2014 was about 20 percent. Of the top four firms, three are Indian: Cipla, Sun Pharma, and Ranbaxy; one firm is an affiliate of a multinational company (MNC), GlaxoSmithKline. Given the highly differentiated nature of the pharmaceutical industry, it is rather difficult to say whether the industry is competitive or not in terms of market share. However, Chaudhuri (2005) has shown that in very narrowly defined markets, the concentration is rather high, with one or two firms accounting for the entire sales in that segment.

A useful categorization of the firms may be found in Green (2007) wherein, by employing multiple criteria of size, sales, exports, and R&D capabilities, the firms are categorized into three groups. This is shown in Table 5.2.

Within the top four firms, the following three stand out in terms of either market share or revenue growth:

1. Cipla has the largest market share at 5 percent of the Indian pharma market with a Moving Annual Total (MAT) of USD 1675.6 million during March 2014.
2. Sun Pharma posted revenue growth of 20 percent, the highest among the major players during the same period.
3. Ranbaxy ranks fourth in the market with a revenue base of USD 734.1 million for March 2014 MAT sales.

5.3 CIPLA AS THE MARKET LEADER

Selecting a specific firm as the market leader among the various domestic pharmaceutical firms has been a difficult exercise. Several of the firms fulfil all three criteria of market dominance, global reach, and innovation. However, we have selected Cipla as the market leader for the following reasons:

1. It is one of the oldest domestic firms in the Indian pharmaceutical industry. It was established in 1935, long before the country became independent. A technically trained entrepreneur founded the firm, thus qualifying Cipla as an example of knowledge-intensive entrepreneurship. The firm has been in existence throughout the various stages of evolution in India's pharmaceutical industry.

Table 5.2 Categorization of India's pharmaceutical firms

Grouping	Number of firms	Description
Group 1	100	Largest firms; include both wholly owned Indian firms and subsidiaries of MNCs; have annual revenues of at least USD 650000; have brand recognition and are engaged in developing R&D capabilities; are responsible for recent wave of cross-border acquisitions and alliances; export to regulated, semi-regulated, and unregulated markets
Group 2	200	Mid-size firms with annual revenues between USD 210410 and USD 650000; have limited investment capabilities and primarily serve the domestic Indian market; are generic drug producers that subsist mainly on reverse engineering of patented off-patent drugs (primarily bulk drugs and APIs); also include niche players specializing in contract research (CRAMS) and contract clinical trials in segments of the market where they have a comparative advantage; export to both semi-regulated and unregulated markets
Group 3	5700	Smallest forms with annual revenues of less than USD 210410; primarily perform contract manufacturing services for MNCs or domestic firms; many have been adversely affected and have been forced to close their doors due to revised Good Manufacturing Practices set by Schedule M of India's Drug and Cosmetic Act 1940 that came into effect from July 1, 2005; those affected cannot meet production standards of regulated market regulators and their production will be limited to the domestic, semi-regulated, and unregulated markets

Source: Green (2007) based on Sampath (2006).

2. Cipla has the largest market share in terms of domestic pharmaceutical sales. Currently (c. 2014) it accounts for about 5 percent of the total domestic sales in the industry. The firm achieved this position and has maintained it since 2007.

3. Cipla is one of the few firms manufacturing medicines for rare diseases such as idiopathic pulmonary fibrosis, pulmonary arterial hypertension, thalassemia, and multiple sclerosis.
4. Cipla has outperformed other global pharma majors by offering patented anti-AIDS drugs at affordable prices.
5. The firm has a line of more than 400 drugs which include anti-asthmatic, anti-cancer, anti-inflammatory, anti-depressant, and anti-AIDS medications. Over the years, the company has developed strong research and marketing capabilities. In recent times, Cipla has attracted considerable media attention because of its efforts to offer anti-AIDS drugs globally at very low prices.
6. Cipla was the first company to develop a drug for the treatment of H1NI flu.
7. Cipla is a highly globalized company with presence in over 150 countries. Global sales contributed about 25 percent of its total sales in 2014–15 and have been growing at a rate of 30 percent per year. The firm has 20 000 employees and over 10 000 product registrations worldwide. Its global reach is unquestionable.
8. Cipla's innovation performance is best judged by its US patenting performance, which is shown in Table 5.3.

As seen in the information above, Cipla has the best patenting record, with a cumulative total of 58 patents, during the five-year period 2010–14 .

Thus, although there are many interesting firms in the pharmaceutical industry that are also strong contenders to be considered as a leader, we have chosen Cipla as it satisfies the criteria of being a dominant player, having considerable global reach, and being highly innovative. We now seek to understand the origins of this leadership position in terms of the framework set out in Chapter 1.

5.4   ORIGINS OF MARKET LEADERSHIP

5.4.1   Firm-Level Factors

5.4.1.1   Vibrant entrepreneurship

Cipla was founded in 1935 by Dr Kwaja Abdul Hamied. Dr Hamieed was educated in both India and Germany. He received his doctorate in chemistry from Humboldt University in Berlin, Germany. He was also a nationalist in that after his higher studies he returned to India to participate in its industrialization process. From the beginning, Dr Hamied

Table 5.3   US patenting by Indian pharmaceutical firms, 2010–14

	2010	2011	2012	2013	2014	Cumulative 2010–14
Cipla Ltd	6	10	18	15	9	58
Ranbaxy	5	10	4	16	18	53
Cadila Health Care	2	11	7	11	14	45
Dr Reddy's Laboratories	5	13	6	6	3	33
Lupin	8	1	5	8	10	32
Wockhardt	1	2	5	5	15	28
Hetero Drugs	12	3	4	4	1	24
Glenmark	1	4	3	12	2	22
Orchid Chemicals	4	0	7	7	1	19
Piramal Enterprises	0	0	1	5	13	19
Suven Life Sciences	2	7	3	4	3	19
Divi's	0	2	2	10	4	18
Piramal Life Sciences	3	9	5	1	0	18
Hetero Research Foundation	0	0	1	9	7	17
Natco Pharma	0	6	2	3	6	17
Aurobindo Pharma	0	3	8	3	2	16
Matrix Laboratories	2	8	4	2	0	16
Sun Pharma Advanced Research	2	2	4	6	2	16

Source: Compiled from UPTO.

stressed the importance of developing local technological capability. He was instrumental in establishing the Council of Scientific and Industrial Research (CSIR) as well as its important, associated laboratory, namely the National Chemical Laboratory (NCL) (Singh, 2010). It is important to recall that the NCL at Pune is generally considered to be the best government research institute in the CSIR fold, especially when seen in its transfer of technology to local business enterprises. Dr Hamied is a rare entrepreneur-turned-scientist. His vision led Cipla to draft its initial corporate strategy. This corporate strategy placed great emphasis on developing local technological capability via two methods: (i) populating the company with technically trained human resources; and (ii) through systematic investments in in-house R&D. This corporate strategy was carried forward by his son, Dr Yusuf Hamied, who became the CEO of Cipla. Dr Yusuf Hamied is also well educated in organic chemistry, having received his doctorate on the subject from the University of Cambridge, UK.[2] Currently, the company is led by a professional from outside the

Hamied family. In short, Cipla received its guidance and spirit from the firm's founding family. The founders were extremely well trained in pharmaceutical chemistry. Their spirit resulted in a strong desire to develop local capability that would result in the ability to manufacture inexpensive, essential drugs. In fact, the company's success in developing cheap anti-retroviral (ARV) drugs to combat HIV infections that are used in countries such as South Africa is, to a great extent, attributed to the leadership provided by the key entrepreneur.

5.4.1.2 Learning, capabilities, and strategies

Cipla's overall strategy has been to make medicines for a whole host of common ailments at extremely affordable prices. The company has earned a great reputation in this area. It is one of the few firms also manufacturing medicines for rare diseases such as idiopathic pulmonary fibrosis, pulmonary arterial hypertension, thalassaemia, and multiple sclerosis. Over the eight decades since its inception, one can identify five major epochs in terms of capability building. These are outlined in Table 5.4.

Compared to other firms in the industry, Cipla has relied heavily on developing and changing its capabilities through internal efforts rather than acquiring competencies through acquisitions abroad. Therefore, Cipla has been characterized by dynamic capabilities accumulated and changed mainly through internal efforts. Three strategies described below are visible in explaining the dominant position the company has acquired over time.

1. *Significant cost leadership* The most notable expression of the firm's cost leadership has been making ARVs available at significantly lower prices. For instance, the Cipla brand of anti-retroviral combination

Table 5.4   Major epochs in the 70-year history of Cipla

Year	Epoch
1935–78	Cipla established to make India self-sufficient in health care
1978–94	Pioneered inhalation therapy to manufacture Metered Dose Inhaler (MDI)
1994–2001	Launched Deferiprone, world's first oral iron chelator
2001–12	Pioneered access to HIV ARVs made available at less than a dollar
2012–	Made cancer treatment affordable with breakthough in reducing the cost of cancer drugs

Source: Company website; India Brand Equity Foundation (2015).

drug was sold in 2000 for USD 800 per patient per annum. On the other hand, the major Western pharmaceutical firms sold the same combination drug for about USD 12000 per patient per annum. Subsequently, Cipla further reduced the price to about USD 300 per patient per annum and then further reduced it to approximately USD 140.[3] This cost leadership is a direct outcome of firm strategy. This strategy was aided by a sectoral system of innovation wherein the Indian patent regime allowed reverse engineering of pharmaceutical products at considerably cheaper prices.

2. *Market differentiation* Cipla has differentiated itself by being the first to manufacture a range of pharma products. According to the company, it was among the first Indian pharmaceutical firms to develop and manufacture APIs, the important raw material for making drug products. In 2015 the firm manufactured over 200 generic APIs. This formidable portfolio covers a broad spectrum of therapeutic categories, reaching out to over 170 countries around the world. As a result of being the first company to manufacture a range of drugs,[4] the company achieved its leadership position.

3. *Focus on new markets* Cipla, relatively speaking, focuses more on domestic markets than on foreign markets. Among the major domestic pharmaceutical companies, it has the lowest export intensity. This is shown in Table 5.5.

In other words, as part of the founder's vision, Cipla concentrated on making essential drugs affordable to the large population in India through cheap prices. However, in recent years, the firm has also been diversifying

Table 5.5   Export intensity of major pharmaceutical firms, 2010–11

	Consolidated net sales	International sales	Exports as % of net sales 2010–11
Ranbaxy Labs	8960.77	6771.74	75.6
Dr Reddy's Labs	7236.8	5940.7	82.1
Lupin	5706.82	3983.08	69.8
Cipla	6130.31	3361.49	54.8
Sun Pharma	5721.43	2898.2	50.7
Wockhardt	3751.24	2709.91	72.2
Jubilant Lifescience	3433.4	2369.11	69.0

Note: Values are in Rs Crores.

Source: Department of Pharmaceuticals (2012).

to new markets abroad. For instance, it now has a wholly owned subsidiary in South Africa, Cipla Medpro. According to the company's Annual Report for 2012–13 (Cipra, 2013, pp. 25–26), '[t]he firm is now evaluating several business models such as capturing value through direct presence in key priority markets including South Africa, US, Europe and Australia.' The company has been diversifying into the exporting of services as well, as shown in Table 5.6.

The firm has institutionalized the process for its forays into new activities by setting up Cipla New Ventures (CNV). CNV has three incubators with specific focus areas:

Table 5.6   Trends in external transactions of Cipla, 1990–2013

	Exports of goods	Exports of services	Other	Total external transactions
1990	111.4	–	–	111.4
1991	95.0	–	–	95.0
1992	177.6	–	–	177.6
1993	199.9	–	–	199.9
1994	240.7	–	–	240.7
1995	309.6	–	–	309.6
1996	397.1	7.6	–	404.7
1997	617.0	7.8	–	624.8
1998	728.1	8.0	–	736.1
1999	1 163.6	28.3	–	1 191.9
2000	1 406.4	28.0	–	1 434.4
2001	1 406.4	28.0	–	1 434.4
2002	4 941.7	25.8	–	4 967.5
2003	5 660.3	69.0	–	5 729.3
2004	8 122.8	544.5	38.9	8 706.2
2005	10 532.1	415.4	32.0	10 979.5
2006	15 136.4	415.6	104.3	15 656.3
2007	17 804.4	764.7	81.6	18 650.7
2008	21 017.4	1 533.9	0.8	22 552.1
2009	27 426.9	2 174.5	0.2	29 601.6
2010	29 005.8	1 537.6	33.4	30 576.8
2011	33 614.9	547.6	14.2	34 176.7
2012	36 920.3	295.5	65.9	37 281.7
2013	44 261.6	604.3	81.3	44 947.2

Note: Rs in millions.

Source: Compiled from Annual Reports of Cipla.

1. CipTec: focused on bridging unmet needs through innovative technology platforms, repurposing of existing drugs, and developing novel combinations.
2. Biologicals: focused on making a disruptive impact in the field of biosimilar monoclonal antibodies and stem-cell-based innovative products and therapies.
3. Consumer Healthcare: focused on leveraging Cipla's market outreach and development of a unique basket of value-added and differentiated Consumer Health products to improve the day-to-day lives of consumers.

Further, Cipla has investments in an Indian company engaged in stem-cell research, a drug company in the US focused on early-stage drug development especially for the treatment of Alzheimer's, and a biosimilar company in China.

The company has also completed a large number of acquisitions both in India and abroad. Some of its more recent purchases (during the period 2000–14) have been:

1. a 100 percent of a Goa-based biotech firm, Mabpharm Private Limited, for an undisclosed amount;
2. a 60 percent stake in Cipla's existing Sri Lankan distributor, for a consideration of USD 14 million (Rs 840 million);
3. 100 percent of Celeris d.o.o., Cipla's distributor in Croatia;
4. a 14.5 percent stake in Quality Chemical Industries Limited, Uganda, for a consideration of USD 15 million; and
5. it entered into a definitive acquisition agreement for 100 percent of the Brazilian company, Duomed Produtos Farmaceuticos.

These acquisitions have helped Cipla in two specific ways: (i) they broaden its external market since new subsidiaries provide the capability to directly serve a number of new markets in Africa, Europe, and Latin America; and (ii) they supplement its source of technology.

This focus on new markets has been an important part of Cipla's strategy. The firm has become an important player in India's pharmaceutical industry due in great part to its ability to serve broader markets.

5.4.1.3 Strong in-house R&D

We have seen that the pharmaceutical industry contributes one of the largest shares of business enterprise R&D, as it is one of the most knowledge-intensive manufacturing industries. Cipla has been investing heavily in in-house R&D. This investment has shown some appreciable increases

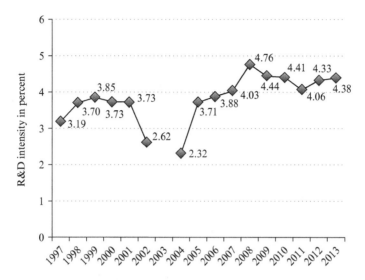

Source: Based on Annual Reports.

Figure 5.3   Trends in Cipla's R&D intensity

in its intensity after TRIPS compliance during India's patent regime in 2005. This is shown in Figure 5.3.

Cipla's R&D is focused towards developing new products, improving existing products and drug delivery systems, and expanding product applications. The three main objectives of the firm's R&D are: (i) developing new drug formulations for existing and newer drug substances; (ii) improving processes for existing APIs and formulation products; and (iii) developing new drug delivery systems[5] for existing and newer active drug substances, as well as newer medical devices, mainly in the area of respiratory medicine.

According to the company's website, in-house R&D has resulted in a number of patents. As was shown in Table 5.3, R&D has resulted in 58 USPTO patents during the period 2010–14 alone. Apart from patents, the following other outputs have been claimed by the firm:

1. 139 Drug Master Files (DMFs), 87 registered ANDAs, and 25 ANDAs under review in the US;
2. approximately 1000 DMFs for a total of 101 APIs; 49 Certificates of Suitability approved;
3. over 700 marketing authorizations in Europe;
4. over 10000 product registrations globally; and
5. 49 products pre-qualified by the World Health Organization (WHO).

5.4.2   Sector-Level Factors

To achieve the leadership it has now, there are five sector-level factors that are extremely important for the growth of India's pharmaceutical industry. These sectoral factors are common to all the firms in the industry. The firms which have been able to benefit and profit from these factors are the ones that emerge as successful. Our main point here is that Cipla has been able to take full advantage of these factors. These five factors are as follows.

5.4.2.1   The Indian patent regime

This is by far the most important institution that supported and enabled Indian pharmaceutical companies to achieve dominant leadership positions. Chaudhuri (2005) has given a succinct analysis of how changes in the Indian Patents Act 1970 have been helpful in enabling considerable technological and innovation capability building in India's pharmaceutical industry. At the risk of repetition, the main points are described in this subsection. An important and distinguishing feature of the Patents of 1970 was that processes only, but not products, were allowed to be patented in India. Furthermore, the term of a process patent for drugs was reduced from sixteen years, as provided in the previous act, to five years from the date of sealing or seven years from the date of filing complete specifications, whichever ended earlier. For non-pharmaceutical patents, the duration was fourteen years. According to Chaudhuri (2005), the Act of 1970 virtually eliminated the monopoly status which the MNCs had enjoyed until then. Domestic firms were able to immediately manufacture a new drug if they could use an older process or develop a new process not mentioned in the patent of the innovator company. Even when they could not, the period of monopoly held by an MNC would be significantly shorter – seven years at the most.

Thus, the complete elimination of product patent protection, together with the provision that only one process could be patented by an applicant, enabled Indian pharma companies to develop considerable technological capability. The pharma companies operated under this facility from 1972 until 2005, when the 1970 Act was amended to make it TRIPS-compliant. TRIPS compliance now requires that both pharmaceutical products and processes require a patent and the term of a patent is twenty years from the time of application.

The long period comprising nearly three and a half decades provided an opportunity for domestic manufacturers to learn the new technology, which involved discovering new drug molecules. This is proved by the fact that even after the introduction of the product patent regime in 2005, and measured by indicators such as sales, net profit, R&D, and patents, none of the domestic manufacturers was adversely affected. In many ways, the pharma companies were able to stand on their own feet as far as innovation capability was concerned. This learning was facilitated to a great extent by three factors, all of which are interrelated: (i) most of the leading firms invested heavily in in-house R&D which enabled them to not only absorb known drug technologies but also to devise new ones, even if only incremental in nature; (ii) the firms had easy access to a copious supply of scientists with good chemistry skills, churned out by India's higher education sector; and (iii) most of the leading firms had clear corporate strategies to emerge as important players. Of these three factors, we now focus on the human resource issue as it is an important facilitating factor for this science-based industry.

5.4.2.2   Supply of advanced human resources for pharmaceutical research

The Indian higher education system (that is, universities) has traditionally been biased in favor of science education. As noted earlier, India has produced more science graduates than engineers. Within the sciences and medicine, chemistry and pharmacy are the two subjects that produce the maximum number of graduates, postgraduates, and doctoral degree holders (Ministry of Human Resource Development, 2014). Historically, this has been the traditional picture. In order to further supply more specifically trained personnel, the central government established a new institution, the National Institute of Pharmaceutical Education and Research (NIPER). It is the first national-level institute for pharmaceutical sciences with the stated objective of becoming a center of excellence for advanced studies and research in pharmaceutical sciences. The University Department of Chemical Technology, University of Mumbai (now known as the Institute of Chemical Technology) has been another important institute that has supplied high-quality chemistry graduates for the industry. Some of the public research institutes under the CSIR have also been important contributors of high-quality human resources in medicinal chemistry. Furthermore, the Department of Biotechnology of the government of India has a reverse brain-drain scheme. The scheme aims at encouraging high-skilled migrants from India to return to their homeland and participate in R&D activities, taking advantage of the skills held by Indian scientists abroad. These skills are applicable to India's biotechnology industry, which to a large extent is dominated by the biopharmaceutical industry.

The patent regime, coupled with the availability of high-quality chemistry graduates, has enabled pharmaceutical firms such as Cipla to emerge as leaders. Given the fact that Mumbai in particular was the center of chemistry education, it has really helped Mumbai-based pharmaceutical firms such as Cipla to enjoy a copious supply of well-trained human resources.

5.4.2.3 Role of public research institutes

Another sector-level factor that is extremely beneficial is the existence of a series of public research institutes (PRIs) dedicated to pharmaceutical research. Three PRIs stand out: the Central Drugs Research Institute (CDRI), the National Chemical Laboratory (NCL), and the Indian Institute of Chemical Technology (IICT). There are three ways in which these laboratories have supported innovative activity in the sector. First, they have generated a number of new drug technologies and have transferred these technologies to the industry with great success (relatively speaking, when compared with other PRIs within the CSIR fold). In this way, the laboratories supplemented the R&D efforts of other private-sector pharmaceutical companies. Second, these PRIs also perform research and provide technical consultancies of various types in medicinal chemistry to clients in the industry. Third, the PRIs have been a source of high-quality human resources in medicinal chemistry by graduating a number of doctoral-level degree-holders in the subject. Many pharmaceutical firms in India have benefited from their long-term association with these PRIs. According to Chaudhuri (2005), Cipla has been one of the regular users of these services, particularly those provided by the NCL and the IICT. Cipla has been highly successful in scaling up the laboratory-scale processes developed by these labs to large-scale manufacturing. Cipla's diversification in anti-AIDS drugs was actually the result of a public–private initiative. In short, the PRIs have supported the innovative activities of Cipla.

5.4.2.4 Fiscal incentives for R&D

In-house or intra-mural R&D is one of the main routes through which firms innovate. In literature on the economics of innovation, it is widely recognized that if industrial R&D is left entirely in the hands of private-sector enterprises, then there is a likelihood of these enterprises under-investing in R&D. This means the amount of R&D undertaken will be less than the socially desirable optimum. The tendency to under-invest is due to the problem of appropriability or the failure of private-sector agents to fully appropriate the returns of their own research. Governments across the world have sought to overcome this problem by providing subsidies to private-sector firms, encouraging them to make continued investments in R&D. India has also been using tax incentives to encourage domestic enterprises to commit more resources to R&D.

This policy on R&D tax incentives has evolved over time, as seen in Table 5.7.

It is evident from Table 5.7 that India has one of the most generous incentive regimes for R&D. The generosity of a tax regime with respect to R&D is measured using a summary measure called the B-Index.[6] The lower the B-Index, the higher the generosity of the tax regime. Recent estimates of the B-Index confirm this view, as shown in Figure 5.4.

It is evident that almost a quarter of the industrial R&D performed in India is subsidized through tax incentives (Mani, 2014). The subsidization rate has been increasing over time as technology generation has globalized. Although the R&D tax incentives are not exclusively targeted at the pharmaceutical industry, being R&D-intensive, it is one industry that has made, relatively speaking, extensive use of the incentives (Mani, 2002). Thus, although the R&D tax policy is a country-level policy, as it pertains to incentivizing R&D, we treat it more as a sectoral-level policy.

5.4.2.5 Proactive government policies

The pharmaceutical sector was supported by a number of general and specific policies. Three specific policies are directly addressed to the industry. These are: (i) the drug policy of 1986; (ii) the pharmaceutical policy of 2002; and (iii) the national pharmaceutical pricing policy of 2012. Of the three, the one that is most relevant today from the innovation point of view is the pharmaceutical policy of 2002. This policy has specific pronouncements on promotion of R&D and human resources development. See Box 5.2.

Another important policy that is highly relevant is related to significant reductions in the time taken for various approvals. In order to compete with global players in pharmaceutical industries, the authorities have simplified the approval process for drugs while the approval time for new facilities has been drastically reduced.

The other sector-specific policies are:

1. Indian government plans to set up a USD 640 million venture-capital fund to boost drug discovery and strengthen pharma infrastructure;
2. memorandums of understanding with the USFDA, Health Canada, etc., to boost growth in the Indian pharma sector by benefitting from their expertise;
3. support for technology up-gradation through the Export Promotion Capital Goods scheme;
4. Pharma Vision 2020, which aims to make India a major hub for end-to-end drug discovery; and
5. HIV/AIDS drugs and diagnostic kits made fully exempted from excise duty.

Table 5.7   Evolution of the policy on R&D tax incentives in India

Union budget	Major change	Scope of change
1999–2000	R&D tax incentives of 125 percent extended up to 2004–05	Under the current law, a weighted deduction of 125 percent of the expenditure made on in-house R&D was available to corporate houses up to March 31, 2000. This has now been extended up to 2004–05. Further, it was proposed to extend a similar concession of permitting a weighted deduction of 125 percent of expenditure for R&D projects entrusted to research laboratories and universities.
2000–01	R&D tax subsidy raised to 150 percent in the Finance Act of 2000	Under this, the incentive was available only to companies engaged in the production of drugs and pharmaceuticals, electronic equipment, computers, telecommunications equipment, chemicals, manufacture of aircraft and helicopters, automobiles and auto parts.
2009–10	R&D tax incentives extended to all industries in 2009–10	The scope of the current provision of a weighted deduction of 150 percent on expenditure incurred on in-house R&D extended to all manufacturing businesses except for a small negative list.
2010–11	R&D tax incentives increased from 150 percent to 200 percent	Weighted deduction on in-house R&D expenditure increased from 150 percent to 200 percent. Further, the weighted deduction on payments made to national laboratories, research associations, colleges, universities, and other institutions for scientific research increased from 125 percent to 175 percent.

Source: Author's compilation based on Union Budget documents cited in Mani (2014).

Thus, pharmaceuticals is one of the few manufacturing industries in India that have benefited from specific policies. This has made the sectoral system of innovation of the industry quite dynamic and open to innovative activity.

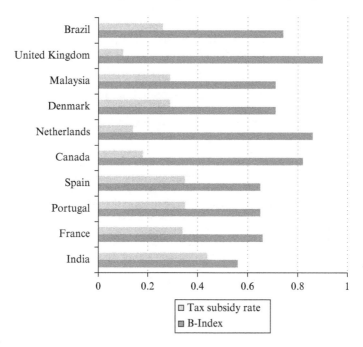

Source: Based on Stewart et al. (2012).

Figure 5.4   Generosity of tax regimes with respect to R&D

5.4.2.6   The role of the increasing domestic demand for drugs

The demand for medicines is expected to rise for three reasons. The first is epidemiological factors, the second due to the diffusion of health insurance, and third is the growth of exports. We discuss each of these separately below:

1. *Increase in the incidence especially of non-communicable diseases (NCDs)* Unfortunate as it may seem, NCDs account for nearly half of all deaths in India (Ministry of Health and Family Welfare, 2011). Cardiovascular diseases (CVDs), cancer, diabetes, chronic obstructive pulmonary disease (COPD), mental disorders, and injuries are the main causes of death and disability due to NCDs. This is bound to increase the demand for drugs to treat these types of ailments.
2. *Diffusion of health insurance* This diffusion is expected to more than double by 2020. An important reason for this is the growth of government-sponsored initiatives such as Rashtriya Swasthya Bima Yojana (RSBY) and the Employees State Insurance Corporation (ESIC). According to a World Bank study (Forgia and Nagpal, 2012), over 300

BOX 5.2   SALIENT FEATURES OF THE PHARMACEUTICAL POLICY, 2002

- In principle, approval to the establishment of the Pharmaceutical Research and Development Support Fund (PRDSF) under the administrative control of the Department of Science and Technology, which will also constitute a Drug Development Promotion Board (DDPB) on the lines of the Technology Development Board to administer the utilization of the PRDSF; and
- The National Institute of Pharmaceutical Education and Research (NIPER) has been set up by the government of India as an institute of 'national importance' to achieve excellence in pharmaceutical sciences and technologies, education, and training. Through this institute, the government's endeavor will be to upgrade the standards of pharmacy education and R&D. Besides tackling problems of human resources development for academia and the indigenous pharmaceutical industry, the institute will make efforts to maximize collaborative research with the industry and other technical institutes in the area of drug discovery and pharma technology development.

Source: Department of Pharmaceuticals, Government of India, http://pharmaceuticals.gov.in/.

---

million people, or more than 25 percent of India's population, gained access to some form of health insurance by 2010, up from 55 million in 2003–04. More than 180 million of these were people below the poverty line. Given these trends, the World Bank study projects that more than 630 million people, or about half of India's population, will be covered by health insurance by 2015. By this time, spending through health insurance is also likely to reach 8.4 percent of total health spending, up from 6.4 percent in 2009–10. In terms of expenditures, Forgia and Nagpal (ibid.) estimated this amount to grow from Rs 45 billion in 2003–04 to Rs 380 billion in 2015. This increase in the diffusion of health insurance is likely to lead to a huge demand for pharmaceutical products.

3. *Increase in exports* Exports of pharmaceutical products have been growing at a rate of 18 percent per annum during the period 1996 through 2014. The increased demand for generics and the high cost of drugs in western countries creating demands for cheap drugs from India is bound to increase further in future.

These three factors together will lead to increasing demands for pharmaceutical products. This is good news for the Indian pharmaceutical manufacturers.

5.4.3   Country-Level Factors

As stated in Chapter 1, there are essentially four country-level factors that facilitate the emergence of industrial leaders. These factors are as follows: (i) active public policies in support of specific industries; (ii) policies to unleash private entrepreneurship; (iii) changes in the education system; and (iv) untapped local markets. The automotive case discussed in Chapter 4 has factors (ii), (iii), and (iv) in common with the pharmaceutical industry.

The only country-level factor that is of relevance, especially for future growth and maintenance of the leadership position for Cipla, is the opportunity to take advantage of the newly launched program, 'Make in India.' The program, which was launched on August 15, 2014, complements the 'National Manufacturing Strategy of 2011,' increases the size of the organized manufacturing sector, and aims to simplify laws and procedures for existing firms to expand and for new firms to come onstream. This program is likely to offer further fillip, encouraging the leading firms in India's pharmaceutical industry to grow and flourish.

5.5   CONCLUSIONS

In this chapter, we have analysed the case of Cipla as a market leader in India's pharmaceutical industry, which itself, as we have argued, is a leader in India's manufacturing industry. Cipla met all three conditions of market leadership: market dominance, global reach, and innovation. It must, however, be pointed out that there are other companies that can also claim to be leaders in the industry, including Ranbaxy, Dr Reddy's Laboratory, and Sun Pharma. But Cipla has had a significantly longer history and has enjoyed greater success in serving both domestic and foreign markets. It has been a trailblazer for pioneering, low-cost, lifesaving drugs and is therefore highly respected in India. We sought to explain the origins of its leadership in terms of firm-level and sector-level factors. Knowledge-intensive entrepreneurship was a key factor. The firm has a very good vision and a corporate strategy focused on being a provider of low-cost, lifesaving drugs both domestically and abroad. Cipla has also taken advantage of three sector-level factors, namely the patent regime, technology contributions from PRIs, and the higher-education sector. In a number of ways, the origins of Cipla's leadership are similar to those discussed in the Tata Motors case. An important factor that is common to both these firms is the knowledge-intensive entrepreneurship behind their respective foundations. Although the founding entrepreneurs wield overall control, the management of both companies is in professional hands. In both cases, the contribution of both sectoral- and country-level factors have been important.

NOTES

1. ANDAs were introduced in the Hatch-Waxman Act and are used by foreign generic drug-makers to challenge a US patent before its expiry. If successful, the applicant gets a six-month (180-day) exclusive right to sell its generic version. At the end of that period, other generic drug companies can enter other versions of the molecule and generally the price of the generic version falls sharply.
2. Dr Y. Hamied worked under the guidance of Alexander Todd, a recipient of the Nobel Prize in the field of Chemistry. See more at: http://business.mapsofindia.com/business-leaders/yusuf- hamied.html#sthash.3zJok0AN.dpuf (accessed June 10, 2015).
3. http://www.ukessays.com/essays/economics/Cipla-business-model-and-tension-between-generics-economics-essay.php#ixzz3cdac5Iuh (accessed June 10, 2015).
4. These 'firsts' may be seen by year on the company's website. See: http://www.Cipla.com/Home/Research-Innovation/CiplasFirsts.aspx?mid=1290 (accessed June 10, 2015).
5. Drug delivery is the method or process of administering a pharmaceutical compound to achieve a therapeutic effect in humans or animals.
6. The B-Index is computed by the following formula: B-Index = (1 – After Tax Cost) / (1 – Corporate Income Tax Rate). 1 – B-Index measures the tax subsidy rate. The higher the tax subsidy rate, the higher the generosity of the tax regime.

REFERENCES

Chaudhuri, Sudip (2005), *The WTO and India's Pharmaceuticals Industry, Patent Protection, TRIPS and Developing Countries*, Delhi: Oxford University Press.
Cipla (2013), *Annual Report, 2012–13*, Mumbai: Cipla.
CRISIL (2014), 'Indian pharma well placed to weather spurt in FDA actions,' *CRISIL Insight*, available at: http://www.crisil.com/Ratings/Brochureware/News/V5-Pharma%20Article%20EdV3.pdf (accessed June 8, 2015).
Department of Pharmaceuticals (2012), *Annual Report 2011–12*, Government of India.
Forgia, Gerard La and Somil Nagpal (2012), 'Government-sponsored health insurance schemes: are you covered?', Report, The World Bank, available at: file:///Volumes/Dilla%20Media/Rise%20to%20market%20leadership/EE%20Book%20RML%202014/CIPLA/Government%20sponsored%20healkth%20schemes.pdf (accessed June 11, 2015).
Green, William (2007), 'The emergence of India's pharmaceutical industry and implications for the U.S. generic drug market,' Report, US International Trade Commission, available at: http://www.usitc.gov/publications/332/EC200705A.pdf (accessed June 9, 2015).
India Brand Equity Foundation (2015), 'Pharmaceuticals, market overview and trends,' available at: http://www.ibef.org/industry/indian-pharmaceuticals-industry-analysis-presentation (accessed June 11, 2015).
Mani, Sunil (2002), *Government, Innovation and Technology Policy: An International Comparative Analysis*, Cheltenham, UK and Northampton, MA: Edward Elgar.

Mani, Sunil (2009), 'Why is the Indian pharmaceutical industry more innovative than its telecommunications equipment industry?', in Franco Malerba and Sunil Mani (eds), *Sectoral Systems of Innovation and Production in Developing Countries: Actors, Structure and Evolution*, Cheltenham, UK and Northampton, MA: Edward Elgar, pp. 27–56.

Mani, Sunil (2014), 'Innovation: the world's most generous tax regime,' in Bimal Jalan and Pulapre Balakrishnan (eds), *Politics Trumps Economics: The Interface of Economics and Politics in Contemporary India*, New Delhi: Rupa, pp. 155–169.

Mani, Sunil (2015), 'India,' *World Science Report*, Paris: UNESCO.

Mani, Sunil and Richard Nelson (eds) (2013), *TRIPS Compliance, National Patent Regimes and Innovation: Evidence and Experience from Developing Countries*, Cheltenham, UK and Northampton, MA: Edward Elgar.

Ministry of Health and Family Welfare (2011), *Annual Report to the People on Health*, Delhi: Government of India, available at: http://www.mohfw.nic.in/showfile.php?lid=121(accessed June 12, 2015).

Ministry of Human Resource Development (2014), *All India Survey on Higher Education 2011–12, Final Report*, Department of Higher Education, Ministry of Human Resource Development, Delhi: Government of India.

Sampath, Padmashree-Gehl (2006), 'Indian Pharma Within Global Reach?', Working Paper #2006-031, UNU-MERIT.

Singh, Harkishan (2010), 'Kwaja Abdul Hamied (1898–1972): pioneer scientist,' *Indian Journal of History of Science*, Vol. 45, No 4, pp. 533–555.

Stewart, Luke A., Jacek Warda, and Robert D. Atkinson (2012), *We're #27!: The United States Lags Far Behind in R&D Tax Incentive Generosity*, Washington, DC: The Information Technology and Innovation Foundation.

6. To market leadership: the evolutionary journey of Hindustan Computers Limited

Arun Madhavan

6.1 INTRODUCTION

In 2006 and for the first time in its history, the global information technology (IT) giant International Business Machines Corp. (IBM) held its annual investors meeting in India, hailing India as the driver of the company's future growth. This was a complete turnaround for a company that had exited the country three decades prior, after a falling out with its government. In IBM's absence, the Indian IT industry had steered its own course and found a niche in the global IT industry. While we cannot say for sure that it was IBM's exit that helped the domestic IT industry to grow, we do know for sure that the homegrown IT firms catapulted India into the position of a global player.

In the mid 2000s, India became the largest exporter of IT services in the world, overtaking Ireland (Mani, 2014). The Indian IT industry is concentrated around export-oriented IT service firms. IT exports, which account for around 15 percent of the country's total exports (as shown in Table 6.1), are a vital source of foreign exchange. The Indian case is a stellar example of how an industry based on new technology can put a developing country on the path of rapid economic growth.

A large portion of India's export of software and related services comprises custom software development and related services (69 percent). Of the remaining IT exports, Business Process Outsourcing (BPO) services make up approximately 21.6 percent while software product development and engineering services account for about 5 percent each (RBI, 2012). The biggest market so far is the United States (US) with 64 percent, followed by the United Kingdom (UK) with 15 percent.

India's IT industry consists of a few large firms and a great number of smaller firms. The top eight firms account for about 44–47 percent of exports and nearly 35 percent of employment (NASSCOM, 2012). This

Table 6.1   Software and related services exports (in USD millions)

	Software and related service	Software and related service exports as a percent of service exports	Software and related service exports as a percent of total exports
2005–06	23 600	40.93	14.50
2006–07	31 300	42.42	15.44
2007–08	40 300	44.61	15.71
2008–09	46 300	43.69	15.70
2009–10	49 705	51.75	17.85
2010–11	53 100	42.60	13.94
2011–12	62 212	43.71	13.76
2012–13	65 867	45.21	14.56
2013–14	69 439	45.84	14.77
2014–15	73 108	47.03	15.48

Source: Database on Indian Economy, Reserve Bank of India.

category includes the Indian firms Tata Consultancy Services (TCS), Infosys, Wipro, and HCL Technologies. There are more than 3500 small and medium firms.

Underlining the significance of domestic firms, Mani (2014) argues that India's sustained leadership in IT services is due to its domestic firms. He contrasts the Indian case with that of Ireland, where multinational corporations lead growth. Given this significance, it is important to see how the leaders of India's IT service sector were created.

A systemic perspective of leadership creation suggests that the process involves being shaped by the system and in turn shaping the system. This chapter attempts to bring out the complex, interactive process that churns out a leader, with focus on the learning process, capability building, and adaptation. For the purpose of this study, I have taken the fourth-largest Indian IT firm, Hindustan Computers Limited (HCL). After TCS, it is the oldest surviving top-ranking IT firm. It was an unchallenged leader in the domestic market during the 1980s. Though HCL's position declined in the 1990s, the company later reclaimed its leadership position. The significance of HCL's resurgence was best captured in these words: 'IBM and the other multinationals are becoming increasingly nervous about the fifth-biggest Indian outsourcer, HCL Technologies' (*The Economist*, 2007). HCL started out as a hardware firm and later moved to software. It is also different from its contemporaries in that it was a technopreneurial venture rather than a subsidiary of an established enterprise.

This chapter has five sections, beginning with this Introduction. Section

6.2 provides a brief history of the Indian IT Industry. Section 6.3 discusses the reasons for selecting HCL as a leader and traces its history. The systemic factors and firm strategies that contributed to HCL's leadership are discussed in Section 6.4. Section 6.5 concludes this chapter with a discussion on some of the important lessons from the case study.

6.2   A BRIEF HISTORY OF THE INDIAN IT INDUSTRY

The Indian IT industry went through three stages of transformation, each defined by change in public policy and technology. The first stage, dating from the 1960s to the late 1970s, was dominated by mainframe technologies. IBM was the main supplier of computing machinery to India during this period.

Following its defeat in the Indo-China war of 1962, the Indian government decided to advance its capabilities in electronics and computing technologies. As a result, it set up the Electronics Committee in 1963 (Grieco, 1984). The committee was of the opinion that instead of buying obsolete technology from foreign firms, India should build its capability to develop the small and medium computing devices that the country needed most. It set a target of ten years for India to develop the technology indigenously.

Soon, a computer division was opened in Electronics Corporation of India Limited (ECIL), a government monopoly in the electronics industry. The aim was to domestically produce minicomputers in place of refurbished systems provided by IBM and International Computers Limited (ICL). Meanwhile, the government began exerting pressure on these firms to share ownership of their subsidiaries with Indians, leading to mounting tension between the government and the firms.

About this time, foreign firms such as Digital Equipment Corporation entered the Indian market through joint ventures with Indian firms. IBM remained an unchallenged leader until the late 1970s when it decided to leave the country due to differences with the Indian government on equity and domestic manufacturing. Meanwhile, demands for computing devices were increasing, because such demands came from not just the public-funded research institutions, but also the private sector and government.

With most of the action happening on the hardware front, software production had a lame start as an activity to complement hardware sales. Mainframe-makers such as IBM had their team of software engineers to build software for customers. The Tata group set up the consulting firm Tata Consultancy Services (TCS), the first fully Indian-owned IT firm, to serve the software needs of its business enterprises in 1968. Apart from renting computing facilities, TCS also began developing custom software for others, including the Indian public sector organizations. It exported software for the first time in 1971 to an oil company in Iran.

The government policy on foreign exchange resulted in hardware manufacturers turning to exports to gain foreign currency. With the foreign currency, the manufacturers could then import components to make computers. The manufacturers exported hardware components for printers and sometimes software as well. A major breakthrough was achieved in 1974 when TCS and Burroughs, the most important computer firm after IBM at that time, entered into collaboration. TCS started providing IT services to Burroughs and its clients while marketing their computers in India. This opened the doors to a large market for IT services outside India, which included custom business software development and maintenance of these applications. Engineers were sent abroad to work due to the lack of communication facilities. Export-oriented software services emerged as a new industry, with TCS almost exclusively serving the market.

The period between the late 1970s and the early 1990s marks the second stage in the evolution of the Indian IT industry. The government realized that the strategy of creating an IT leader through ECIL was a failure and allowed other firms to emerge, even in the private sector. Globally, it was a period of great technological change heralded by microprocessor technology. This shift in technology and policy saw the emergence of many new computer firms in India. Among them was HCL.

The demand for computers in the domestic market shot up in the mid 1980s, which gave a boost to the hardware industry. This was complemented by a rise in demand for software in India, as shown in Table 6.2. Software

Table 6.2   Production of IT goods and services (in USD millions)

Year	Computer hardware (domestic)	Software and related service (domestic)	Software and related service exports	Total software and related service
1981	34	0.26	7	7
1985	125	6	28	34
1990	584	114	114	229
1991	425	110	145	256
1995	622	478	725	1 203
2000	745	1 958	6 008	7 966
2001	746	2 246	7 206	9 452
2005	2 268	5 669	21 769	27 438

Source: As reported in Pradhan (2007).

and the related service sector started getting more government support in terms of easier import, foreign-exchange access, dedicated communication links, etc. Foreign firms such as Texas Instruments and Citibank recognized India's potential in IT services and established operations in India. The establishment of operations by these foreign firms signaled India's software capabilities to the world. Patni Computer Systems (PCS) and Infosys were the new Indian entrants during this period.

The third stage in the transformation of India's IT industry began in the mid 1990s and was marked by a major shift in favor of software. The liberalization of the Indian economy almost wiped out the Indian computer hardware industry. At the same time, it invigorated the software export sector. This created new leaders such as Infosys, Wipro, and Satyam, but TCS continued to be the top IT service exporter. With the emergence of Indian IT firms, the role of foreign-owned and jointly owned firms was diminished.[1]

6.3   HINDUSTAN COMPUTERS LIMITED: AN EVOLUTION OVER 30 YEARS

6.3.1   Why HCL?

HCL meets the parameters of domestic market share, global presence, and innovativeness set for this study. During its early days as a microcomputer vendor, HCL was the number one computer firm in the Indian market. However, it evolved with developments in the national and international markets and became an IT service company. Though it was a late entrant in India's IT services sector, it became one of the leading groups of companies. HCL showed significant growth performance even during the global economic recession of 2007–09. Among the top five IT services firms, it was the one that showed the highest growth performance. As the software service industry is targeted in the global market, domestic market size is not an important consideration in determining the leader.

HCL is an export-oriented firm with a global presence. Its customers are from developed countries. The company also operates service delivery centers outside India. The latest annual report suggests that HCL has a presence in 31 countries across the globe. Joint ventures and acquisitions of foreign firms were integral to its growth strategy, which in turn increased its global presence (see Section 6.4.2.2 for a detailed discussion).

Considering that it is a service firm, none of the conventional indicators can be used to measure the innovativeness of HCL. The very fact that it is successfully competing in a globalized and highly competitive market-place vouches for its innovativeness. Moreover, it has shown higher growth performance vis-à-vis its counterparts in India and achieved growth even during the recent global recession.

An important process involved in innovation is learning. How HCL learned and adapted to a dynamic environment is discussed at length below.

6.3.2   The Origin of HCL

DCM (Delhi Cloth & General Mills), one of India's leading business groups, set up DCM Data Products, a new division for electronic data processing equipment in the late 1960s. It was headed by a 23-year-old engineer, Shiv Nadar (De, 2010). In 1972, it launched indigenously designed electronic calculators. Its impressive sales established Shiv Nadar's reputation as a marketing genius. In 1975, DCM produced India's first microprocessor-based calculator that signaled India's entry into the microcomputer industry.

Despite this success, the team at Data Products did not enjoy the support it wanted from DCM's leadership. The members were young and believed in the potential of a microprocessor-based industry. Shiv Nadar and his colleagues decided to leave DCM to set up their own company. But their greatest problem was capital. Fortunately for the team, an electronic calculator company came forward requesting them to market its product. The team set up Microcomp, a technology product marketing company, with a pooled capital of Rs 187 000 (USD 21 000). The company was set up in one of the founders' grandmother's house that was located in a posh residential area of New Delhi.

Shiv Nadar and his team successfully marketed the product across India, leveraging on their prior experience and their partner company's network. The partnership was quite successful and brought in good revenue. They were also able to obtain a bank loan of a few hundred thousand rupees (Borpuzari, 2011).

In a government-regulated environment, obtaining a license to import components was not easy. Microcomp approached Uttar Pradesh Electronics Corporation Limited (UPTRON), a public sector electronics company in Uttar Pradesh, which had an unused manufacturing license. Microcomp and UPTRON formed a joint venture called Hindustan Computer Limited in 1976 with a 26 percent equity participation by UPTRON to manufacture microcomputers.

6.3.3   First Period of Growth and Early Globalization (1976–89)

In 1978, HCL launched its first microcomputer, almost at the same time as Apple launched theirs in the US. In 1980, HCL introduced a new version with a 16-bit processor. The company also began to develop software in response to demand from local customers. In 1983, it developed a database management system and networking operating system for microcomputers while the respective technologies were being developed in the west. The same year, HCL brought out its own word-processing software that added value to the company's microcomputers.

HCL was not the only player in the computer hardware business in India during this period. The major incumbents were mainframe and minicomputer manufacturers. IBM was the leader. Other players included foreign firms such as ICL, Digital Equipment Corporation, and the state-owned ECIL. By 1978–80, microcomputers were leading the market. Forty percent of the total computer installations in the country went to HCL and 27.5 percent went to DCM (Grieco, 1984, p. 41). The remaining 32.5 percent went to other micro, mini, and mainframe computer vendors.

With its success in India, HCL decided to take its business abroad. In 1980, it announced a joint venture with the Economic Development Board of Singapore. The new subsidiary, Far East Computers Limited, manufactured microcomputers in Singapore. In addition to providing computer hardware, it also offered IT services to clients in Singapore and nearby regions. HCL started a software development center in Madras, India. The air connectivity between Madras and Singapore allowed HCL to undertake development in India and send code on floppy disk by air. This marked the beginning of HCL's transition from a hardware company to a solution provider. While marketing and trading were core strengths of HCL, it invested substantially in research and development (R&D) to gain a competitive edge.

One of HCL's most important innovations was the development of the *Magnum* series workstation computers with a Motorola 68030 processor and customized Unix Operating System in 1988. This brought HCL customers from lead markets such as the US.

HCL's Unix hardware and software solutions were so successful that the company decided to test its fortune in the American market, based on the recommendations of the consulting firm, McKinsey & Company. HCL America was founded in 1989 to sell its workstations in the US. It opened single-person marketing offices across the US (*Computerworld*, 1989) with a US manufacturing partner. However, the project did not take off as expected due to the fact that the power supply unit designed for the workstation was not given government clearance. This failure, combined with the health issues of one of the company's partners in charge of operations, forced HCL to wind up its operations in the US. However, HCL's Unix capabilities had been established by that time, and requests from American clients persuaded HCL to continue its operations as a software service provider in the US (De, 2011).

With increasing demand and decreasing restrictions on firm entry and import, more Indian firms emerged in the Indian computer hardware industry.[2] Wipro and Usha Microprocessors Controls entered the market with their own microcomputers. In 1984, Minicomp, another Indian vendor, launched India's first IBM-PC-compatible machine. IBM PC soon became the de facto standard for personal computers across the world. HCL and others followed suit with their own PC-compatible machines for a lesser cost. The price of the computers fell from an average of Rs 500 000 in the early 1980s to Rs 80 000 by the mid 1980s (Sivakumaran, 2000). The adoption of the PC model eliminated a few old-timers such as Hindtron, which specialized in minicomputers. Despite the new competitors, HCL continued to lead the market and became the largest IT firm in India in 1986.

6.3.4   The Uncertain Times (1990s to early 2000s)

In the early 1990s, India was caught in a major foreign-exchange crisis. This resulted in further liberalization of the economy and restrictions on foreign investments were relaxed. The liberalized import regime allowed the entry of new Indian firms such as Sterling Computers that imported computer kits from Taiwan and sold them in India. Unlike HCL, which had its own system design, these new firms brought limited value addition. Manufacturing within India became an unattractive option, as semi-assembled or fully assembled systems could be imported from Taiwan and other East Asian countries. A price war among hardware vendors had already resulted in reduced margins; with liberalization, it became worse.

The growing software industry began to exert pressure on the hardware industry. It demanded public policies that favored the lowering of hardware costs. The tax barriers for importing computing devices were further reduced. Availability of large grey markets for hardware was also an issue for the government. The computing hardware market in India was opened to foreign, multinational players.

To keep afloat, HCL needed a new strategy. The company required a globally competitive partner in IT manufacturing. This led to a joint venture between HCL and Hewlett Packard (HP) in 1991, with 26 percent equity for HP. Both firms were already in collaboration, using HCL's expertise in Unix for technology development. All hardware-related businesses of HP and HCL in India were brought under one umbrella. The partnership was unique in that HP embarked on a joint venture as a minority shareholder for the first time in its history. It turned out to be a fruitful partnership for both firms. HP needed a platform to engage in the Indian market. HCL's extensive network in India, its marketing capabilities and brand identity gave HP the jump-start it needed. As for HCL, it needed a partner to make it globally competitive in the hardware market. A new state-of-the-art computer-manufacturing unit was set up with an investment of USD 3 million in the joint venture.

The joint venture between HCL and HP came to an end in 1997. By that time, the Indian government's policy on foreign equity participation had changed, allowing 100 percent foreign ownership in the place of the earlier limit of 40 percent. The tariff on fully assembled computers was also reduced.

6.3.5   Growing by Going Global (From the Early 2000s)

HCL had to reinvent itself in the post-liberalization scenario. Shiv Nadar, who had initially been against joining the race for low-tech IT services such as Y2K rectification, began to rethink his position.

When the joint venture between HCL and HP was formed, HCL's R&D and consultancy services were regrouped under HCL Consulting Limited. This new HCL entity focused on R&D outsourcing, software-related services, and other types of services such as remote infrastructure management. It also provided Unix development services to HP. When the partnership ended, HCL reorganized its hardware business and system integration under a new firm, HCL Infosystems. Software and related services were brought under HCL Consulting, later renamed HCL Technologies Limited. The focus of HCL Technologies was overseas businesses, while HCL Infosystems focused on India and other emerging economies.

For its re-emergence, HCL required capital inflow. In 1999, HCL issued its first Initial Public Offering (IPO) on the Indian Stock Exchange. The market responded positively to HCL's IPO, raising substantial capital for the company. With that, HCL entered a new growth phase.

HCL's new growth plan was focused on the export of software and related services. HCL Technologies led this growth. However, HCL did not have the early bird advantage this time around, and the company had to catch up with incumbent firms such as Wipro and Infosys.

To hasten this growth, Shiv Nadar went into a buying spree with the funds available. He created new joint ventures and acquired firms across the globe. Despite this, HCL did not exhibit a growth trend. However, this changed in 2005, when Nadar brought in Vineet Nayar as the new CEO. Internal reforms were Nayar's immediate priority. A disconnect between management and employees, as well as deteriorating employee morale were major challenges. To address these concerns, he brought about significant management and operational changes within HCL under a new initiative, 'Employees First, Customers Second.' The strategic objectives of the reforms were 'to provide a unique employee environment, to drive an inverted organizational structure, to create transparency and accountability in the organization and to encourage a value-driven culture' (Hill et al., 2008). The initiative was quite successful in rejuvenating the company from within (ibid.). In 2008, in the midst of the global financial crisis, HCL resumed its efforts to acquire foreign firms. In a major breakthrough, the company outbid Infosys, the second-largest Indian IT firm, and acquired Axon, one of the leading consulting firms based in the UK. In 2012, HCL found its way onto the Forbes Global 2000 list, following other Indian IT firms such as TCS, Infosys, and Wipro.

6.4 SYSTEMIC FACTORS AND HCL'S STRATEGIES

HCL's emergence from a garage start-up to becoming a world leader resulted from a combination of firm-specific characteristics and systemic factors. HCL evolved its strategy in response to changes in the environment that elevated it to a leadership position. The company's ability to learn and adapt stands out as a key determinant of its success. A sectoral system of innovation approach is adopted here for the analysis.

6.4.1 Entrepreneurship

HCL's story is also the story of Shiv Nadar. In the 1970s, he spotted an entrepreneurial opportunity with the advent of the microprocessor and the domestic demand for computers. He built a team with the necessary technical and marketing capability to successfully exploit the opportunity. The entrepreneurial story of HCL and Shiv Nadar is comparable to other garage entrepreneurs of Silicon Valley who rode the microcomputer wave.

As HCL's experience in entering the US computer hardware market and its late entry into IT services exemplify, entrepreneurial decision-making involves taking wrong steps. The ability to learn and change helped Mr Nadar achieve entrepreneurial success. HCL's experience also provides a case for infant industry protection.

Most Indian IT service firms have an important entrepreneur such as Shiv Nadar behind them. In most cases, the entrepreneur is the link between the firm and the foreign market. Often, he is an expatriate Indian who found a market in his country of residence and decided to establish a firm in India. HCL's case is different as it started out as a domestic firm that later expanded onto the global market. The transition of leadership from the founding figure to the next generation of leaders has now become a challenge for the early-generation firms as demonstrated by Vineet Nayar's assumption of leadership and redefinition of HCL Technologies. (See Section 6.4.2.1 for a detailed discussion.)

6.4.2 Capability Building Strategies

HCL adopted different capability building strategies at various stages of its growth. The company went from learning by doing to joint ventures and acquisitions.

6.4.2.1 Learning
HCL was committed to constantly upgrading its capabilities. Initially, it attracted the best talent in the country and focused on in-house technology development. HCL independently designed microcomputers, developed software, and invested in R&D to respond to the needs of its customers. When competition intensified in the 1980s, the company retained its leadership through continuous technology development. HCL has reportedly been one of the most R&D-intensive firms in India right from the start, spending 10–15 percent of its revenue on R&D (Lall, 1982). The company's achievements with Unix, R&D outsourcing businesses, etc., indicate that learning has been an important source of capability building for HCL.

Not all of the company's learning has to do with technology. HCL's resurgence in the mid 2000s stemmed from gaining other types of knowledge within the organization.

In 1985, when Vineet Nayar joined HCL at the age of 23, HCL was at the peak of its success and Nayar became one of its leading marketers. He was contemplating leaving the company during a downturn in the early 1990s. However, Shiv Nadar proposed the idea of a setting up a new HCL subsidiary under Nayar's leadership to provide IT infrastructure management solutions that would be in demand in the domestic market. Nayar went on to form a team, and HCL Comnet was established. It soon became one of the most successful businesses under HCL.

When Shiv Nadar began scouting for new leadership to head HCL Technologies, Vineet Nayar was his natural choice. Nayar took on the mantle on the condition that he be allowed to bring about drastic changes within HCL Technologies, which was losing clients and whose employees were leaving the company in droves. With his experience in the service business, Nayar knew that people matter to clients. He introduced some of Comnet's practices to HCL Technologies with the goal of improving the management process and employee self-esteem. Business units were reorganized and new IT systems were brought in from Comnet to automate operations. The attrition rate began to drop.

The new systems were aimed at bringing greater transparency in functioning as well as improving the flow of information and knowledge within the organization. Management solicited ideas from employees to strengthen the firm. A culture of transparent feedback was also implemented. Some of the changes were symbolic; many were pragmatic. These efforts brought results in the form of new business. Vineet Nayar introduced outcome-based pricing for customers, meaning they needed to share their revenue with HCL Technologies only if it brought about improvement in their businesses. This meant that HCL Technologies was responsible for its customers' businesses and shared their risks. HCL Technologies also decided to improve transparency with its customers. The company shared pricing and other information with its customers to win their confidence.

These changes were not copied from outside HCL Technologies. Rather, they came from Comnet, one of HCL Technologies' subsidiaries. HCL Technologies leveraged the successful strategies of Comnet for the benefit of the entire firm. The autonomy given to subsidiaries meant that there was diversity in terms of strategies, which enhanced learning. At the same time, Nayar realized that too much diversity was hurting the organization. To bring about coherence, joint ventures were dissolved and subsidiaries were merged, unifying HCL Technologies. However, exceptions were made. For example, after acquiring the British consulting firm Axon, HCL Technologies retained it as an independent firm, HCL Axon, and merged a part of HCL Technologies with it. Thus, HCL Technologies retained the unique culture of Axon, which was a source of diversity.

6.4.2.2   Joint ventures and acquisitions

Forming joint ventures was an important aspect of HCL's strategy for survival and growth. Its very origin can be traced to a joint venture. After the UPTRON collaboration, the next joint venture was between HCL and HP. It was a survival strategy, considering the changing situation in the Indian hardware sector, and it was an important learning opportunity for HCL. As part of this initiative, four senior managers from HP were posted in India to lead manufacturing, customer service, engineering, and R&D. Teams of ten HCL–HP engineers were sent to HP's plant in Germany for three to twelve months at a time (Brewer and Nollen, 1998). This improved HCL's skills and knowledge in technology, manufacturing, and

Table 6.3   Acquisitions and joint ventures from 2005

Feb 2012	Joint venture	India	HCL Eagle Limited with Great American Insurance Company, USA
Feb 2012	Joint venture	India	State Street HCL Services with State Street Corporation, USA
Mar 2010	Acquisition	USA	RKV's Unemployment Insurance Practice
Aug 2009	Acquisition	South Africa	SAP biz of South Africa's UCS group
Dec 2008	Acquisition	UK	AXON
Sept 2008	Acquisition	UK	Liberata Financial Services
Sept 2008	Acquisition	USA	Control Point Solutions, Inc.
Feb 2008	Acquisition	USA	CapitalStream
Jun 2005	Joint venture	India	NEC HCL with NEC Japan
Feb 2005	Acquisition	Ireland	AnswerCall Direct Contact Centre

Source: Various annual reports of HCL Technologies.

customer support. HP also brought system integration capabilities to the joint venture. In the mid 1990s, HCL Technologies floated joint ventures with US firms such as Deluxe Corporation (1996–99), James Martin & Co (1996–99), and Perot Systems (1996–2003) to gain a foothold in the global IT services sector, including Y2K-related business. The company continues this strategy of joint venture formation today.

After its highly successful IPO in 1999, HCL Technologies pushed for more aggressive growth based on acquisitions. These acquisitions were made to expand business and markets, as well as capability building. For example, the company acquired Apollo BT Contact Centre in the BPO sector, which was not one of HCL Technologies' strong areas. HCL Technologies completed seven acquisitions around the globe between 2005 and 2012, as shown in Table 6.3.

The company's largest acquisition was Axon. It made HCL Technologies one of the world's most important players in enterprise consulting. The acquisition of Axon brought new capabilities to the firm. HCL Technologies was no longer a provider of IT services alone; it became a business service provider that used information technology to improve its clients' businesses. It also became a provider of comprehensive enterprise computing solutions with services ranging from high-end consulting to call centers. The Axon acquisition placed HCL Technologies in a very advantageous position in the global market.

Similarly, HCL Technologies' acquisition of Deutsche Software in 2001 had the effect of adding knowledge relating to software for financial sectors. HCL Technologies also acquired various BPO firms to expand its capability. Apart from new capabilities, joint ventures and acquisitions also brought new clients to HCL Technologies. The acquisition of Gulf Computers Inc. was done with the intent to gain access to its government clients. Not all acquisitions delivered results and some of the acquired businesses were later closed. It should be noted that each of the joint ventures lasted less than a decade, after which one of the partners took over the business.

6.4.2.3 Intellectual property rights and capability building

The number of technology-related patents held by a firm is an indicator of innovation in technology development. Interestingly, HCL does not have any, and until 2012 it had not filed any applications with the United States Patent Trademark Office (USPTO). While the number of patents held by leading Indian IT firms is low, HCL's lack of patents is glaring, considering that it has included R&D since its inception. HCL's lack of patents may be explained by the fact that patenting software innovations did not come into existence until recently. Also, HCL undertakes R&D for other technology firms. The client firms retain rights for the work completed. Therefore, HCL has not been able to take credit for all of its technology innovations and the resulting knowledge generated.

While HCL did not benefit from patents, it did benefit from the early lack of property rights over software innovation. Unix technology, developed by AT&T, was distributed freely due to the conditions of the anti-trust settlement imposed on the firm in 1958. Unix technology was distributed in source form so that anyone could learn how it worked. HCL seized the opportunity to learn this technology, and it came up with the world's first Unix port on Motorola 68030 processors. In 1983, AT&T was relieved of the settlement conditions and rushed to commercialize Unix. HCL then licensed Unix from AT&T and began to offer it as part of its hardware.

6.4.3 Technology Change and New Opportunities

Reorganization of industry is inevitable in the face of technology change. Microprocessor technology and developments in computing peripherals pushed IBM's mainframe model to the sidelines[3] in the 1970s. The complex computer architecture of the mainframe era was replaced by simple designs with microprocessors. New garage firms such as Apple and HCL designed computers with inexpensive microprocessors and other mass-produced components. Smaller firms that built computers using components from multiple suppliers replaced large, vertically integrated firms such as IBM. New independent firms began to develop software for these computers.

As the microprocessor technology was nascent, it was easier for a new entrant such as HCL to use and adapt it to its advantage. The ability to learn a technology is a prerequisite for leveraging opportunities that the technology brings in, and HCL had a supply of trained human resources in the country (see Section 6.4.4 for more details). HCL's entry was also eased by the low cost of components and simpler engineering processes. It could produce these computers with very little capital.

Technology change also affects demand. With the advent of microprocessor technology, computers became cheaper, yet more powerful and multi-purpose. The technology opened new markets for computers in small businesses, homes, etc. As the microprocessor technology improved, it found applications in high-end business environments. Workstation computers, built using microprocessor technology, replaced mini and mainframe computers in high-end business computing. HCL also introduced multi-user, network-based operating systems such as Unix to its enterprise clients.

Another aspect of technological change was the modularization of both hardware and software that allowed new specializations to emerge. This led to a greater division of labor in IT production, and that provided opportunities for innovation and the emergence of new firms. In the 1970s, modularization of computer hardware helped HCL to emerge as a computer manufacturer through sourcing components from other firms. Later, modularization in the software segment enabled HCL to develop software components for other firms, for example, developing components for a Unix Operating System used by HP. Growth of the IT services sector in both scale and scope was facilitated by standardization and modularization of software components. It enabled firms such as HCL to provide several services with varying degrees of technological sophistication in the creation and maintenance of IT infrastructures. HCL's specialization in remote infrastructure management is an example of such services. Today, IT infrastructures include a large number of hardware and software components that originate from diverse sources.

6.4.4 Role of Academic Institutions

Indian academic institutions played a major role in the emergence and growth of HCL. These institutions provided key human resources for IT firms, including HCL, aiding the company's ambitious pursuit of growth. HCL's founders were trained at premier technical institutions such as the Indian Institute of Technology (IIT). The management resources HCL needed came from leading management institutes such as the Indian Institute of Management (IIM). HCL hired the best students from IIM with excellent offers.

The IIT and IIM have extensive networks with academic institutions in several developed countries, established through research collaboration, movement of researchers, etc. In fact, many of these institutions were set up in collaboration with developed countries. The fact that the engineers of DCM Data Products and HCL were familiar with microprocessor technology around the same time as it was introduced in the developed world proves that there was an efficient flow of information between the developed world and India.[4]

Academic institutions were early consumers of mainframe computers and microcomputers in India. They had the capability to operate the computers and develop the software they needed. HCL found its early customers in these institutions.

As the industry grew, the demand for skilled human resources also grew. The educational and training institutions in both the public and private sectors met this increasing demand. The government approved the setting-up of new engineering colleges and increased the number of seats offered to students. The private sector responded to the demand by setting up independent training institutions such as NIIT, Aptech, and others. These private institutions trained students from non-technical disciplines in IT. As the range of IT services expanded, it created job opportunities for people with diverse skill-sets and even low skills. Therefore, it wasn't only the premier educational institutions that mattered for the Indian IT industry, but a large variety of other training institutions as well.

The Indian academic organizations did not play a major role as technology providers for the local industry. However, this need not be taken as an indication of their low technical capabilities.

6.4.5 Role of Demand

As the earlier discussion on the history of HCL indicates, the domestic demand for small computers led to the emergence of HCL. While the burgeoning computer market generated greater demands for software, there was more value in building computers.

In 1984, the young Rajiv Gandhi became the Prime Minister of India and under his leadership, the IT sector received a major boost. His government proposed a new Computer Policy that favored the adoption of computers in public institutions to increase their efficiency. In 1985, the Rangarajan Committee, constituted to modernize the banking system in India, decided to adopt the Unix Operating system and Motorola processor based computers in Indian banks. HCL introduced the Horizon series of computers, with Motorola chips and their own custom Unix operating system called Hicix. Meanwhile, Wipro developed Unix for Intel's processors.[5] Other vendor companies followed suit.

Entry into leading markets was a learning experience for Indian firms. User feedback from these markets gave them pointers for future innovation. Entering the Singapore market in the early 1980s gave HCL such an opportunity (Evans, 1995, p. 190). The technologies developed by the company for the Singapore market later became a success in India. Its attempt to gain entry into the US, the largest and the leading market, with an American partner in 1989 was a failure, but it brought a new business opportunity for HCL in R&D outsourcing and IT services in general.

The growing demand for computers in the domestic market combined with a policy-induced lowering of entry barriers heightened the competition among firms. Reduced import duty and easy availability of computer kits from East Asia forced HCL and Wipro, the leading hardware manufacturers, out of the hardware business. These firms turned their attention to software.

Standardization and commoditization of hardware and software, along with rampant piracy, diminished the domestic software demand. Software from multinational companies dominated the standardized software market. The market for custom software in India was small. Beginning in the 1970s, demand for maintenance of custom software in mainframe computers grew in the developed countries, particularly the US. TCS and a few other firms addressed a large portion of this demand. HCL did not have expertise in this area, and its attempts to enter the market through joint ventures did not succeed. Software exports surged in the 1990s in response to demands to fix the Y2K bug. The business triggered by Y2K came to an end by 2000. The period of growth that followed resulted from software exports and other services for Unix-based network environments, internet-related technologies, etc. India was prepared to deliver these services and software, as there had been a high demand for some of these technologies in the country during the 1980s and 1990s. HCL had the capabilities to meet the new demands, which gave the company a jump-start in the lucrative market of software exports. In short, domestic software demand, which developed in complement to its hardware business, was the source of HCL's growth post-2000, though growth was driven by global demand rather than domestic.

6.4.6   Public Policy and the IT industry

The Indian IT Industry was shaped by two policy regimes, pre- and post-liberalization. The protection provided during pre-liberalization lead to the emergence of the Indian computing industry, including HCL. The post-liberalization period saw the collapse of the computer hardware segment that served the domestic market and spurred the growth of the export-oriented software segment. The three aspects of public policy – demand generation, protection of domestic firms, and industry promotion – significantly influenced the pathways of the IT industry and those of HCL. The demand-related policy was discussed in an earlier section. The other two aspects are discussed in this section.

6.4.6.1   Protectionism and the ascension of local industry

Indian public policy was focused on creating a single national leader in computer manufacturing through ECIL until the very end of the 1970s. During the second half of the 1970s, without bringing any formal change to this policy, the government tacitly allowed Indian firms in the public and private sectors to set up microcomputer businesses. But at the same time, it continued to restrict entry through licensing. This, in effect, created a greenhouse for new firms.

Unlike many other entrants, HCL was not a part of any major business house with established credentials. HCL would not have even made an entry in this restricted environment were it not for its clever strategy of striking a deal with the public sector company UPTRON. Other early players in microcomputers include business houses such as DCM, Tata's Nelco, etc., and public-sector firms such as Keltron.

When restrictions on the entry of hardware firms were relaxed in the 1980s and demand grew, more Indian firms entered the hardware market. HCL remained a leader not only because of the early-starter advantage it had, but also because it continually improved its capabilities.

The government never had a protectionist policy for the IT services industry, including the software sector. On the contrary, it promoted software exports. In the early days, software was disregarded as it was thought to be of negligible value among other components of the computing system. The domestic market for software was also small. The public policy objective was to build capability in computer hardware. However, the protectionist policy that governed the hardware industry also helped domestic hardware firms to build their capability in Unix and IBM PC technologies.

Arora (2012) argues that protectionism and local demand did not help much, as the technological skills generated in the process were not essential for the kind of work undertaken by the Indian IT services export sector. However, at least HCL's story is different. The company built its capability through serving domestic demand and leveraged it to go global. HCL's global entry via Singapore was facilitated by its capability in microcomputer technology. Complementary capability developed by the company in software enabled it to venture into software exports beginning with Singapore. HCL's effort to enter the US market in the late 1980s was again driven by its capability in Unix systems[6] that also came from serving the domestic market (due to government demand in the banking sector). HCL entered higher-value R&D outsourcing for firms such as HP around the Unix system (perhaps a pioneer of R&D outsourcing service in India). R&D in services accounted for nearly a quarter of HCL's total revenue until around 2010. While the company's hardware capabilities could not survive the global competition, its complementary skills in software did succeed.

It is questionable whether HCL would have grown in the absence of protection from foreign firms and competition among domestic firms, both constrained by public policy. An easy entry into the microcomputer sector would have made it less profitable, rendering the sector non-viable as seen in the post-liberalization period. Would HCL have invested in learning advanced technological capabilities such as the Unix system in such a competitive situation? We can only speculate on this, but the chances seem low. What is unique about HCL is that its technocratic leadership did not shy away from reinvesting part of the rent from protection in learning, even though the company wasn't forced to do so by external factors.

6.4.6.2   Public policy support for the IT services industry

Government policy, right from the start, was favorable for the growth of the IT services sector. The necessity to earn foreign exchange pushed firms to undertake IT services as early as the 1970s. The Computer Policy of 1984 and the Software Policy of 1986 recognized the need to let the software sector grow, independent of computer hardware. Software export firms were allowed to import hardware without paying duty. The policy also aimed to improve access to national and international computer networks through satellites for software exports from the country.

The government set up the Software Technology Parks society in 1988 to host export-oriented software and IT service firms. Besides a common infrastructure, these firms provided satellite communication links and power-supply facilities. Firms registered under the scheme were allowed tax exemption for five years. The exemption continued until the end of 2010.

6.4.7   Co-Evolution and HCL's Strategies

The story of the Indian IT Industry and HCL is one of co-evolution of the many actors involved. It begins with the electronics policy conceived during the mainframe era of the 1960s. This policy was expected to create an Indian version of IBM. Till the country could achieve this, import of hardware was allowed to continue. But to offset the loss of foreign exchange, importing firms were required to export as well. Hardware manufacturers such as IBM in India exported computer peripherals such as printer parts. However, due to the poor manufacturing capability of India and the increasing capability in software development, the exports shifted from peripherals to software. Thus, India became an exporter of IT services. In the computing industry of the time, software was a low-value activity, which made it easy for India to enter the global market. Once there, the Indian IT firms built a reputation for themselves with the quality of their work. TCS, in particular, played an important role in building India's credentials in the sector.

Microprocessor technology rendered the policy of the 1960s obsolete. ECIL's inability to achieve the policy objective signaled its failure. The government responded by allowing private Indian firms to enter the hardware sector. HCL came into existence in this context. The policy of the mid 1980s gave a boost to the local hardware and software industry by increasing demand. The domestic market was protected in favor of local firms. The capability of Indian firms in hardware and software development improved. With its aggressive marketing and continuous technological improvement, HCL became a leader in the domestic market.

As computers became cheaper, domestic demand continued to increase. With advances in microprocessor technology, standardized hardware platforms such as IBM PCs and software platforms such as Unix Operating Systems emerged. These helped software developments evolve into an independent activity. HCL's capability in software also expanded with the changing demand.

During the 1980s, the government recognized India's software export potential. It adopted proactive policies to promote the sector. It took measures to attract foreign firms such as Texas Instruments to India. In 1988, firms in the software and related services sectors formed the National Association of Software and Services Companies (NASSCOM) that became one of the most influential industry associations in the country.

As activities in the software sector gained momentum, the demand for human resources grew. Educational institutions in the private and public sector responded to this demand.

The foreign-exchange crisis in the 1990s, which led to liberalization, hurt hardware-oriented firms such as HCL because they depended heavily on imported components. The crisis also forced the government to extend further support to software and IT services exports to earn foreign exchange. It was also a time of a sudden surge in demand due to Y2K bugs in mainframe software. Though the Y2K bug did not require much technical capability, it was labor-intensive. The Indian IT Service sector benefited from this demand and created new leaders such as Infosys and Satyam.

HCL, which was not into mainframe technology, did not take advantage of the Y2K business. The company concentrated on a joint venture strategy to save its hardware business. Leveraging on its software capabilities developed during its growth phase, HCL entered the R&D outsourcing market. Industry bodies such as NASSCOM lobbied for pro-IT service policies such as reduction in duty for hardware, which further weakened the Indian hardware sector.

The Indian IT services sector continued to grow even after Y2K, catering to new demands. In leading markets such as the US, workstation technologies began to replace mainframes. Towards the end of the 1990s, development in internet technology, particularly the World Wide Web, led to the dot-com boom. Improvements in communication technology allowed for IT-enabled services such as call centers and BPOs. India's human resources were available to cater to all these needs.

Being a latecomer in IT services, HCL needed a different strategy to move forward. Acquisition was identified as a means of leapfrogging over the competition. Funds generated from the company's successful IPO in 1999, combined with the favorable policies towards outward foreign direct investment from India during the 2000s helped HCL to achieve its strategic objective (Satyanand and Raghavendran, 2010).

Foreign firms have now learned to manage the global service model pioneered by the Indian IT firms. The foreign firms started employing cheap labor forces from various countries, including India, to deliver services abroad. This poses a challenge for Indian firms. HCL has a different business strategy to counter this. It is moving towards becoming a business service firm that provides a wide range of services. It aims to act as a single provider for services ranging from low-tech call centers to high-end business consulting.

HCL also brought in a new model of pricing to the market, where the firm takes the responsibility of improving the client's revenue. In this model, the risk and the cost to clients adopting a new solution is reduced. At the same time, the model provides an opportunity for HCL to make continuous financial gains from its clients' growth. Years of providing services to foreign businesses has given IT service firms such as HCL insight into client businesses, which may have also given the firms the ability to take up these challenges.

6.5   DISCUSSIONS AND CONCLUSION

HCL's case gives an insight into the complex evolutionary pathways of Indian IT firms. An important characteristic of an organization is its ability to respond to changing environments. HCL showcases the diverse responses required for a firm to stay afloat and grow in a catch-up economy, amidst rapid technological change and policy evolution. Its experience also sheds light on what shaped the Indian IT sector into what it is today.

6.5.1   Learn and Change

If there is one lesson to be taken from HCL's case, it is on how important it is to learn and change in order to be a leader. It also shows how the learning strategies of a firm evolve as it grows. HCL chose a nascent technology domain to make its entrance. Hence, the lack of accumulated knowledge did not pose a challenge. What mattered was its capability to learn and construct new knowledge in technology. Although HCL grew in a protected environment, it continued its learning through R&D.

Venturing into foreign markets meant new challenges, which HCL converted into opportunities for learning. HCL responded to the challenges by introducing new services such as an offshore development center, improved hardware design, etc. (Evans, 1995). Joint ventures were another strategy that helped the company expand its capability and enter new markets.

As HCL's financial capabilities improved and public policies became favorable, it switched to an aggressive strategy for capability expansion through acquisition across the globe. By virtue of its sheer size, HCL was able to acquire firms that provided higher value services, as illustrated in the case of Axon. In order for HCL to survive in a market that was getting highly competitive, it had to acquire Axon.

The role of open access to technology should also be noted. HCL's first phase of growth and capability building was facilitated by open technologies, such as microprocessor-based systems, in the place of proprietary mainframe architecture and Unix software.[7] Capabilities that HCL developed around these open technologies enabled the company to enter the global market. Recent developments in free and open-source software have to be appreciated in this context.

Learning enables a firm to change in response to changing situations.

At every stage of its evolution, HCL demonstrated its ability to change. When its hardware business slumped, it moved to IT services. And now the company is moving beyond IT services to become a business service firm.

6.5.2   Hardware to software to business service: an evolutionary strategy

A common criticism of the Indian IT industry is that it is biased towards low-value IT services. While some attribute this to the low capability of Indian firms, others point a finger at the weaknesses in public policy, which did not favor a domestic market, as well as at the backwardness of the IT hardware sector.

Understanding the experience of HCL helps us to better appreciate the orientation of the Indian IT industry towards IT services as a strategic choice. Given the circumstances, HCL (and other firms in the industry) found it better to focus on IT services. The capability to do this was derived from their earlier activities. Increased global demand, improved communication systems, and the availability of human resources facilitated the change. Unlike its hardware business, IT Services gave HCL the opportunity to work with leading companies. It resulted in better learning opportunities for HCL. In addition, the co-creation mode of software service helped the flow of knowledge from user to producer. The producer was required to have only the capability to provide the services.

With its experience in Unix development, HCL's move towards IT services was not just a matter of technological capability. Low-value, high-volume IT services provided an easy path to growth. The case of Axon shows that growing by size (rather than value) has some advantage.

Foreign firms have also started taking advantage of India's systemic advantage in IT services by setting up subsidiaries. HCL and the other Indian IT firms are countering this challenge by positioning themselves as business service firms. The ability to counter these challenges has been made possible by the learning that happened during the IT services period. Indian IT firms have gained expertise in different sectors, such as finance, retail, etc., a benefit of providing IT services to clients in these sectors. Today, Indian IT firms are trying to create new services based on the knowledge thus gained. Acquisition of business consultancy firms abroad is a strategy to accelerate this transformation. Thanks to the huge income earned from IT services, such acquisitions are no longer a distant dream.

6.5.3   On the Role of the State

An oft-debated topic which has opinion heavily divided is the role of the government in the growth of the Indian IT services sector. Arora (2012) argues that policies were ineffective and inconsistent. He dismisses various policies relating to the software sector as 'ameliorating bad existing policy.' He particularly highlights the failure of policies related to hardware.

An appreciation of public policy as an interactive learning process is lacking in the discussion on the role of public policy. It is true that India's policy objectives with regard to hardware failed and that the origin of the IT services sector was incidental. Still, it needs to be acknowledged that policies, particularly those that apply to the high technology industry, are susceptible to failure in the event of a major technological breakthrough. India's strategy for the computer industry was first drawn up prior to the advent of the microprocessor. As there was no domestic capability in computer hardware, a public enterprise was set up. The development of microprocessor technology substantially reduced the complexity of computing systems and led to a new industrial dynamic, which eventually saw the government amend its policy to allow private-sector involvement. As a result, many private-sector firms ventured into the industry, especially into the microcomputer segment. The government's computer policy had its origin in the strategic objective of ensuring powerful computing systems were available. By the early 1980s, the technological gap was considerably reduced due to technical changes and domestic capability building. Thus, the strategic objective was not relevant any more. However, the government failed to build a sustainable domestic computer hardware industry while developing substantial system integration and software capabilities.

The potential of software exports was evident to the government as early as the 1970s. Setting up India's first export processing zone in 1973, along with export obligations on large computer vendors, led to the birth of the nascent software export industry in the country. This experience led to a policy shift towards promotion of software exports in the 1980s. By the 1990s, the government had withdrawn its support to the hardware sector in favor of software exports. What needs to be appreciated about India's IT policy is the agility with which it evolved, responding to global and local changes. As the case of HCL illustrates, the policy co-evolved based on a lot of factors and has, in the process, created global players such as HCL.

NOTES

1. There has been a change in the trend recently. Foreign firms have started gaining a large share in India's software exports.
2. Questions may be raised as to whether increased demand or reduced restrictions promoted the entry of new firms. Considering the fact that nearly 30 firms had obtained licenses for manufacturing microcomputers by the end of the 1980s and only four entered production, we have to assume that increased demand was the key factor.

3. For detailed discussion of the technological change toward microcomputers and how it changed the IT industry (then referred as the data-processing industry), see Grieco (1984, ch. 3).
4. Microprocessors became commercially available by 1971. DCM introduced their microprocessor-based system in 1975.
5. While HCL worked on Motorola processors, Wipro worked on Intel processors.
6. The Unix system includes advanced workstation computers to run the Unix Operating System and a customized version of Unix for the particular hardware.
7. The term 'open' is not used here as in 'open source.' It refers to easier access to technological knowhow through various sources such as component manufacturers, journals, standardization bodies, documentation, code etc.

REFERENCES

Arora, A. (2012), 'The Indian software industry and its prospects,' in Jagdish N. Bhagwati and Charles W. Calomiris (eds), *Sustaining India's Growth Miracle*, New York: Columbia University Press, pp. 166–211.

Borpuzari, P. (2011), 'Boots on fire,' July 30, available at: http://entrepreneurindia. in/people/successinc/boots-on-fire/9411/ (accessed February 21, 2013).

Brewer, T.L. and S.D. Nollen (1998), 'Knowledge transfer to developing countries after WTO: theory and practice in information technology in India,' Report to the Carnegie Bosch Institute, Working Paper 98, 14, available at: http://cosmic. rrz.uni-hamburg.de/webcat/hwwa/edok01/cbi/WP98-14.pdf.

Computerworld (1989), 'Start-up company makes passages from India with Unix,' *Computerworld*, XXII(23), 83.

De, R. (2010), 'Shiv Nadar: the winner of the Dataquest Lifetime Achievement Award 2010,' December 31, available at: http://archive.dqindia.com/content/ top_stories/2010/110123101.asp (accessed February 21, 2013).

De, R. (2011), 'A pioneer and a philanthropist,' February 4, available at: http://www. dqchannels.com/dq-channels/news/135487/a-pioneer-philanthropist (accessed February 9, 2013).

Economist, The (2007), 'Hungry tiger, dancing elephant,' *The Economist*, April 7, available at: http://www.economist.com/printedition/2007-04-07.

Evans, P.B. (1995), *Embedded Autonomy: States and Industrial Transformation*, Princeton, NJ: Princeton University Press.

Grieco, J.M. (1984), *Between Dependency and Autonomy: India's Experience with the International Computer Industry*, Berkeley, CA: University of California Press.

Hill, L.A., T. Khanna, and E. Stecker (2008), 'HCL technologies (A),' Harvard Business School Case, 408-004.

Lall, S. (1982), 'The emergence of third world multinationals: Indian joint ventures overseas,' *World Development*, 10(2), 127–146, doi:10.1016/0305-750X(82)90043-2.

Mani, S. (2014), 'Emergence of India as the world leader in computer and information services,' *Economic and Political Weekly*, 49(49), 51–61.

NASSCOM (2012), *Strategic Review 2012*, New Delhi: NASSCOM.

Pradhan, J.P. (2007), 'National innovation system and the emergence of Indian information and software technology multinationals,' available at: http://papers. ssrn.com/sol3/papers.cfm?abstract_id=1515648.

RBI (2012), 'Survey on computer software and information technology services exports: 2010–11,' *RBI Monthly Bulletin*, October 11, 1957–1965.

Satyanand, P.N. and P. Raghavendran (2010), 'Outward FDI from India and its policy context,' available at: http://academiccommons.columbia.edu/catalog/ac:128868.

Sivakumaran, P. (2000), 'The PC in India: the desktop story,' September 12, available at http://archive.dqindia.com/content/industrymarket/100091220.asp (accessed February 21, 2013).

7. Market leadership in the Brazilian automotive industry: the case of Marcopolo

Luiz Ricardo Cavalcante and Bruno César Araújo

7.1 INTRODUCTION

In the mid 1950s, Brazil initiated an effort to start large-scale motor vehicle production in the country. The so-called 'auto plan' was part of the Import Substitution Industrialization (ISI) policy which was based on attracting foreign capital and technology. The plan provided financial incentives to multinational automobile companies to produce vehicles in the country (Shapiro, 1989; Baer, 2002). These multinational companies were therefore present in Brazil long before the 1990s, when the country liberalized its economy and integrated it with international markets. As a result, in the early 2010s, there were no nationally owned market leaders in light vehicles, heavy-duty trucks, or bus assembly segments in the country.

There were, however, important national leaders in niches such as the bodywork and road implements segments. This is the case with Marcopolo, which is a bus bodywork manufacturer, and Randon, a leader in road implements manufacturing. As shown in this chapter, some idiosyncratic factors regarding the Brazilian market led the large auto manufacturers to give up contesting Brazilian incumbents in these segments. This allowed Brazilian companies to grow hand-in-hand with the local automotive market and dictated the customer–supplier relationship patterns. Moreover, these companies have recently found their own way to internationalization, especially towards developing countries.

This chapter focuses on Marcopolo, a Brazilian bus bodywork manufacturer[1] that may be considered one of the incumbents mentioned in the previous paragraph. Marcopolo's net revenues reached USD 1.4 billion in 2014.[2] The company exports to more than 100 countries and its market share in Brazil was around 40 percent in 2014. Today, Marcopolo has four production units in Brazil, thirteen production units abroad, and employs approximately 17 000 people around the world (Marcopolo, 2015). In the early 2010s, Marcopolo represented around 8 percent of the world bus bodywork market (Zignani and Deiro, 2011). These numbers are directly related to the company's ability to innovate and provide customized products to meet its clients' needs. In fact, just before it formed a joint venture in India with Tata Motors, a Brazilian business magazine described Marcopolo as 'the bus Embraer'[3] (Revista Exame, 2007).

All of these features, which contribute to Marcopolo's dominant position in the domestic market as well as its global reach and innovativeness, fit the definition of market leadership provided in the first chapter of this book. Marcopolo is a remarkably interesting case of market leadership in a non-traditional segment in Brazil and represents one of the most internationalized Brazilian companies. The company may be considered a 'polar type' (Yin, 2013), providing interesting insights for market leadership and internationalization processes of firms in emerging countries.

The aim of this chapter is to analyse the factors that have led to Marcopolo's market leadership position. The five main steps of the research included: (i) an analysis of the dynamics of the bus bodywork manufacturing sector and its sectoral innovation system; (ii) a bibliographic review of Marcopolo, as the company has been the subject of several case studies in Brazil; (iii) a systematization of the data on the company; (iv) in-depth interviews to capture the company's strategies and trajectory; and (v) an analysis of the role played by the sector as well as firm- and country-level factors that led the to company becoming a market leader. From a methodological standpoint, this chapter is a case study based on a bibliographic review and in-depth interviews. It is interesting to understand and explain the case by contrasting different sources through triangulation. It was possible to rely on four hours of recorded interviews with the Director of Strategy and Development and the Manager of Corporate Development Engineering, as well as abundant written material including financial reports, press, and academic articles. In line with the sources of market leadership indicated in Chapter 1, this work is structured into four sections as well as this Introduction. Sector-level factors are discussed in Section 7.2 and firm-level factors in Section 7.3. Country-level factors, which involve government support and public policy instruments, are the subject of Section 7.4. The main findings and remarks on this chapter are highlighted in Section 7.5.

7.2   SECTOR-LEVEL FACTORS: AN OVERVIEW OF THE DYNAMICS OF THE GROWTH OF THE BUS BODYWORK MANUFACTURING INDUSTRY

7.2.1   Bus Bodywork Manufacturing: Technological Requirements

The automobile industry encompasses a wide range of activities, from vehicle assembly (the most typical activity of the sector) to auto parts production. In addition to light vehicles and auto parts, the automobile industry involves the assembly of heavy-duty trucks and buses as well as the manufacturing of vehicle bodies, interiors, and trailers.

In the case of bus manufacturing, some companies like Daimler (which owns or has shares in Mercedes and Setra for example) or Volvo and Scania integrate chassis, motor, and bodywork production. These companies are primarily included in the heavy-duty-truck- and bus-manufacturing sector. On the other hand, companies that manufacture only bus bodyworks belong to the motor-vehicle-body-, interior-, and trailer-manufacturing sector. These companies may produce coaches, urban buses, and medium, micro, and minibuses, or a mix of these products.

Other than the segment of micro-buses, in Brazil most bus transportation companies acquire buses through two separate purchase transactions: one with the chassis manufacturer and another with the bodywork manufacturer. This allows several combinations between chassis and bodywork, and provides some flexibility for customization of the bodywork itself. This flexibity is an important feature of the Brazilian market, as will be discussed in later sections of this chapter.

Technological requirements for bus bodywork manufacturing may vary from product to product. As coaches are often used for long-distance journeys, this type of product may have a luggage hold separate from the passenger cabin, comfortable seats, and a toilet. Therefore, technological requirements for manufacturing coaches is typically different than requirements for the production of, for example, urban buses. In addition to fuel consumption, emissions reduction, and alternative fuels, which are not directly related to bodywork manufacturing, technological challenges for product innovation involve concerns such as: (i) maximizing seating capacity within legal constraints; (ii) reducing weight to maximize laden capacity; and (iii) stability. These concerns are strictly associated with the use of new materials (such as aluminum) that result in lighter structures, and improved aerodynamics, since these structures must be stable and durable. While these challenges apply to all types of buses, coaches have additional requirements involving comfort issues such as seats, air conditioning, and noise reduction, along with design flexibility considerations to match different market requirements.

In Brazil, flexibility of customization according to the needs of the bus transportation companies is considered the most important 'order winner' in the sense of Slack and Lewis (2003) (Di Serio et al., 2006). Indeed, the decision criteria for the purchase of a bus include: (i) the possibility of customization; (ii) the cost, which includes not only the purchase price, but also the total cost of ownership including maintenance and resale value (which is, in turn, related to quality); and (iii) the conditions for the acquisition, for example, financing.

Hence, the challenge for bodywork manufacturers is to leave room for customization at affordable prices for customers. The solution found was to combine some characteristics of job shop and batch production (in other words, small manufacturing operations that handle small to medium-size customer orders or batch jobs). All firms have some product families ('generations,' as named by Marcopolo), which are related to the concept of platform in the automotive industry. The customizations demanded by clients are made at the final stage of the assembling process. Technically, there are internal 'mini-assembly lines' operating in parallel, according to production orders, which feed the final assembly of the bus body itself, an extremely labor-intensive process.

Since bus bodywork manufacturing is a technologically mature segment, product innovations tend to be incremental. In this sense, technological requirements for bus bodywork manufacturing are lower in comparison with light and heavy vehicle assemblers. In fact, it is the tight process control that keeps costs at a reasonable level and is a key factor for competitiveness. Process innovation is essentially associated with the adaptation of models and techniques originally developed for the light-vehicles industry such as lean production, modular consortia, just-in-time (JIT) and *kanban*.[4]

However, the adaptation of these models had to deal with some restrictions. The first is that production of bus bodyworks is more customized than production of light vehicles. The second is a segmentation of 'tiers of suppliers.' While the first tier supplies complete systems (such as chassis, motor, air-conditioning system, seats, and windows), the second tier supplies components to the first tier while the third tier suppliers produce isolated, low value-added pieces. Despite the spread of lean production techniques, several bodywork manufacturers are vertically integrated with first tier suppliers. In Brazil, as opposed to the European case, the existence of only a few specialized suppliers in the bodywork manufacturing segment imposes the need for vertical integration. On the one hand, this allows more room for customization, but on the other hand, JIT and lean production techniques have become a key factor for cost reduction and competitiveness.

7.2.2   Bus Bodywork Manufacturing and the Automobile Industry in Brazil

In Brazil, multinational companies (MNCs) dominate the bulk of the automobile industry.[5] Scale requirements and the massive presence of MNCs (since the mid-twentieth century) left practically no room for national automobile, light truck, and utility vehicle manufacturers in Brazil.[6] In fact, Chevrolet, Citroën, Fiat, Ford, Honda, Hyundai, Iveco, Mitsubishi, Nissan, Peugeot, Renault, Toyota, and Volkswagen manufacture automobiles, light trucks, and utility vehicles in the country. Similarly, heavy-duty truck producers[7] in Brazil tend to be MNCs. This is the case with Daimler, Volkswagen, Ford, Volvo, Scania, and Iveco. Among large heavy-duty truck producers, only MAN and Renault are not present in the country. It is noteworthy that bus bodywork assemblers (such as Marcopolo) are not included in this sector since they do not produce frames or motors.

Daimler, Scania, and Volvo produce chassis and motors for buses and coaches in Brazil, being, in this sense, close partners to Brazilian bodywork manufacturers. These companies have always focused on the heavy-duty trucks as their prime market and consider the bus-assembling market as a spin-off.

In Brazil, the auto parts industry[8] involves both national (smaller) and multinational (larger) companies, but the latter's leadership is quite clear. In fact, as stressed by Santos and Pinhão (2002, p. 16), in Brazil in the late 1990s 'almost all large domestic companies were acquired.' The leadership of MNCs might be credited to the hierarchy of preferences of assemblers mentioned by Humphrey and Salerno (1999, p. 48). MNCs have a clear preference for their traditional global suppliers, leaving local suppliers as the least preferable resort.

Three of the automobile industry sectors are by far the most important in Brazil's automobile industry. These sectors correspond to the codes 29.1, 29.2, and 29.4 in the Brazilian National Classification of Economic Activities (CNAE), as shown in Table 7.1. In fact, they comprise almost 95 percent of net sales and about 85 percent of the employees of the automobile industry in Brazil. In turn, the remaining sectors (CNAE codes 29.3 and 29.5) represent almost half the number of companies, but only 5 percent of net sales and about 15 percent of the number of employees. In the case of motor vehicle body, interior, and trailer manufacturing (CNAE code 29.3), there are 1014 companies with net sales reaching USD

Table 7.1 Automobile industry in Brazil: number of companies, net sales, and number of employees, 2012

CNAE Code	Description	Number of companies	%	Net sales (USD million)	%	Number of employees	%	Sales/employee (USD thousands)
29	Automobile, light truck and utility vehicle manufacturing and heavy duty truck and bus manufacturing	3 868	100.00%	135 174	100.00%	549 499	100.00%	246.0
29.1	Automobile, light truck and utility vehicle manufacturing	20	0.52%	72 283	53.47%	110 100	20.04%	656.5
29.2	Heavy duty truck and bus manufacturing	16	0.41%	16 630	12.30%	29 065	5.29%	572.2
29.3	Motor vehicle body, interior and trailer manufacturing	1 014	26.22%	6 671	4.93%	67 140	12.22%	99.4
29.4	Motor vehicle parts and accessories manufacturing	1 987	51.37%	39 279	29.06%	330 748	60.19%	118.8
29.5	Rebuilding of engines for motor vehicles	831	21.48%	311	0.23%	12 446	2.26%	25.0

Note: Data refer to companies with number of employees greater than or equal to five.

Source: Brazilian Institute of Geography and Statistics (IBGE); elaborated by the authors.

*Table 7.2   R&D investments and percentage of innovative firms,
             automobile industry in Brazil, 2011*

Code (CNAE)	Description	Internal and external R&D exp./net sales	Percentage of innovative firms
29.1 + 29.2	(Automobile, light truck and utility vehicle manufacturing) + (Heavy duty truck and bus manufacturing)	1.57%	75.02%
29.3 + 29.5	(Motor vehicle body, interior and trailer manufacturing) + (Rebuilding of engines for motor vehicles)	0.64%	20.24%
29.4	Motor vehicle parts and accessories manufacturing	1.21%	34.08%

Source: Brazilian Innovation Survey/Brazilian Institute of Geography and Statistics (IBGE); elaborated by the authors.

6.7 billion and about 67 000 people are employed. Average net sales per company are around USD 6.6 million. These firms tend to be national and are typically considered 'family businesses.' Moreover, in comparison with CNAE codes 29.1, 29.2, and 29.4, bodywork manufacturing is clearly a more labor-intensive industry, as demonstrated by the ratio of net sales to employees indicated in Table 7.1.

As shown in Table 7.2, bodywork manufacturing is less R&D-intensive than light and heavy vehicle manufacturing.

The ratio of R&D expenditures to net sales reaches 1.57 percent for light and heavy vehicle assembling and 1.21 percent for the auto parts industry, but remains as low as 0.64 percent for the motor vehicle body, interior, and trailer sector.[9] The analysis of the percentage of innovative firms in each sector (also shown in Table 7.2) leads to the same conclusion.

In short, bus bodywork manufacturing (compared with light vehicle manufacturing) is a relatively labor-intensive, smaller (comprising only 5 percent of the automobile industry net sales), and less R&D-intensive industry as innovation tends to be incremental. Lower technological requirements and higher labor intensity of the bus bodywork industry leaves room for the presence of emerging countries in the sector. In fact, according to the International Organization of Motor Vehicle Manufacturers, world production of heavy buses reached almost 345 000 units in 2013 and the world leaders were China (173 000 units), India

(44 000 units), and Brazil (40 000 units).[10] These countries represented approximately 75 percent of world production in 2013.

7.2.3 The Path of the Bodywork Manufacturing Sector in Brazil

Two 'waves of entry' mark the establishment of bus bodywork companies in Brazil. The first wave was in the late 1940s and early 1950s and the second wave was in the 1990s and early 2000s.

At the beginning of the twentieth century, electrical trams began to spread in Brazil, replacing animal-powered vehicles. American, British, and Canadian firms usually supplied these trams. After the Second World War, however, an imports shortage created the opportunity for a national industry that essentially assembled bus bodyworks on truck chassis and provided spare parts. This movement was simultaneous with the industrialization and urbanization of the country. Essentially, this is the environment that marked the creation of Marcopolo, Busscar, and Comil, which began manufacturing buses in 1949, as well as Ciferal, which began its operation in 1955. The creation of these companies took place during the so-called 'import substitution industrialization' (ISI) model adopted in Brazil between the 1930s and the 1980s (see Baer, 2002).[11]

The influence of the descendants of European immigrants is quite clear in these reported cases. Marcopolo was created by Italian descendants, Busscar by Swedish descendants, and Ciferal by an Austrian who emigrated to Brazil. Three out of the four companies created during the first wave were located in the southern region of Brazil: Marcopolo, Busscar, and Comil. Ciferal, on the other hand, was located in Rio de Janeiro.[12]

Interestingly, while the bulk of the Brazilian industrialization process took place in the southeastern region (which includes São Paulo and Rio de Janeiro), bus bodywork companies tended to concentrate in the south. This trend is probably associated with a more entrepreneurial spirit of the immigrants together with skills they (or their families) had in metal-mechanics. Indeed, many Italian immigrants who moved to the Caxias do Sul region, in Rio Grande do Sul, were mostly from Piemonte and Veneto and had skills and experience in the metal-mechanic industry. The local market in the south of Brazil was, in the beginning, large enough to provide the necessary scale to the bus bodywork companies and the transportation costs between the southern and the southeastern regions of Brazil created a sort of natural market protection for these companies.

The initial concentration of these companies in the south of Brazil contributed to the formation of a cluster of firms in that region which remains today. A self-reinforcing presence of sectoral capabilities which would fit Myrdal's (1957 [1960]) cumulative causation theory took place, so that the clustering of auto parts companies in the state of Rio Grande do Sul relied on the availability of skilled labor, and local universities focused on engineering as a response to the increasing demand. This movement seems to have been a consequence, and not a cause, of the concentration of bus bodywork companies in the south of Brazil. There is no evidence that lower labor costs might have influenced the location decisions at the time.

Between the mid 1950s and the 1990s, no large plant was installed in Brazil. However, in 1991 and 1995 San Marino Neobus and Metalbus, respectively, were created in Caxias do Sul. In 1998 a Spanish company founded in 1889 (Irizar) installed a unit in São Paulo and in 2003 a spin-off of Comil resulted in Mascarello, installed in Cascavel (in the southern state of Paraná). The location of these plants is indicated in Figure 7.1.

As shown on the map, bus bodywork manufacturers tend to cluster in the southern region of the country, which represents around 17 percent of Brazilian GDP, while the southeastern region, which hosts only two plants, concentrates 56 percent of GDP. This suggests the existence of a sectoral and regional innovation system in the southern region, since a more 'natural' choice (due to agglomeration economies) would be the southeast.

Historically, the early establishment of important bus bodywork manufacturers and the lack of interest by large multinational auto companies in this segment led the supplier–customer relationships to be dictated by national firms. Since the beginning, bodywork manufacturers have offered highly customizable sets of bus bodies/chassis to their prime clients, namely, bus transport companies. In turn, bus transport companies attributed high value to flexibility, which became a competitive advantage. Moreover, almost all bus transport companies have their own insurance and maintenance structures. This means that if global heavy vehicle assemblers wish to contest the bodywork manufacturing market in Brazil by providing complete buses, they will have to deal with customers who value customization and flexibility and for whom after-sales services are not so important.

Today, the main bus bodywork companies are Marcopolo/Ciferal,[13] Caio/Induscar, Neobus,[14] Comil, Mascarello, Busscar, Irizar (Spanish capital), and Metalbus. According to de la Rosa et al. (2015), in 2014 Brazilian bus production reached 28 429 units (24 628 for the domestic market and 3801 for the external market). The leading company in Brazil (Marcopolo) kept its market share between 40 percent and 50 percent during the 2000s. The second-largest market share is Caio/Induscar, which focuses on the urban bus segment. Neobus and Comil represented, in 2010, around 10 percent of the Brazilian market each.

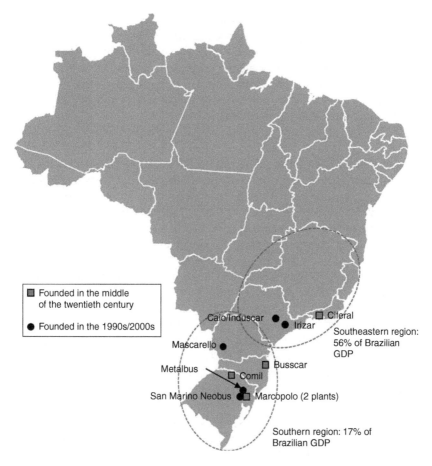

Source: Elaborated by the authors.

Figure 7.1   Bus bodywork manufacturer locations in Brazil

7.3   FIRM-LEVEL FACTORS: MARCOPOLO'S LEADING POSITION IN THE BODYWORK MANUFACTURING SECTOR

7.3.1   Marcopolo's Trajectory

Marcopolo was founded in 1949 by eight partners. Although it was not a spin-off of any other pre-existing company, most founders had previous experience in assembling, auto mechanics, and repairing. The company was created under the name 'Carrocerias Nicola' (see Cadó, 2001). Paulo Bellini, who originally worked in accounting and was, for a long time, its president, joined the company in 1950. He is a descendant of Italian immigrants. The Nicola brothers left the company between 1960 and 1967 to create a van-manufacturing firm and in 1971, the name of a bus model was given to the company, 'Marcopolo SA Carrocerias e Ônibus' (Marcopolo Bodyworks and Buses Corporation).

The first bus bodywork produced by the company was handmade in wood and adapted from truck bodyworks. The capacity was 26 passengers and it took 90 days for the bus bodywork to be produced. In 1952, the company began using the first steel structures. This was a relevant innovation for the firm, as these structures reduce the weight of vehicles and allow for maximizing laden capacity. Then in 1954, the first intercity bus equipped with reclining seats was launched. The company went public that same year, changed its name to 'Carrocerias Nicola SA,' and began the construction of a new plant. According to Cadó (2001), shares in the company were sold to relatives and friends at that time, resulting in some 'love money funding' during the early years of the company. In the mid 1950s, the availability of chassis specially designed for buses considerably reduced the manufacturing time. In 1957, Brazilian suppliers began producing chassis, which, up to that time, had been imported as completely knocked down (CKD) vehicles.[15] This movement is clearly associated with the ISI model adopted in Brazil at the time.

Several new models were launched in the 1970s, such as the modular urban bus, *Romeo and Juliet*, whose rear section could be removed to adjust the required number of seats, and an electrically-powered urban bus. Additionally, some models incorporated flat-bed seats and air conditioning. The company acquired Elizário, a bodywork assembler located in Porto Alegre (the capital of the state of Rio Grande do Sul) in 1971, and they acquired Nimbus, a bodywork assembler, also located in Caxias do Sul, in 1977. In 1979, Marcopolo installed a unit in Betim in the state of Minas Gerais.

Although Marcopolo had gone public in 1954, it wasn't until 1978 that its shares began being traded on the São Paulo Stock Exchange (Bovespa). Trading shares on the exchange market represented the engagement of a different growth strategy, involving riskier initiatives. Hence, the company called new partners to share risks as well as benefits. Currently, Marcopolo's capital structure comprises Brazilian and foreign shareholders. However, foreign shareholders do not own ordinary shares. Rather, they hold the majority of preferential shares.

The 1980s are widely considered a 'lost decade' for the Brazilian economy. The crisis affected Marcopolo in particular at the beginning of the decade. Between 1981 and 1983, production was reduced from 12 267 units to 6695 units. Notwithstanding the economic impact, the crisis encouraged the company to seek out new forms of commercialization, such as leasing and sales consortia. However, the negative economic environment of the early 1980s in Brazil did not prevent the establishment of a new plant in 1981 (the so-called 'Ana Rech'), the release of new models (some of which became a reference for the sector, for example the 'low-driver' model), and the vertical integration process (whereby, in 1984, the auto parts company 'Marcopolo Distribuidora de Peças Ltda' was created and in 1987, MVC Plastics Components was installed in São José dos Pinhais, in the state of Parana[16]).

In the 1990s, the company kept releasing new models including 'low-entry' and 'double-decker' buses. It was during the 1990s that Marcopolo developed its production scheme. The organization of production at Marcopolo follows, in essence, a kind of Toyota Production System (TPS) adapted to bus bodywork manufacturing with a high degree of vertical integration. Pieces and modules are assembled during a final stage, which is extremely labor-intensive, to meet customization demands. The process is guided by lean production and JIT principles. Internal inventory and logistics costs as well as transfer prices are strictly controlled.

This adaptation was highly successful. Between 1986, when the implementation process of the Japanese techniques began, and 1994, inventory costs dropped 70 percent and the production cycle was significantly reduced. The mastery of process technologies is a key capability for competitiveness, both in Brazil and abroad.

During the 2000s, Marcopolo considerably expanded its presence abroad, as will be described in the next section. Moreover, Marcopolo acquired Ciferal in 2001 and 39.6 percent of Neobus shares in 2007, consolidating its leadership in the Brazilian market.

Di Serio et al. (2006) elaborate an importance–performance matrix for Marcopolo. In both the coaches and urban buses segments, the order-winner factors are customization, quality, resale price, purchase price, and financing. In the first three factors, Marcopolo is better than its competitors; it is equal to its competitors regarding the financing conditions; and it is worse in the price factor. In sum, in terms of market positioning, Marcopolo does not offer the cheapest bodywork, but it is the company that provides the greatest possibility for customization. During one of the interviews, it was mentioned that the company offers up to 3 million different combinations of buses, as well as the best quality and the best resale value, even though its product is more expensive than the average.

In the early 2010s, Marcopolo was the third-largest bus bodywork manufacturer in the world. According to the company's financial statements, net revenues reached USD 1.4 billion in 2014. As mentioned in the previous section, Marcopolo's market share in Brazil oscillated between 40 and 50 percent during the 2000s. The company's 2010 in-country market share reached 66.5 percent for intercity buses (coaches), 37.8 percent for urban buses, 42.0 percent for microbuses, and 46.9 percent for minibuses. In 2014, Marcopolo produced 17 793 units (Marcopolo, 2015).

7.3.2 Towards a Global Company

The early 1960s marked the first export experience of Marcopolo. The target was Uruguay, a neighbor of the state of Rio Grande do Sul. And in 1971, Marcopolo started exporting technology and CKD bodyworks to Venezuela.

Exporting CKD kits is standard practice in the automobile industry as a whole, as local governments tend to impose heavy taxes on CBU imports in order to stimulate local assembling and job creation. According to Martins (2003), while freight costs and average import taxes for CBU exports reached, in the early 2000s, USD 5500 and 25 percent, respectively, for CKD these figures are USD 1200 and 0 percent to 5 percent. In this sense, the mastery of CKD reassembling technology was a key capability for the internationalization process of Marcopolo. Indeed, the company used the former Elizário plant to simulate its first CKD exports to Venezuela (Hexsel, 2004).

In spite of some experience of exporting CKD and SKD bodyworks to some countries in prior decades, it wasn't until the early 1990s that Marcopolo intensified its internationalization process with plants abroad. This movement seems to have been a consequence of the perception that the technology licensing contracts established up until the 1980s would eventually encourage the emergence of new competitors who could assimilate the company's technology. As a result of this perception, in 1991 Marcopolo acquired a bodywork plant in Portugal.

Indeed, Marcopolo had in mind an 'advanced observatory point' in Europe, in a country that shares the same language spoken in Brazil. Moreover, the company was concerned about the restrictive regulations to imports and foreign direct investments (FDIs) the upcoming European Union could eventually impose on non-member countries. Initially, Marcopolo sent entire parts to be assembled in Europe and the plant was totally controlled by the company.

In 1998, Marcopolo's second plant abroad was installed in Argentina to assemble CKD vehicles exported from Brazil. The FDI experiences in Portugal and Argentina might be considered the start of a learning process, given that the absence of local partners as well as the low levels of integration with local suppliers would become problems to be faced in the future. Additionally, Martins (2008) argues that in the case of Portugal, Marcopolo's products did not fit the local market.

In 1999, the third plant abroad, Polomex, was installed in Mexico. This plant was originally the result of an acquisition by Marcopolo and was 100 percent controlled by the company. Subsequently in 2001, 26 percent of the shares were sold to DaimlerChrysler.[17] According to Martins (ibid.), '[a]ll the mistakes made in Portugal and Argentina were corrected in Mexico.'

During the 2000s, Marcopolo deepened its internationalization process and seemed to find its own way to succeed in foreign markets. The most remarkable characteristics of this phase are: (i) growth towards developing countries (with the exception of Australia); and (ii) joint ventures with local leaders or renowned chassis manufacturers, bringing prestige as well as knowledge about the market, distribution channels, and suppliers network.

Developing countries are the most promising ones in terms of future growth, and, in many cases, are under-explored by traditional auto companies. Moreover, these markets sometimes have customer characteristics that are similar to the Brazilian ones, particularly when it comes to the high value attained through customization. In this sense, the 'order-winners' are basically the same as in the Brazilian market. Specifically, the case of Saudi Arabia is emblematic, as Marcopolo had the ability to develop bodyworks to fit some religious requirements. Currently, Marcopolo has plants in all BRICS countries. Table 7.3 summarizes the internationalization process of Marcopolo.

A noticeable change occurred in the local content of Marcopolo's foreign plants from the middle of the 2000s onwards. Over time, Marcopolo's plants located abroad tended to become similar to its Brazilian plants, specifically regarding virtualization and process management. There are two factors primarily responsible for the process changes. The first is the appreciation in value of the Brazilian Real.[18] As a result of that appreciation, production costs in Brazil rose steadily in foreign currency. The second factor is the evolution of the internationalization process. Some studies suggest that the case of Marcopolo adheres well to the gradualist paradigm of internationalization, with increasing involvement with foreign partners (Rosa, 2006; Stal, 2007). This increasing involvement is beneficial from at least three points of view: (i) financial, because it allows the company to avoid exchange-rate risks affecting critical costs; (ii) market positioning, as it allows a better understanding of the market and supply chain; and (iii) institutional image, as a result of greater integration with global and/ or locally renowned partners, which facilitates entry into countries with stricter FDI regulation and higher local content requirements. As a result,

Table 7.3 Marcopolo's internationalization process

Year	Country	Name	Strategy	Current status
1991	Portugal	–	Acquisition of a local firm. The plant in Portugal would be an advanced standpoint in Europe. No local partners directly involved.	The plant was shut down in 2009.
1998	Argentina	Metalpar Argentina	Greenfield investment for CKD assembling. No local partners involved. Low integration with local suppliers.	After a standby, the plant is active. Since 2007, the plant is a joint venture with Metalpar Chile, but Marcopolo is a minority partner.
1999	Mexico	Polomex	Acquisition of a local firm. However, in 2001, Marcopolo sold 26% of the shares of that plant to DaimlerChrysler.	Active.
2001	South Africa	Marcopolo South Africa (MASA)	Acquisition of a local firm. Joint venture with Scania.	Active.
2001	Colombia	Superpolo	Joint venture with Volvo.	Active.
2001	China	Auto Components	Joint venture with Iveco.	Active, after a standby.
2006	Russia	Russia Buses Marco	Joint venture with a local firm, RusAutoProm.	Currently a joint venture with Kamaz.
2006	India	Tata Marcopolo Motors	Joint venture with Tata Motors.	Active.
2008	Egypt	GB Polo	Joint venture with GB Polo. The idea was to replace the Portuguese plant taking advantage of a Free Trade Agreement between Egypt and Europe.	Standby, due to the political crisis.
2011	Australia	Australian Volgren	Acquisition of 75% of Australian Volgren.	Active.

Source: Elaborated by the authors based upon several references used in this chapter.

Marcopolo currently controls thirteen plants abroad and four plants in Brazil.

A benchmark of this higher integration with foreign partners is the joint venture with Tata Motors in India. Tata Marcopolo Motors was created in 2006 to manufacture fully built buses and coaches for India and other selected international markets (Mani, 2011, p. 20; the case of Tata Motors is discussed in Chapter 4). Initial investments were estimated at USD 13.3 million with total investments estimated at USD 70 million. Marcopolo holds 49 percent of Tata Marcopolo Motors, while 51 percent is held by Tata Motors. Local suppliers were to be fostered in this project. Tata Motors is responsible for providing chassis and for commercializing the buses, while Marcopolo provides the production technology and develops new products.

Besides these movements, by the 2000s Marcopolo had already consolidated its position as a large bus exporter. Marcopolo's buses circulate in more than 100 countries. Its presence in Portugal and Mexico, for example, allowed the company to benefit from free trade agreements in the European Union and from the North American Free Trade Agreement (NAFTA) area, and to export to several more developed countries in these continents. The same happened in Africa, where the company could benefit from the Southern African Development Community (SADC).

7.3.3 Sources of Capability Building

Marcopolo's internal sources of capability building may involve, 'for example, R&D activities and learning-by-doing. Its external sources encompass purchasing technology, joint ventures, and mergers and acquisitions.

Marcopolo conducts R&D aimed at product development. The formal name for the department is the 'Corporate Engineering Division.' This department is centralized in Caxias do Sul, employs approximately 100 people, and is responsible for structural and complex projects such as the new 'generations' or platforms of bodies. As such, this department is different from other local engineering departments, which are specific to plants and focus on the production processes and less complex customizations. Local engineering employs around 200 people in plants around the world.

According to data collected during the interviews, in 2011 the company invested around USD 27 million in R&D. Although this number refers only to the investments made in Brazil, where revenues are limited to the domestic plants, it is possible to estimate an R&D–revenues ratio of around 2 percent, as shown in Table 7.4.

The rise to market leadership

Table 7.4   Marcopolo's R&D expenditures

	2008	2009	2010	2011
R&D expenditures in Brazil (USD million)	17.00	16.55	22.33	27.48
Net operational revenues in Brazil (USD million)	845.76	694.13	1 182.66	1 467.59
R&D intensity (R&D/revenues)	2.01%	2.38%	1.89%	1.87%

Source: Based on Marcopolo's data and financial statements, elaborated by the authors.

Marcopolo's average R&D intensity during the period between 2008 and 2011 (2.04 percent) is more than three times the average of motor vehicle body, interior, and trailer manufacturing in Brazil (0.64 percent) and above the average for automobile, light truck, utility vehicle, heavy-duty truck, and bus manufacturing (1.57 percent). However, in the latter sector, R&D is still in the hands of MNCs (Malerba and Nelson, 2011, p. 1654).

The Corporate Engineering Division has two teams. One team is in charge of design and the other is in charge of engineering developments. In terms of prospective development of new products, Marcopolo's R&D can be divided into three time horizons: short, medium, and long term. There are about five researchers whose work is to prospect the major trends in bus manufacturing and to consider the implications of these trends in engineering. The medium-term development is related to the need for relevant changes or adaptations in existing production platforms, which generally require new designs, prototypes, and tests, such as aerodynamic testing, stability, and damping. For aerodynamics tests, Marcopolo uses extensive simulations in CAD/CAM as well as the wind tunnel of the Aerospace Technical Centre (CTA) of the Aeronautics Technological Institute (ITA) located in São José dos Campos, using prototypes for these tests. Finally, short-term development is related to incremental innovations to meet customization needs such as new seats, windows, and doors.

The management of innovation projects in Marcopolo is centralized in the Corporate Engineering Department. Naturally, there are interactions with other departments such as commercial areas and operations management. However, these interactions serve as suggestions and feedback mechanisms, and should not be characterized as interdepartmental development teams.

Nevertheless, bus bodywork manufacturing is a segment where it is possible to predict, with reasonable accuracy, the technological routes. Developments tend to be marginal and targeted at the needs of customization, as well as reducing the cost of operation and maintenance, which, like the production process, is consistent with the market positioning of the company. Examples of such developments are aerodynamic concerns to reduce fuel consumption and the introduction of various accesses to the chassis without the need to disassemble the body in order to reduce maintenance costs. Another development was the mounting of the bodywork using screws instead of braze, which both reduces maintenance cost and increases the possibilities of customization. An interesting example of this application is the aforementioned case of the buses with removable roofs in Saudi Arabia.

However, one could wonder what makes Marcopolo so special in its segment. Since bus bodywork manufacturing is a technologically process-driven mature segment, why don't competitors simply catch up with Marcopolo's performance?

Actually, other competitors organize the manufacturing process in a remarkably similar way to Marcopolo. It is not in fact difficult to divide production into mini assembly lines that converge in the end. However, production management is not only a sequence of steps, as it involves capabilities and strategies. No Brazilian competitor achieves the degree of vertical integration that Marcopolo has, nor do they have access to several components produced by Marcopolo because the company does not sell to its competitors. There is strict cost control and transfer pricing, and inventories are particularly low because the production is practically simultaneous to the demand. According to the interviews, logistics costs account for no more than 3 percent of the total cost. Furthermore, Marcopolo has the highest degree of flexibility to meet the demand for customization in Brazil as well in the other countries in which it operates.

External sources of capability building are mainly related to Marcopolo's relationship with customers and suppliers as well as benchmarking of its main competitors (by taking part in exhibitions, for example), but the company does not directly buy external technology. In particular, the relationship with customers and suppliers and the need for product adaptation to different market requirements and regulation standards works as an important innovation driver. Castilho (n.d.) argues that bus bodywork product customization in Brazil began domestically, as buses are largely used for short- and long-distance trips and these vehicles must adapt to different conditions. According to Verol and Campos Filho (n.d.), the 1980s mark the beginning of the efforts to adapt products to external markets. In 1988, for example, Marcopolo exported shuttles to the United States. These buses had to be adapted to a niche for medium distances (up to 250 km) and to match local standards. Still according to Verol and Campos Filho (n.d.), not only customers but also suppliers took part in these efforts as new materials were required. This experience is reported as an extremely important source of learning and it served as a reference for future developments. Accordingly, the case of buses exported to Saudi Arabia, which, for example, had to have separate sections in the same bus for men and women, is another example of how requirements for exports created incentives for innovation. Interestingly, Malerba and Nelson (2011, p. 1648) argued that catching-up firms usually have a hard time trying to replicate the organizational, managerial, and institutional aspects of productive practices of benchmarking firms. In Marcopolo's case, however, the capacity of adapting to indigenous conditions was itself a factor that contributed to its leadership position.

In spite of its relatively high R&D intensity, linkages with universities and public laboratories seem to be less important sources of capability building. In fact, differently from Embraer, which strongly relied on a public university created to provide skilled labor and R&D services for the aerospace sector (the aforementioned ITA), Marcopolo and the other automobile companies in the southern region of Brazil mainly preceded the supply of skilled labor by local universities.

Moreover, there seems to be no cooperative culture among companies located in the region, at least in the automotive sector. These companies are basically competitors and do not cooperate in innovative projects. In fact, some of these companies are spin-offs of existing ones and are not welcome by the previous incumbents. As university–enterprise linkages are rather weak in terms of innovative projects, cooperative innovation projects tend to be nonexistent among companies in the bus bodywork sector, since they are generally intermediated by local universities. The exception is the cooperation between companies that do not compete directly against one another, for example the case of the cooperation between Marcopolo and Randon, a Brazilian road implements company. These two companies share vehicle proving grounds in Caxias do Sul, where both companies have industrial plants.

As shown previously in this section, Marcopolo widely uses acquisitions and joint ventures to spread its plants around the world, following a trend mentioned by Carvalho et al. (2010, p. 5), according to whom 'Brazilian firms are reaching overseas markets in a large variety of ways, but acquisitions have been widely broadcasted.' However, there is no evidence that these movements were intended to acquire technologies. This perception converges with Carvalho et al. (ibid., p. 20), who argue that among Brazilian internationalized firms, 'technology seeking investments are rather scarce.'

To guarantee intellectual property of innovations in aerodynamics, design, and comfort items, Marcopolo used invention, utility model, and industrial design patents. The company is by far the leader in Brazil, as the number of invention and utility model patents granted to Marcopolo is five times greater than the number of invention and utility model patents granted to the second company (Busscar). Furthermore, the number of Marcopolo's patents is more than twice the rest of bus bodywork companies in the country put together. The analysis of industrial design patents leads to a similar conclusion. These data make clear the offensive technological strategy adopted by Marcopolo according to Freeman and Soete's (1997) typology. Regardless, one must consider that patenting and other formal strategies for intellectual property protection may result in disclosure of technology, so they are not a perfect proxy for the outputs of technological activities from Marcopolo. Additionally, it was mentioned during the interviews that verticalization is also a technology protection strategy, since many innovations are related to materials, and if these items are outsourced, they may become available to competitors as well. In other words, in several instances, Marcopolo prefers industrial secrecy and verticalization as an intellectual property protection strategy, especially when legal uncertainty is taken into account.

The adoption of lean production principles in Marcopolo is combined with a high degree of verticalization and many of its suppliers are firms controlled by the company. However, there is no vertical integration between motor and chassis producers and bus bodywork manufacturers in Brazil. This environment is completely different from the European one, for example. In Europe, it is rather easy for a large auto manufacturer to become a bus manufacturer as well, since they may outsource many stages of production. Moreover, the European market is not used to customization, which leaves room for economies of scale.

In fact, according to Zignani and Deiro (2011), Marcopolo produces nearly all the parts used in the manufacturing process (seats, foams, windows, doors, hydro-sanitary installations, handbag compartments, plastic components, air conditioning, and audio and video systems). The exceptions are, of course, chassis and motors, which may represent between 50 and 60 percent of the bus total cost.[19] This ratio varies according to the type of bus. While urban buses have simpler (and less expensive) bodyworks, coaches usually have more expensive bodyworks. Bus bodywork assembling is different from motor and chassis production (as well as from light-vehicle manufacturing) because of the customization requirements. In contrast, motor and chassis are usually produced at a large scale. This makes bus bodywork assembling a different business and explains why motor and chassis manufacturers do not often integrate their processes with bodywork production to assemble the entire bus.

Examples of suppliers controlled by Marcopolo include MVC Plastic Components, Wsul (seats), and Spheros (air conditioning manufacturer).

Interestingly, companies like MVC supply components not only to Marcopolo, but also to other automobile assemblers (such as Nissan) and aircraft assemblers (such as Bombardier), as well as wind-power companies, for example. That makes the company a sort of outsider in the automobile industry, where outsourcing is a clear trend (Collins et al., 1997). In this sense, Marcopolo differs from Embraer, which, according to Marques and Oliveira (2009), has not been able to consolidate its supply chain within Brazilian national borders. While Embraer's internationalization led to an increase of its import content from 68 percent in the 1980s to approximately 95 percent in the 1990s, Marcopolo used vertical integration to consolidate its supply chain in Brazil. Furthermore, its international plants also rely on local suppliers.

7.4   COUNTRY-LEVEL FACTORS: GOVERNMENT SUPPORT AND PUBLIC POLICY INSTRUMENTS

During the 2000s, Marcopolo accessed credits provided by the Brazilian Innovation Agency (FINEP) in 2002, 2005, and 2007, and accessed fiscal incentives for R&D during 2006, 2007, and 2008. The company argues, however, that innovation financing depends on innovation projects, and their innovation projects suitable for FINEP's requirements do not happen on a yearly basis. From the company's standpoint, the public policy instrument most used by Marcopolo was credit at more favorable conditions provided by the Brazilian Development Bank (BNDES). During the 2000s, this instrument was accessed each year.

However, much more important to Marcopolo (and for the whole sector as well) is buyers' credit, both domestically and abroad. Domestically, the National Equipment Financing Authority (Finame), a financial program aimed at the purchase of machinery equipment at more favorable conditions for buyers, provided by the BNDES, has played a very important role for capital goods producers in general. Internationally, export financing through the Export Finance Program (Proex) has been crucial for the company's exports, since it equalizes borrowers' interest rates for foreign clients with international standards. Interest rates in Brazil have traditionally been high. Hence, without the support of a program like Proex, exporting firms would face considerably reduced competitiveness from the financial side. These instruments, although benefiting Marcopolo, do not specifically target the company or even the sector. Yet their importance to the company suggests that, in some cases, focusing financial policy instruments on product demand might have a more relevant impact on the company's performance than the supply-sided ones.

In any case, there is no evidence that government support and public policy instruments explain the leadership position of the firm. Not only are these instruments rarely mentioned in previous analyses of the company, but Marcopolo's technological development and internationalization process do not seem to have relied on them. It seems more appropriate to state that Marcopolo and other Brazilian bus bodywork companies benefit from public policies originally designed for light-vehicle manufacturers, as in the case of providing access to credit at more favorable conditions, provided by the BNDES. As a result, at the national level, public policies could not be considered as proactive since they did not promote the birth of the leading company. It might even be argued that public policies were reactive, as they supported Marcopolo only after it had already emerged as a leader. But it seems more accurate to say that the bulk of these policies were not aimed at this sector and Marcopolo simply took advantage of the availability of these instruments, which were, in fact, not designed for bus bodywork manufacturing, as (for example) the BNDES credits.

7.5   MAIN FINDINGS AND FINAL REMARKS

The aim of this work was to analyse the factors that explain the industrial leadership of a Brazilian bus bodywork manufacturer. From a methodological point of view, the chapter was a case study based on a bibliographic review and on in-depth interviews.

All in all, the main hypothesis of this work, that at some point in the past some idiosyncratic factors regarding the Brazilian market led the large auto manufacturers to give up contesting Brazilian incumbents in the bus bodywork sector, was confirmed. In fact, the lower technological requirements and higher labor intensity of the bus bodywork industry left room for the establishment and leadership of emerging countries like Brazil, India, and China in the segment. From that point onwards, path dependency and capability building consolidated this leading position.

At first, the development of Marcopolo in an enclave around which metal-mechanic firms clustered helped the company to develop its techno-logical capabilities. After that, however, Marcopolo seems to have focused on the development of these skills, investing in R&D and vertical integ-ration. On the other hand, cooperation between companies in bus bodywork manufacturing and support from universities and research centers cannot be considered factors that explain the leading position currently occupied by Marcopolo. Even the mergers and acquisitions in which Marcopolo was involved were driven by market reasons and did not aim at technology transferring. Although there is a kind of bodywork-manufacturing cluster in Caxias do Sul, there is no evidence of cooperation culture among firms. Typically, new firms are spin-offs of incumbent firms and are perceived as competitors that could appropriate the technological capabilities accumulated by the companies that originated them. This explains the low levels of cooperation between firms observed in the region. However, it was possible to verify the existence of some cooperation activities between Marcopolo and other companies in the automotive sector that do not belong to the bus bodywork-manufacturing segment.

The analysis of the trajectory of the company revealed that Marcopolo tried to keep ahead of the official rhetoric of public policies and market trends in Brazil. Indeed, the company went public when initial public offerings (IPOs) were a very rare financing option in Brazil, began to export at a time when the country emphasized import substitution, and was among the first national companies to own production facilities abroad. The internationalization process of the company was marked by successive approximations, a trial-and-error process which has been gradually involving more and more local suppliers. Although the main positions of Marcopolo abroad are in developing countries, in 2012 the company acquired four production units in Volgren, Australia.[20]

As evidenced throughout this work, the company has grown into a niche where it could dictate the relationship patterns between suppliers and buyers. Currently, the prime customers of the bus bodywork manufacturers – bus transportation companies – appreciate the possibilities for customization and maintain their own maintenance facilities. This means that for an MNC to contest the leadership of Marcopolo offering full buses (body, chassis, and engine), it will have to deal with customers used to customization and flexibility and for whom the post-sales services such as maintenance, for example, are not as important.

However, the presence of large, multinational manufacturers of complete buses in Brazil is a threat to local businesses, especially when one considers the sluggish demand in developed countries. In this case, products would be offered at lower prices, even without the customization possibilities of the domestic market, and MNCs could eventually stop supplying chassis for Marcopolo. Thus, the biggest challenges for Marcopolo in the near future appear to be associated with process technologies, modularity, and product platforms, in order to reduce costs. Additionally, in the case of tough competition with MNCs, Marcopolo and other major local producers may need to start producing chassis and engines or to identify alternative suppliers of these components. In this sense, Marcopolo's alliance with Tata Motors seems to be a strategic one.

The case of Marcopolo may provide important insights for policy-makers in Brazil, who have been putting strong emphasis on the segment of light vehicles since the mid-twentieth century and failed to consolidate a nationally owned company leader in this segment. In contrast, a nationally owned global leader emerged in a relatively neglected segment, as far as explicit industrial policies are concerned. Marcopolo's leading position was consolidated over a long time; one could hardly predict it would be a global player in the early days of the company. In fact, Marcopolo's leading position results from clearly riskier decisions and strategies that paid off, but one can only understand the company's current position through the combined and contextualized analysis of these decisions and strategies.

NOTES

1. Bus manufacturing may include coaches, urban buses, medium-sized, micro, and minibus production. In this chapter, the word 'bus' refers to this range of vehicles.
2. Throughout this chapter, Brazilian Real (BRL) was converted into US dollars using the corresponding annual average exchange rate.
3. Embraer is a Brazilian aerospace company which is among the largest of the world.
4. See Womack et al. (1990) for a detailed description of these processes and how they changed the auto-manufacturing industry.
5. Formally, according to the Brazilian National Classification of Economic Activities (CNAE Version 2.0), the automobile industry encompasses 'automobile, light truck and utility vehicle manufacturing and heavy duty truck and bus manufacturing' (CNAE 29). The Brazilian CNAE is compatible with Standard Industrial Classification (SIC).
6. CNAE 29.1 (Automobile, Light Truck and Utility Vehicle Manufacturing).
7. CNAE 29.2 (Heavy Duty Truck and Bus Manufacturing).
8. CNAE 29.4 (Motor Vehicle Parts and Accessories Manufacturing).
9. Although these data are only available for the aggregate Motor Vehicle Body, Interior and Trailer Manufacturing plus Rebuilding of Engines for Motor Vehicles (CNAE 29.3 and 29.5), net sales of the last one are too small and do not affect significantly this conclusion.
10. Available at: http://oica.net/wp-content/uploads/buses-2010.pdf (accessed December 14, 2011).
11. It is noteworthy that the ISI model relied on a protected market to attract multinational investments in light-vehicle manufacturing, for example. In the case of bus bodywork manufacturing, however, mostly national companies benefited from market protection.
12. In 1992 the plant was moved to Duque de Caxias, also in the state of Rio de Janeiro.
13. As described in Section 7.3, Marcopolo acquired Ciferal in 2001.
14. Marcopolo acquired 39.6 percent of Neobus shares in 2007.
15. Vehicles can be traded as completely built up (CBU), partially knocked-down (PKD), semi knocked-down (SKD), and completely knocked down (CKD). From CBU to CKD, the local value added tends to increase and freight costs tend to decrease.
16. This plant began its operations in 1989.
17. The plant was originally installed in Aguascalientes and, after the joint venture with DaimlerChrysler, was transferred to the latter's plant in Monterrey.
18. The average nominal exchange rate fell from BRL 3.07/USD in 2003 to BRL 2.35/USD in 2014, after a minimum of around BRL 1.50/USD in the early 2010s.
19. According to the bus dealer's documents, the final price of an urban bus (including taxes) in Brazil is, on average, around USD 215 000; in this case, the bus bodywork costs USD 100 000, while the rest refers to motor and chassis. A long-distance coach may cost around USD 230 000, and half of this cost refers to the bodywork.

20. These movements continued after the first versions of this work. Indeed, in February 2013 Marcopolo acquired 19.99 percent of New Flyer, which has production facilities in Canada and the United States.

REFERENCES

Baer, Werner (2002), *A Economia Brasileira*, 2nd edn, São Paulo: Nobel.

Cadó, L.C.D. (2001), 'Marcopolo S/A: Uma Empresa Frente à Conjuntura Econômica Pós-Real,' Porto Alegre: Universidade Federal do Rio Grande do Sul / Curso de Pós-Graduação em Economia / Mestrado Profissional em Economia.

Carvalho, F., I. Costa, and G. Duysters (2010), 'Global players from Brazil: drivers and challenges in the internationalization process of Brazilian firms,' working paper #2010–016, United Nations University (UNU) / Maastricht Economic and Social Research and Training Centre on Innovation and Technology (MERIT).

Castilho, M. (n.d.), 'O Futuro da Inovação em Carrocerias de Ônibus no Brasil: Um Panorama da Evolução do Negócio, Produto e Serviço,' in *Design Thinking*, pp. 92–125.

Collins, R., K. Bechler, and S. Pires (1997), 'Outsourcing in the automotive industry: from JIT to modular consortia,' *European Management Journal*, 15(5), 498–508.

Freeman, C. and L. Soete (1997), *The Economics of Industrial Innovation*, 3rd edn, Cambridge, MA: MIT Press.

Hexsel, A.E. (2004), 'O sucesso internacional da Marcopolo: uma visão com base em recursos,' *Revista Eletrônica de Administração*, 10(4), 1–22.

Humphrey, J. and M. Salerno (1999), 'Globalization and assembler–supplier relations: Brazil and India,' *Actes du GERPISA*, 25, 40–63.

Malerba, F. and R. Nelson (2011), 'Learning and catching up in different sectoral systems: evidence from six industries,' *Industrial and Corporate Change*, 20(6), 1645–1675.

Mani, S. (2011), 'The Indian automotive industry: enhancing innovation capability with external and internal resources,' in P. Intarakumnerd (ed.), *How to Enhance Innovation Capability with Internal and External Sources*, ERIA Research Project Report 2010-9, Jakarta: ERIA, pp.1–39.

Marcopolo (2015), 'Informações Consolidadas,' Caxias do Sul: Marcopolo, February 20, available at: http://ri.marcopolo.com.br/ptb/2571/Relatrioda Administrao2014.pdf (accessed March 6, 2015).

Marques, R.A. and L.G. Oliveira (2009), 'Sectoral system of innovation in Brazil: reflections about the accumulation in the aeronautic sector (1990–2002),' in F. Malerba and S. Mani (eds), *Sectoral Systems of Innovation and Production in Developing Countries: Actors, Structure and Evolution*, Cheltenham, UK and Northampton, MA: Edward Elgar, pp. 156–204.

Martins, J. (2003), 'Expansão Internacional de Empresas Gaúchas,' Marcopolo, Presentation to the Rio Grande do Sul House of Representatives.

Martins, J. (2008), 'Internacionalização da Marcopolo,' Marcopolo, Presentation to the Associação Brasileira da Construção Metálica ABCEM.

Myrdal, Gunnar (1957 [1960]), *Teoria Econômica e Regiões Subdesenvolvidas*, Belo Horizonte: Editora da UFMG (Biblioteca Universitária).

Revista Exame (2007), *A Embraer do ônibus*, available at: http://exame.abril.com.br/revista-exame/edicoes/0909/noticias/a-embraer-do-onibus-m0147800 (accessed June 6, 2013).

Rosa, J.R de la, J.A. Valiati, and T.A. Deiro (2015), 'Divulgação dos Resultados de 2014,' Presentation, February, Caxias do Sul: Marcopolo.

Rosa, P.R. (2006), 'Internacionalização da empresa Marcopolo S.A.: um estudo de caso,' Dissertação (Mestrado), Universidade Federal do Rio Grande do Sul, Escola de Administração, Programa de Pós-Graduação em Administração, Porto Alegre.

Santos, A.M.M.M. and C.M.A. Pinhão (2002), *Overview of the Auto Parts Sector*, Rio de Janeiro: BNDES.

Serio, L.C. di, L.H. Oliveira, and R.M. Rebelo (2006), 'Estratégia de Operações e Competitividade Global: o Caso da Maior Fabricante Mundial de Carrocerias de Ônibus,' in *Proceedings of the 30th Meeting of ANPAD*, Annual Meeting of the National Association of Graduate Studies and Research in Administration, Salvador, available at: http://www.anpad.org.br/enanpad/2006/dwn/enanpad 2006-gola-0506.pdf.

Shapiro, H. (1989), 'State intervention and industrialization: the origins of the Brazilian automotive industry,' *Business and Economic History*, second series, 18, 26–30.

Slack, N. and M. Lewis (2003), *Operations Strategy*, Upper Saddle River, NJ: Prentice-Hall.

Stal, E. (2007), 'A mudança na estratégia internacional da Marcopolo: efeito do câmbio ou da globalização?' *Revista da ESPM*, 14, 16–29.

Verol, M.A. and L.A.N. Campos Filho (n.d.), 'Marcopolo: Evolução na Estratégia deInternacionalização,' available at: http://www.google.com/url?sa=t&rct=j&q =&esrc=s&source=web&cd=1&cad=rja&ved=0CCEQFjAA&url=http%3A% 2F%2Fibmecrjni.wikispaces.com%2Ffile%2Fview%2FCaso%2BMarcopolo.doc &ei=M4I2UIj9Cajs0gGnjIEQ&usg=AFQjCNFgjTPbYHxeh0aS9e82PhOAkVo B7Q (accessed August 23, 2012).

Womack, J.P., D.T. Jones, and D. Ross (1990), *The Machine that Changed the World*, New York: Basic Books.

Yin, R.K. (2013), *Case Study Research: Design and Methods*, 5th edn, Applied Social Research Methods, London: Sage Publications.

Zignani, C. and T.A. Deiro (2011), Institutional presentation, Marcopolo Investors Relations, April.

8. Market leadership in Brazil's ICT sector: the cases of Totvs and Positivo

Bruno César Araújo and Rodrigo Abdalla Filgueiras de Sousa

8.1 INTRODUCTION

Since the early 2000s, the potential of emerging countries to transform the dynamics of the world's economies in the near future in unanticipated ways has been extensively discussed. Two stylized facts illustrate such increasing interest. First, developing nations have achieved consistently higher rates of economic growth than the developed countries, especially after the financial crisis that arose in 2008. Second, developing nations have had a progressively growing participation in the global market. Currently, the number of the world's largest companies that were originally established in emerging countries is increasing; many of them are from Brazil, India, and China.

Along with expected changes in regional distribution of the world's wealth, technical progress is a key factor in understanding the transformation of economic transactions. From this perspective, information and communications technology (ICT) exhibits a large and profound potential to transform social and economic relationships. ICT is at the core of the globalization process and generates positive externalities on overall productivity. Furthermore, ICT firms usually have very intensive Research and Development (R&D) activities that produce innovations, reinforcing positive effects all over the economy.

In Brazil, the largest firms in software and hardware segments are, respectively, Totvs and Positivo Informática (Positivo). Totvs specialized in developing Enterprise Resource Planning (ERP) systems, while Positivo focused on personal computer (PC) manufacturing. Moreover, both are nationally owned firms that have recently ventured into the global markets. In this sense, they are market leaders as defined in the first chapter of this book, having a dominant position in the domestic markets, some global reach, and being innovative.

What factors explain the market leadership of these Brazilian enterprises in such competitive markets, where Brazil is not a traditional player? To answer this question, we develop two case studies, combining information from previous studies, annual reports, financial statements, sector analysis from specialized consulting companies, and other relevant documents, as well as in-depth interviews with company executives and sector specialists from the Brazilian National Development Bank (BNDES).

In both cases it is likely that national idiosyncrasies, such as public policies and institutional frameworks, initially supported the emergence of each company as a market leader. From that point forward, strong marketing capabilities helped forge business models and consolidate the leadership of these companies in their market segments. However, the market-leadership positions in Brazil have not been enough to put these companies technologically ahead of their competitors. This interpretation is in line with the framework presented in Chapter 1 of this book.

Notwithstanding that economies of scale and scope are essential sources of competitive advantage in the ICT sector, both of these cases indicate a combination of two factors that could counterbalance initial scale and scope advantages of foreign-owned firms. First, governmental support has been crucial, although it has used different approaches. Totvs's leadership position was reinforced by financial support from the BNDES, while Positivo benefited from trade protectionism, under the 'infant industry' argument. Second, both companies achieved market leadership through the development of customized products and solutions for specific market segments that had not been properly addressed by world industry leaders.

8.2 TOTVS'S LEADING POSITION IN THE BRAZILIAN ERP SEGMENT

Currently, Totvs is the ERP leader in Brazil, holding 50 percent of the market with more than 26000 customers in 23 countries. Its net revenues reached USD 736 million[1] in 2011 (compounded annual growth rate (CAGR) of 18.4 percent per annum between 2006 and 2011). Totvs employs around 9000 workers, most of them in Brazil. It is also the largest developer of business management applications located in an emerging country and the sixth-largest ERP developer in the world. It offers vertical solutions in ten segments: design and construction, distribution and logistics, agribusiness, legal, educational, financial services, manufacturing, healthcare, outsourcing services, and retail services. It is considered 56th of the 100 best-performing IT companies in the world (according to *Business Week*) and is among the top 1000 R&D investors in the world (according to Booz & Co). Today, Totvs remains interested in growth through mergers and acquisitions (M&As), especially with vertical developers. Totvs has made significant efforts to unify and control its distribution channels. The firm's international growth strategy remains targeted at Latin America and Africa, considered emerging regions for ERP. In the following subsections, the origins of Totvs's leadership will be explored, beginning with sector-level factors.

8.2.1   Sector-Level Factors

8.2.1.1   ERP: dynamics and technological requirements

ERPs are systems that integrate internal and external management information across an entire organization, embracing finance and accounting, manufacturing, sales and service, customer relationship management, etc.[2] ERP systems automate activity with integrated software applications, facilitating the flow of information between all business functions inside boundaries of the organization and managing connections to outside stakeholders, for example supply-chain management.

The most important features of ERP applications are: (i) price; (ii) ease of use; (iii) system reliability and compliance with current legislation; (iv) compatibility with other ERP systems (particularly for supply-chain management); and (v) 'good dialogue' with internet and cloud computing features.

ERP business models are mostly based on the software-as-a-service (SaaS) model. This means client firms will not only buy ERP applications on a 'once and for all' basis; they will demand maintenance and updates. According to this model, customers rely on updated applications from technological and legislative perspectives, and developers may have a stable source of revenue. However, it demands continuous improvements in software applications and its possible interactions, as well as research on adaptation of tax legislation changes whenever necessary.

Typically, ERP markets are segmented in two dimensions: (i) size of client firms; and (ii) sectoral peculiarities of client firms. Regarding size, large firms tend to demand specific ERP solutions, and integration with suppliers' systems is generally important. Inversely, small firms tend to demand rather generic solutions, but they are very concerned with price, billing, and 'package' flexibility.

Thus, development requirements are very different to meet the demands of such distinct segments. For large firms, customization is important, so the ability to understand clients' peculiarities and develop solutions is a competitive advantage. For small firms, price competitiveness may be achieved with scale. Hence, if a software house is able to develop solutions that fit many firms, the final price may be lower. Moreover, small firms may not be interested in whole ERP solutions; some 'modules' of the solution may be enough. This is the case for small firms interested in fiscal ERP modules to meet Tax Authority requirements, but not necessarily interested in inventory management modules. Indeed, the internet has been a very efficient way to deliver 'packages' in a flexible and cheaper way.

The client firms sector is another important segmentation due to some sectoral peculiarities. Understanding these sector-level specific features allows development of ERP solutions that may be front-of-mind for a large number of firms in a specific sector, hence achieving scale and reducing costs. ERP solutions that fit specific sector-level needs are called 'verticals.' Vertical development is midway between customization and large-scale software development. It requires some specific knowledge of distinct segments, ranging, for example, from dental clinics to wholesale.

Gartner[3] points out major technological trends and challenges in ERP for the next few years. These trends include:

- cloud computing;
- systemic and sophisticated analysis of data;
- client computing (powerful servers, client desktops);
- 'green information and communications technology (ICT)': logistics optimization, electronic management of documents, videoconferences;
- pod-based data centers;
- social computing;
- security and intelligence.

8.2.1.2   ERP in Brazil

According to Gartner,[4] the Brazilian market for ICT in general is estimated at USD 15 billion, with estimated cumulated accumulated growth of 11 percent per year. In 2015, Brazil represented 45 percent of the Latin American ICT market, and 2.2 percent of the world market (ABES, 2016, using data from the International Data Corporation (IDC)).

According to Totvs's financial statements (Totvs, 2012), the Brazilian ERP market was estimated at USD 1.5 billion per year. In 2011 Totvs had around 50 percent of this market. This is very different from the world scenario, where the leading companies are SAP, Oracle, and Microsoft, as depicted in Table 8.1.

Although the Brazilian market is relatively small compared to the world market (2 percent), it has great growth potential because only 9 percent of Brazilian firms have adopted ERP solutions while economic growth has fostered dissemination of ICT technologies in general. Moreover, tax

Table 8.1   Market shares in the Brazilian and world ERP markets

Company	Brazil (total)	Brazil (SME)	World
Totvs	50.0%	72.0%	n/a
SAP	24.4%	11.2%	24.0%
Oracle	5.6%	5.6%	18.0%
MS Dynamics	n/a	n/a	11.0%
Others	20.0%	11.0%	47.0%
Total size of the market (in USD billion)	1.5	n/a	Between 21 and 50*

Note: n/a = not available.

Sources: Totvs (2012) and http://whatiserp.net/erp-report/erp-market-share-and-vendor-evaluation-2011/ (accessed January 3, 2013). *According to http://www.quora.com/What-are-the-most-common-ERP-systems-used-by large-companies (accessed January 3, 2013).

law requirements, such as compulsory adoption of the Electronic Invoice System in many states in Brazil, have affected growth. Although not as big as SAP and Oracle, Totvs is currently the sixth-largest ERP developer in the world. Totvs's market share is even larger when considering only the small and medium enterprise markets, the firm's main focus and the fastest-growing segment in ERP.

The question is why a domestic ERP firm eventually had a market advantage over multinational enterprises (MNEs) in Brazil? One possible reason is that, until recently, global players such as SAP and Oracle seemed to target only large firms, many of them multinational companies (MNCs) that already employed their solutions. This strategy left room for local firms to explore growing local demand, especially from small or medium-sized enterprises (SMEs). Over time, Totvs developed an adequate business model based on SaaS and reliability regarding updates on tax and labor legislation changes. Moreover, it has invested in flexibility of its solutions and relies on well-established distribution networks, especially in medium-sized cities. These factors may explain Totvs's leadership position. This model has been replicated in other countries, especially in Latin America. In the next section, we discuss the factors that led Totvs to its current position.

8.2.2   Totvs's Trajectory to Market Leadership

In 1969 a services bureau called SIGA (*Sistema Integrado de Gerência Automática* – Integrated System of Automatic Management) was established by Mr Ernesto Mario Haberkorn in Sao Paulo, SP. The SIGA system allowed centralized enterprise management, whose main purpose was to automate administrative processes. In 1983, with the advent of microcomputers, Microsiga Software SA (Microsiga) was established by Mr Haberkorn in a partnership with Laercio Cosentino. Microsiga is the forerunner of Totvs. Currently, Mr Cosentino is the CEO and Chairman of the Board of Totvs. Microsiga's main purpose was to develop management software for personal computers, targeting the SME segment.

According to the company, during the 1980s and mid 1990s, Microsiga grew through reliance on franchise systems and strategic alliances with major global companies including Dell, Microsoft, IBM, Intel, Oracle, Novell, and Progress. This reliance facilitated promotion of Microsiga's products as well as benchmarking.

In 1998, the company began to develop vertical solutions. Verticals are key pillars to Totvs's market strategy, allowing the company to offer business management solutions suited to the needs of customers in specific segments without losing scale advantages.

In 1999, Advent International Corporation (Advent) became a foreign partner with a 25 percent share in the company. The company changed its status to an open capital company, preparing for an initial public offering (IPO).

From 2003 forward, the company experienced a process of vigorous growth and increasing profit margins. As part of its growth strategy, the company embarked on aggressive M&As. Microsiga went on to acquire several other companies in Brazil and abroad, contributing to its growth strategy.

In 2005, Microsiga admitted the Brazilian Development Bank's branch, BNDES Participations (BNDESPar), as a partner for BRL 40 million (USD 16.4 million). BNDESPar is responsible for managing the Bank's shares in publicly or privately owned companies or groups. From the government's standpoint, BNDES's support for Totvs was part of its Prosoft program, a support program for the software segment, to be discussed later. From the firm's standpoint, BNDES's support was crucial for the continuation of its M&A strategy. With support from BNDESPar, the company acquired Logocenter, Brazil's fourth-largest software developer at that time, making Microsiga 40 percent larger. BNDESPar's support also enabled the company to repurchase Advent's participation. In the same year, Microsiga changed its name to Totvs, the company's current brand.

In March 2006, Totvs went public on Bovespa (the Sao Paulo Stock Exchange), meeting the 'Novo Mercado' standards, which meant attaining the highest level of Corporate Governance requirements. With the IPO,

Totvs raised USD 214 million, cash resources that allowed Totvs to acquire RM Sistemas SA, an ERP developer, in 2006.

Admitting BNDES as a partner changed, per se, the asset structure of the group, a trend subsequently reinforced with the successful IPO. Totvs grew from a company whose growth relied basically on profit reinvestment, to a company with over a third of its assets held by third parties. Through this financial strategy, Totvs internalized skills in segments that did not act, eased the pressure of competition, and strengthened its distribution network.

In 2007, Totvs acquired Midbyte (vertical developer, retail segment), BCS (legal segment), and entered into a joint venture with Quality Software SA to create TQTVD Software Ltd for production of middleware for digital television (DTV). In 2007, Totvs also established EuroTotvs, based in Portugal. TQTVD was established to diversify technology and business focused on DTV, while an affiliate, EuroTotvs, aimed to broaden the company's international integration into Europe.

In August 2008, Totvs took its biggest step to date, merging with Datasul SA, its strongest domestic competitor. This acquisition enabled increased targeting of medium and large enterprises. It's worth pointing out that Datasul was the ninth-largest ERP developer worldwide, larger than Totvs at the time. The merger with Datasul involved BRL 700 million (USD 434 million). The BNDES provided 57.7 percent of the funds for the operation.[5] By itself, this merger would mean a great leap in the scale of Totvs's production and market access. In fact, the combination Datasul/Totvs meant a structure of 130 franchises in Brazil, 18 international franchises, and a network of over 600 vendors. Together they held 21 000 clients and 38 percent of the national market. Later in 2008, Totvs restructured its franchise system and released the TotvsUp system (currently called TotvsByYou), a web-based client relationship platform. This platform enables the hiring of services and the development of solutions in a modular and remote way, reducing costs for customers. This kind of initiative is in line with global trends in ERP, which involve providing SaaS via the web.

8.2.3   Totvs's Internationalization Process

Regarding overseas expansion, Totvs performs Greenfield foreign direct investments (FDIs), M&A, and partnerships with foreign enterprises. Foreign enterprise partnerships seem to be the preferred method of internationalization by Brazilian companies, as provided in Cavalcante and Araújo (2017) and Carvalho et al. (2010). It should be noted that Totvs expanded its international presence through the merger with Datasul, which already had some international presence.

The first step towards internationalization through offices abroad was taken by Microsiga, in Argentina, during1997. The next step was purchasing part of Sipros, a Mexican ERP company, which resulted in Microsiga Mexico in 2003. Already under the brand of Totvs, the group established EuroTotvs in 2007 in Portugal, with a view to entering the European market (especially Portugal and Spain). The group also has an office in the United States (US). In 2011, Microsiga announced a franchise in Lima, Peru, to serve the SME market segment in manufacturing, services, retail, and distribution and logistics. Prior to merging, Datasul had a presence in Argentina, Mexico, and the US. Notwithstanding its expansion, Totvs's international presence is not significant in terms of relative importance to total sales. Precise information is not available, but market specialists argue that no more than 5 percent of Totvs's sales come from abroad (Valor Economico, 2010).

Indeed, Totvs recognizes that it is very hard to compete in Eastern markets, European markets, and North American markets for distinct reasons. Competing in Eastern markets imposes the technological challenge of dealing with 2-byte characters, which implies higher costs. The European market has its own regional leaders (such as SAP), which are the 'front of mind' option for many business segments. In North America, not only are there large 'front of mind' companies such as Oracle, Microsoft, and SAP, but there are also very strong vertical developers that are highly competitive due to the large scale of the American market.

Hence, Totvs focuses on the Latin American and African markets. These markets have very similar characteristics to the Brazilian market, such as low penetration rates of PCs in the SME segment, high growth rates of the ERP market, few competitors, a context of economic fluctuations, and constant changes in legislation. The African market has great growth potential and Totvs is leveraging Portugal's EuroTotvs to serve Portuguese-speaking African countries initially. According to Totvs, growth rates of the ERP market in some Latin American and African countries may reach 30 percent per year by 2020. In a Totvs director's words, 'Totvs wants to be in Latin America what SAP is in Europe. For example, the German SAP has 85 per cent of the Austrian ERP market.'

8.2.4   Firm-Level Factors

8.2.4.1   Totvs's marketing capabilities

It is not easy to draw a clear line dividing marketing and technological capabilities; indeed, they are strongly tied to each other. For example, focusing on SMEs demands less customized ERP solutions, but in turn SMEs may demand a higher degree of flexibility in commercial terms.

In short, Totvs has put some effort into developing a rather flexible SaaS scheme for its clients, aggregating their needs as much as possible in verticals and modular solutions, with everything supported by a strong brand. These features are detailed as follows.

1. *Software-as-a-service (SaaS) approach* Provision of software as a service is a global trend and refers to a form of distribution and marketing according to which suppliers are responsible for all necessary delivery system infrastructure (servers, connectivity, information security) and customers use the software via the internet, paying fees for recurring use.[6] In the case of ERP systems, the main advantage to customers is that they can rely on system upgrades and adjustments due to changes in tax legislation. For the SaaS companies, the advantage is straightforward, since they may rely on recurring revenues.

    In fact, Totvs ensures that its clients will have new versions of their software every two years, and all changes in tax legislation will be promptly updated without additional cost.[7] This has proved to be a marketing differential, since Totvs's main competitors charge for these updates, and changes in tax legislation take some time to be implemented. As a result, almost half of Totvs's revenue (45 percent of USD 736 million) comes from maintenance.

2. *Customization through verticals* Commercially speaking, Totvs offers two dimensions of customization for SMEs: verticals and stages of development of managerial capabilities. The management development cycle is divided into four phases: control (accounting, cost reduction), productivity (automation, customer service), relationship (beginning of customer relationship system (CRS) implementation), and business collaboration (full CRS). To some extent, division of the management development cycle was a way to develop 'vertical' solutions aimed at these different stages.

3. *Flexible commercial approach* Totvs has developed many ways to offer and charge for its technological solutions. For this flexibility, intensive use of the internet has been crucial, following a worldwide trend. A client may purchase an ERP solution best suited to its needs by choosing modules available for sale online. Two examples are the TotvsOcean and TotvsByYou projects.

    TotvsOcean allows modularization of Totvs ERP solutions via the web. The TotvsByYou project is a collaborative platform via cloud computing used by Totvs clients and software and apps developers. The TotvsByYou environment allows for knowledge and experience sharing, as well as template files and even apps and software modules.

4. *Capillarity and distribution* Totvs inherited a sound distribution network from Microsiga, Datasul, and others. Of course, the internet is a very flexible way to deliver Totvs's solutions, but one must remember that many of Totvs's clients are first-time users who may prefer traditional selling approaches. Hence, a consolidated and unified distribution network may constitute a marketing differential.
5. *Strong branding* Strictly linked to the previous feature, Totvs has invested a lot in branding and advertising since the consolidation of the group. This is consistent with the objective of being the 'front of mind' brand in ERP, especially for SMEs. Of course, Totvs inherited part of the prestige and recognition of previous brands (Microsiga, Datasul, RM, Logocenter, and others).

8.2.4.2   Totvs's technological capabilities: internal sources

Technological capabilities are developed to support business strategies. In this sense, Totvs's path for technological development has been oriented by the need for the development of verticals, commercial flexibility, and more recently, the use of cloud computing and social network resources.

Broadly speaking, Totvs's technological development personnel are in charge of three tasks: (i) elaborating a broad 'road map' for future developments, based on customer feedback, market research, and benchmarking; (ii) updating and adding new functions to existing versions (currently, adding social network functionalities; there are other improvements pointed out in the road maps); and (iii) providing tax legislation updates. One must remember that new versions of Totvs's software must be provided every two years. Another challenge for Totvs's developers is related to the fact that Totvs is a merged group of ERP developers with self-developed software languages.

Totvs is a heavy investor in R&D. In 2011, the group invested the equivalent of more than USD 100 million in R&D, which represented 13.7 percent of its net revenues. Totvs has been increasing its R&D investments, both in absolute and relative terms to its revenue. Indeed, it has consistently invested more than 10 percent of its net revenues in R&D since 2007. Totvs is currently considered one of the five largest R&D investors in Brazil and is among the top 1000 worldwide, according to Booz & Co.

For comparison, according to the Brazilian Innovation Survey (PINTEC), in 2008 shares of net revenues invested in innovative activities (not only R&D) were 2.9 percent (2.5 percent in industrial sectors and 4.2 percent in selected services). With regard specifically to R&D, manufacturing invests, on average, 0.64 percent of net sales in these activities and 2.54 percent in selected services sectors. Specifically, the 'IT Services' sector invests around 1 percent of its net revenue in R&D, the same percentage as the subsector 'Development and Licensing of Computer Programs.' Thus, Totvs has a prominent position with respect to its industry when it comes to R&D investments.

8.2.4.3   Totvs's technological capabilities: external sources

Totvs does not rely solely on its own capabilities to develop solutions, although its own technology efforts are the most important. For development of their systems, Totvs also has partnerships with some universities and research groups.

In Brazil, Totvs has some partnerships in the fields of computer science and in areas related to business management (HR, logistics, supply-chain management). Regional units of the group are empowered to lead partnerships with universities. An example is the partnership between Totvs Rio and the ILOS Institute (Institute of Logistics and Supply Chain), from the COPPEAD-UFRJ (the Instituto de Pós-Graduação e Pesquisa em Administração at the Federal University of Rio de Rio de Janeiro, otherwise known as the COPPEAD Graduate School of Business), with the aim of sharing knowledge in logistics. Another example is the partnership with the research group on integrated management systems, the Department of Computer Science from UNISUL (the University of Southern Santa Catarina, a Brazilian state).

Abroad, Totvs partnered with Stanford University and San Jose State University (SJSU) in 2010. The partnership with Stanford University aimed to identify new business in the US market. Stanford University surveyed the strengths and weaknesses of the group and its systems, and pointed out technologies in which it must invest in the future. The partnership with SJSU aimed to develop the platform 'Totvs ByYou,' as discussed above.

Another important external source for technological capabilities is M&A. Mergers and acquisitions have expanded the capabilities and scope of the services offered, especially those with vertical developers.

8.2.5   Country-Level Factors

Totvs's linkage to the rest of the sectoral innovation system is rather weak, except for some aforementioned links with universities. However, what was very important for consolidating its national leadership was government support through the BNDES, especially for the group's M&A strategy.

Totvs's growth was contemporary to some important changes in the Brazilian support system for the software segment. Software was considered a priority in the Industrial, Technological and Foreign Trade Policy (PITCE) released in 2003 by the Brazilian government. Under this new institutional environment, the BNDES modified Prosoft, its support program for the software segment originally released in the late 1990s. The most important modification was the change from product-based to firm-based support. This change was crucial for supporting internationalization initiatives and services operations – one must remember that, strictly speaking, software developers were increasingly becoming service firms – as well as M&A.

According to Totvs, its first contact with the BNDES happened in 1997 as part of a private-equity operation. On two occasions, the BNDES was crucial to the group's growth path. First, in 2005 the BNDES sponsored the purchase of Logocenter (the fourth-largest Brazilian software house at the time), and Microsiga grew 40 percent larger as a result. As a counterpart, BNDESPar became a partner of the group, buying 16.7 percent of its shares for USD 16.4 million. Moreover, this operation enabled Microsiga to repurchase Advent's shares in the company (25 percent of total). Additionally, BNDES support was crucial for the Totvs IPO in 2006. After the IPO that raised the equivalent of USD 211.5 million in local currency, Totvs would buy RM Sistemas, another competitor in the ERP segment.

The second occasion was the merger with Datasul in 2008, at the time the ninth-largest ERP developer worldwide and the largest in Brazil. The purchase of Datasul was estimated at USD 381.7 million. The BNDES contributed USD 220.3 million, with half the funds as a loan with special conditions, the other half as debentures.

Whether Totvs's support from the BNDES was a 'pick-the-winner' kind of policy is a matter of tough debate. On the one hand, it is clear that Totvs's growth strategy would not have been possible without the BNDES's support. Intentionally or not, through the BNDES the government could foster a 'national champion' at least in the Brazilian market, during a global consolidation wave in the ERP segment.

On the other hand, Totvs was already one of the Brazilian ERP leaders before the arrival of the BNDES as a partner. According to Totvs's IPO prospectus – a good document to analyse the company's pre-2006 situation – the group's market share in 2004 was 29.4 percent in Brazil and 12.2 percent in Latin America (Totvs, 2006). Moreover, the company was already the market leader in the 10–499 employees segment. Its revenues reached around USD 60 million in 2004, prior to the arrival of the BNDES and acquisition of Logocenter.[8] One could argue that, as happens with any sector in Brazil, Totvs could access the BNDES as a large enterprise. The choice of admitting the BNDES as a partner was Totvs's solution to the classical debt–equity finance dilemma. Other firms choose to rely solely on debt – Positivo is one example choosing this strategy.

During an interview with BNDES staff, it was argued that Prosoft support was also used by Totvs's competitors. Linx, a Brazilian ERP developer for the retail segment (USD 120 million in revenue for 2012), is a direct competitor of Totvs's, and BNDESPar is also among its partners. As in Totvs's case, BNDESPar supported Linx's IPO in 2013. In the same type of situation, Senior Solution, an ERP developer for the financial sector (USD 23 million in revenue for 2012), went public in 2013.

Finally, and most important, the BNDES is not the only way in which the government has supported Totvs. The group is a heavy user of innovation tax incentives. Tax incentives covered 9 percent of Totvs's R&D in 2007 and 12.7 percent in 2008, corresponding to USD 3 million and USD 6.3 million in the form of indirect subsidies, respectively.[9]

8.3 POSITIVO: LEADER IN THE PC-MANUFACTURING SEGMENT IN BRAZIL

Positivo is the current leader of PC manufacturing in the Brazilian market. According to its financial statements, Positivo is the fourth-largest PC manufacturer in Latin America and the eleventh-largest worldwide. The company produced 2.4 million PCs in 2011 (2.05 million in Brazil and the rest in Argentina), achieving net revenues of approximately USD 1.1 billion.[10] Positivo was the market leader in Brazil for seven uninterrupted years (beginning in 2004) with an average market share of 14 percent (based on five years, 2009–14). In 2011, Positivo's retail market share was 19 percent and 46 percent in government procurement. Success in the government procurement market reflects the company's low-cost/low-end strategy. However, its performance in the corporate segment is far less effective: it has held steady around 3 percent. Regarding the Argentinean operation, Positivo BGH sold 360000 notebooks in 2011, achieving leadership in its first year of operation with 22.0 percent of market share. Currently, Positivo has three production sites in Brazil and one in Argentina. The company has over 4000 employees in Brazil. Again, we will explore the origins of leadership, beginning with the sector-level factors.

8.3.1 Sector-Level Factors

8.3.1.1 PCs: technological requirements
For the purposes of this work, the PC-manufacturing segment encompasses the assembling of desktop computers and notebooks that include a wide range of products, such as desktop and mobile workstations, all-in-ones, servers, tablets, and ultraportable PCs. Due to convergence, firms originally from the computer, consumer electronics, and telecommunications

industries have been competing in all segments. The new frontier for competition is the *smart phone*[11] segment. Although smart phones are not at the core of the current analysis, firms' capabilities to innovate and compete in this segment may be crucial to their survival in the long run.

Standardization plays a very important role in the ICT sector. Standards are necessary to assure compatibility and interoperability among a great variety of systems, subsystems, equipment, and network elements. The coordination between different technologies allows the emergence of new or improved products and services. Hence, standardization enables as well as constrains the behavior of various actors in the sector, currently and in the future. According to Fomin et al. (2008), ICT firms are highly motivated to engage in standardization. Successfully setting ICT standards means significant competitive advantages to companies that have supported them, generating lock-in effects for customers and lock-out effects for possible competitors.

Additionally, standardization in the ICT industry has allowed modularization, which is a method of subdividing a system into modules that can be independently designed, tested, and implemented. Modules with standard interfaces may be reused multiple times in different contexts, driving new systems and functionalities. Benefits of modularizations are reduction in production costs (due to economies of scale), flexibility in design of new systems, and scalability.

Because of modular design and standardization, parts and pieces that compose ICT systems, such as personal computers, have become exchangeable. On the one hand, modularization allows multiple combinations of parts and pieces to form the final configurations of PCs, a process referred to as 'customization.' On the other hand, PCs produced by different manufacturers, with similar technical specifications, and which have very little differentiation between them,[12] are designated as 'commoditizations.' For firms engaging in the consumer market, lack of differentiation in final products have been compressing profit margins since the mid 2000s. In turn, diminishing profits have been forcing the consolidation of firms in the sector, seeking economies of scale.

As a consequence of the lock-out effect of standardization, the number of companies in the semiconductor industry that supply parts and pieces for ICT systems is limited. Therefore, much of the value added in a PC is captured by the semiconductor industry. For instance, Dedrick, Kraemer and Linden (2007) assessed the contributions of value added from the main phases of production processes for certain kinds of ICT equipment. Their study revealed that, for a notebook, value added by the assembling and integration phases corresponds to approximately 1.5 percent of the retail price without taxes, while value added by manufacturing parts and pieces represents more than 15 percent. Furthermore, according to their study, components account for approximately 85 percent of a PC's factory cost, which is about 60 percent of the retail price without taxes.

Moreover, innovation in PC manufacturing is essentially technologically driven and is heavily dependent on the semiconductor industry, whose aim is to progressively produce more powerful processors, faster components, larger storage, and newer peripherals. Sometimes innovation occurs in a cooperative way between PC manufacturers and semiconductor firms, especially during project and design phases. Innovations produced solely by PC manufacturers are usually restricted to the industrial design and marketing of their products. According to Pavitt's (1984) taxonomy, PC manufacturing would be classified as scale-intensive, along with other sectors that assemble consumer durable goods. However, PC manufacturing includes features of specialized suppliers since it may spread technical progress to other sectors. Demand-pull of new features appears indirectly, through increased requirements from software applications.

8.3.2 Market Structure

Since the mid 2000s, the PC-manufacturing segment has achieved astonishing growth and has become progressively concentrated. As displayed in Table 8.2, annual PC production has increased 162 percent since 2004, achieving more than 350 million units per year. The table primarily reflects diminishing costs due to economies of scale and modularization. At the same time, the market share of the world's five largest firms has increased by 17 percentage points, from 42 percent in 2000 to 59 percent in 2011. As mentioned in the previous section, this indicator points to ongoing consolidation in the sector, which followed shrinking of profits.

In 2011, five MNCs controlled almost 60 percent of the global PC market: Hewlett-Packard (US, 17 percent), Lenovo (China, 13 percent), Dell (US, 12 percent), Acer (Taiwan, 11 percent), and Asus (Taiwan, 6 percent). Despite the effects of consolidation and tight profit margins, competition has remained fierce since 2000, as ten different companies have been alternating among the top five positions of the world's biggest firms in the sector. This group includes the five aforementioned firms as well as Compaq (acquired by Hewlett-Packard), IBM (acquired by Lenovo), NEC (Japan), Toshiba (Japan), and Fujitsu (Japan). Gartner reported that, as of the third quarter 2012, Lenovo had surpassed Hewlett-Packard to become the world's largest PC manufacturer for the first time.

According to International Data Corporation (IDC), Brazil is currently

Table 8.2   *Annual PC production (million units) with market share of five largest firms (globally) and Brazilian PC sales (2000–11)*

Year	World PC production (millions)	Market share of top 5 firms	Total PC sales in Brazil (millions)
2000	135	42%	3.6
2001	128	42%	4.0
2002	132	44%	4.3
2003	169	41%	4.5
2004	189	44%	4.6
2005	219	47%	6.3
2006	239	48%	7.7
2007	271	53%	10.7
2008	302	56%	11.9
2009	306	58%	11.1
2010	351	58%	13.8
2011	353	59%	15.4

Sources: Gartner (2000–11)[13] for world data; Meireles (2011) and International Data Corporation (IDC) for Brazilian data.

the third-largest PC market in the world,[14] behind China and the United States. In 2011, annual sales reached 15.4 million units, a figure four times greater than in the year 2000.

It is important to mention a crucial transformation that has been occurring in the Brazilian market since 2005. Not only have total sales been increasing exponentially, illegal and gray markets have been proportionally decreasing. Until 2004, illegal and gray sales corresponded to more than 70 percent of total sales. Although the latest revisions of the institutional framework contributed to this transformation (as will be discussed later), other relevant factors also help to explain this phenomenon: (i) economic growth; (ii) income distribution; (iii) credit; (iv) appreciation of the exchange rate; and (v) internet diffusion. The result is that, during 2004–11, the informal market sales shrank to 25 percent while official sales soared tenfold in just seven years (from 1.2 million in 2004 to 11.5 million in 2011). In other words, the official market was increasing at an average 38 percent CAGR.

Brazil's PC market is disputed by all major multinational brands and also by national firms. All domestic companies take advantage of tax incentives, which require local assembling of products, while multinational firms may select one of the following strategies, varying according to their business planning:

*Table 8.3   Net sales and number of industrial firms with five or more
employees in Brazil by economic activity, 2010*

CNAE code	Description	Number of firms	Net revenue (USD million)	Number of employees
26.1	Manufacture of electronic components and boards	519	2327[a]	22822
26.2	Manufacture of computers and peripheral equipment	319	12831[b]	49035

Notes:
a.   BRL 3886 million, in Brazilian currency.
b.   BRL 21428 million, in Brazilian currency.

Source: IBGE (2010a).

1.   direct importing, when price is competitive regardless of tax incentives for local production or if the product has a strong brand;
2.   outsourcing production to contract equipment manufacturers (CEMs) already established in Brazil (such as Flextronics and Foxconn); or
3.   establishing an assembly line in Brazil.

    With respect to market environments in Brazil, the semiconductor industry is very restricted in size and scope, limiting opportunities for local development of new products for global markets. Table 8.3 provides information about hardware manufacturing in Brazil. CNAE[15] codes shown are: (i) 26.1, manufacturing of electronic components and boards; and (ii) 26.2, manufacturing of computers and peripheral equipment. It may be verified from Table 8.4 that there is weak linkage between these economic segments in Brazil, as the net revenue of (i) above accounts for less than 20 percent of the net revenues of (ii), albeit parts and components correspond to 85 percent of PC factory costs.
    The figures presented in Table 8.4 demonstrate that innovation developed in the hardware-manufacturing segment in Brazil is not internationally competitive. Less than 2 percent of firms stated that they had developed new products or processes for global markets. Moreover, R&D intensity, an indicator of innovation effort measured by R&D expenditures to net revenue ratios, shows that Brazilian hardware manufacturing is also very distant from international investment levels. Average R&D intensity in the US and Europe is in the ranges of 4 percent to 8 percent for IT equipment, and 14 percent to 15 percent for IT components (Turlea et al., 2011). These indicators in Brazil in 2008 were 2 percent and 3 percent, respectively.

Table 8.4   R&D expenditures by percentage of innovative firms and ICT sector in Brazil, 2008

CNAE code	Description	R&D exp./net revenue (2008)	% of innovative firms (2008)	% of firms that developed new products to global markets (2006–08)	% of firms that developed new processes to global markets (2006–08)
26.1	Manufacture of electronic components and boards	1.98%	46.5%	0.27%	–
26.2	Manufacture of computers and peripheral equipment	2.82%	46.8%	1.35%	0.45%

Source: IBGE (2010b).

Despite these facts, innovations have been occurring in the Brazilian PC market, given that about 47 percent of hardware manufacturers in Brazil affirm to have introduced some kind of local innovation in 2008. Therefore, with regard to innovation, market leadership is built upon the development of customized solutions to regional and specific markets, using industrial design techniques (in the fields of aesthetics, ergonomics, and interfaces) and taking into account cultural preferences. There are also opportunities to innovate through the introduction of new services (for example, technical assistance and embedded software) and engagement in new markets.

8.3.3   Positivo's Trajectory

Curso Positivo (in English, Positivo Course) was founded in 1972 by a group of teachers as a preparatory course for admission exams to Brazil's higher educational system (colleges and universities). Supporting the main business, the founders also established a printing shop to produce textbooks with adequate quality and content. Both firms were located in Curitiba, capital of the southern state of Parana.

Curso Positivo's current portfolio comprises a full range of educational services including preparatory courses, primary and secondary schools, a university, a technological center, and a cultural institute. Currently, the group has approximately 25 500 students. Since its inception, with its products and services, approximately 10 million students have attended.

Positivo Informatica was created in 1989. As the computer and IT branch of the Positivo Group, it was closely related to the institutional framework in Brazil at that time. The Brazilian computer market was closed to imports, and national production could not meet demand. The new company was started with the initial objective of manufacturing computers to support the educational and publishing businesses of the group. In the following year, it also engaged in public tenders and bidding processes to supply computers and IT solutions to government-owned companies and institutions. Although officially called Positivo Informatica, the company will be designated simply as Positivo hereinafter for simplification.

In 1994, Positivo started developing educational technologies that supported the creation of a wide range of educational products such as software, portals, and learning tables. Currently, these products are used in more than 10 800 public and private schools in Brazil, and are exported to more than 40 countries.

2004 was a turning point in Positivo's history, marking its true spin-off from the group. In that year, the company engaged with retail businesses for PCs. Conceptually simple, the implemented strategy proved successful: the company established partnerships with the largest retailers in Brazil (supermarkets, department stores, etc.) to distribute low-cost/low-end computers designed for the emerging middle class in Brazil. Use of sales channels already familiar to customers had a significant effect, which positively impelled sales. Within just nine months of retail operations, Positivo became the largest computer manufacturer in Brazil, and computer sales accounted for 85.1 percent of the company's net revenue in 2004.

One year later, Positivo also engaged the corporate market, offering a full series of desktops, notebooks, and servers. In 2006, the company became listed in Bovespa (São Paulo Stock Exchange) through an IPO that raised USD 281 million[16] from national and foreign investors, more than the company's net worth of USD 146.5 million[17] at that time.

In 2008, Positivo began implementing two new strategies: vertical integration and regional decentralization. The company began production of desktop motherboards in Curitiba, Positivo's original plant. Additionally, it established two new facilities, one located in Ilheus (northeastern region) and the other in Manaus (northern region). In the following year, Positivo began production of notebook motherboards and desktop memory boards. Currently, the plant in Curitiba assembles desktops, notebooks, memory boards, and cabinets; the plant in Manaus, desktops and notebooks; and the plant in Ilheus is in charge of LCD monitors. Near the end of 2008,

Positivo's controlling group refused an offer to sell the company to competitor Lenovo for BRL 18.00 per share,[18] roughly twice the price of stocks traded at Bovespa at the time.

During 2009, Positivo initiated its M&A strategy by acquiring Kennex, a Brazilian competitor brand. In 2010, it became international by forming a corporate joint venture with BGH, an Argentinean company in the consumer goods segment. Each partner had acquired 50 percent of Informática Fueguina SA (IFSA), the vehicle for the joint venture, whose management was also shared. Under the Positivo BGH brand, the corporate purpose of the joint venture was to sell desktops, notebooks, all-in-ones, e-readers, and tablets in the Argentinean and Uruguayan markets. In 2011, Positivo acquired Crounal, a Uruguayan company.

In any case, Positivo's margins are rather low; the ratio of Earnings Before Interest Taxes, Depreciation and Amortization (EBITDA)/Gross Revenue is 3.4 percent. This is likely to be the reason why the company has tried to diversify its businesses. The company released a content portal, called *Mundo Positivo* (in English, Positivo's World), focused on Brazilian lower-middle-class families, providing access to magazines, newspapers, videos, books, music, games, and other software applications. Positivo then began production of tablets,[19] complementing its hardware portfolio. Recently, Positivo announced its entry into the smart phone market.[20] *Mundo Positivo* may be considered an adaptation of Apple's App Store for Positivo's products, where applications are in Portuguese and customers are charged in local currency.

8.3.4 Firm-Level Factors

8.3.4.1 Positivo's marketing capabilities
Positivo has innovated by unveiling new markets (one of the possibilities pointed out by Fransman's model) that were unexplored or underexplored by existing competitors. This is especially relevant in the retail and government segments. From 1989 to 2004, Positivo acquired expertise in PC manufacturing and public tendering processes, which proved to be an important foundation for the company's next move. When Positivo engaged in retail business in 2004, the company's marketing strategy focused on developing low-cost/low-end products for the emerging middle-class in Brazil. Moreover, access to easy credit by this consumer class was a very important maneuver used by Positivo to increase sales and retain clients. Both retail business and government tendering have been supporting Positivo's leadership throughout the years.

Positivo puts strong effort in brand management. Through significant investments in branding, the company has been able to consistently receive marketing awards such as 'front of mind' in computer and notebook categories. Brand investments comprise both advertisements in newspapers and magazines, TV commercials, and trade marketing such as point-of-sale promotions and events.

Finally, Positivo is also diversifying its portfolio, which now comprises desktops, notebooks, educational tables, an internet portal, tablets, and more recently, a line of smart phones using the Android platform.

8.3.4.2 Positivo's technological capabilities: internal sources

Since 2010, the company has been investing an average of USD 11.9 million per year[21] (about 1.1 percent of net revenues) in R&D, mostly as compensation for tax incentives (as discussed below). Using an industrial design approach (aesthetics, ergonomics, and interface techniques), the company has been developing a wide range of new products. First, it launched 'Positivo Faces,' desktops with customizable cabinets bundled with an application that allowed consumers to produce their own 'face.' It then produced a new line of notebooks that featured some design elements. Other products include 'Positivo PCTV Digital,' equipped with an analog/digital TV board, and 'Positivo Fácil,' bundled with an application for first-time users. Positivo entered the tablet segment with 'Positivo Ypy,' specially designed for the Brazilian market after extensive research of local consumers. The company also produced other incremental innovations focusing on local customers, such as soft-touch keyboards that may also be regarded as a kind of customization.

All in all, the R&D strategy of Positivo targets incremental innovation, customization, and design improvements, with the goal of consolidating its position in the low-cost/low-end segment. No major high-tech developments should be expected from Positivo. Indeed, Positivo has only nine industrial patents and models of utility at the Brazilian Institute for Industrial Property (INPI), which refer to educational systems and computing algorithms. Currently, this segment is responsible for about 2.0 percent of Positivo's net revenue.

8.3.4.3 Positivo's technological capabilities: external sources

M&A and joint ventures are not an important source of capability building. However, Positivo has established relationships with some of the most important IT research centers in Brazil: BRISA, in Sao Paulo; CESAR (Centro de Estudos e Sistemas Avançados de Recife), in Recife; and IRT (Instituto Recôncavo de Tecnologia), in Ilheus. All of these are private research institutes and most of Positivo's projects with these centers refer to the development of Digital TV technologies.

Positivo also has an agreement with Positivo University, a company owned by the Positivo Group, for mutual cooperation and exchanges in the science and technology fields of the ICT sector, which involves the outsourcing of R&D, the provision of technological and scientific services, education, training, and technology transfer, and the use of laboratories.

In any case, it should be noticed that the developments that arise from these partnerships tend to be technologically marginal, as the company itself is not engaged in a technologically challenging strategy. Nevertheless, many of these links to research centers are to meet the IT law's legal requirement for investments in R&D.

8.3.5   Country-Level Factors

The most important systemic links for Positivo are not those established with competitors or suppliers, but those marketing-related alliances: retail chains and technical support structures. Concerning the first factor, the company took advantage of solid commercial relationships with the biggest retail chains in Brazil, which are largely responsible for selling consumer goods to the emerging middle class as well as financing these purchases. As a result, Positivo claims to have the widest and least concentrated distribution network in the country, making products available at more than 8800 points of sale. Positivo has also benefited from these close ties with retail chains by receiving constant access to information on consumer demand. By controlling point-of-sale inventories, the company has been capable of responding rapidly to customer needs and preferences.

Positivo also built the largest technical support network in the country, covering every Brazilian city. The company also implemented a Customer Care Center that provides a direct link with consumers for solving simple issues such as computer set-up.

8.3.5.1   Evolution of the institutional framework of the ICT sector in Brazil

The most important system factor for Positivo however, is the institutional framework of the ICT sector in Brazil. While the computer industry is global, the institutional environment in Brazil is quite peculiar. Therefore, based on the concept of the ecosystem presented in Section 8.2, the dynamics of the ICT sector in Brazil have been affected by these idiosyncrasies. A brief description of PC manufacturing's trajectory in Brazil, as well as the main characteristics of the current institutional framework, may clarify its influence on Positivo's current market leadership.

In Brazil, the dynamics of the ICT sector have been highly dependent on public policies. The federal government has been adopting some kind of public policy for ICTs since 1984. In its first version, national markets were closed to imports under the 'infant industry' argument. After an outcome that combined high prices, the existence of illegal markets, and the slow diffusion of computer technology, a new version of the public policy was implemented in 1991. Designated as *Lei de Informática* (in English, information technology law or IT law), it significantly changed the previous institutional framework. On the one hand, seeking more efficiency in the Brazilian market, it authorized competition with foreign companies. On the other hand, it offered tax incentives for a period of eight years to companies established in Brazil, both national and foreign, which carried out local R&D programs. A third version (in truth, a revision of the second version) was implemented in 2001. A summary of the main characteristics of each period is presented in Table 8.5.

Table 8.5   Summary of ICT public policies in Brazil

Phase	First	Second	Third
Period	1984–91	1991–2001	2001–present
Policy	Close national market to imports	● Promote local production ● Stimulate local R&D	
Main goals	Protect infant computer industry	● Substitute imports ● Develop local capabilities in Science & Technology (S&T)	Idem
Instrument	Control of trade	Tax incentives	Tax incentives (revised)
Main characteristics	Creation of small national firms	Assembly lines of multinational firms	Technological convergence of telecom, IT, and media
Outcomes	● High prices in official market ● Existence of illegal markets ● Slow diffusion of technology	● Negative balance of trade ● Low value added in Brazil ● Limited effects for R&D	● Rapid demand growth in the consumer market ● Faster diffusion of technology ● Reduction of illegal markets ● More negative balance of trade ● Still low value added in Brazil ● Still limited effects for R&D

Source: Authors' elaboration.

The current institutional framework was expected to expire in 2019. Nonetheless, in 2014, it was renewed for a decade more and is now valid until the end of 2024. A transition to a fully open market is expected to occur during 2025–29, using a decreasing tax incentive scheme. The existing model consists of three instruments at the federal level:

1. Tax incentives of 12 percent to 15 percent on domestic sales of PCs and other products for firms that comply with local production and investment in R&D.
2. High import fees for final goods (16 percent) and low import fees for parts and pieces (2 percent).
3. As of 2005, tax exemptions of 9.25 percent for personal computers used in households, both imported and locally produced.

The combination of the first two instruments accounts for a difference of as much as 30 percent in PC retail prices when compared to direct imports. Depending on the existence of additional tax incentives at the State level, the difference in tax percentage between PCs assembled in Brazil versus imported may go up to 50 percent. A more detailed discussion of the Brazilian institutional framework for the ICT sector may be found in Sousa (2011).

8.4   MAIN FINDINGS AND FINAL REMARKS

This chapter presented two case studies in the Brazilian ICT sector. One company is an ERP software developer (Totvs) and the other is a PC assembler (Positivo). Both are leaders in their segments in Brazil, and have some international presence.

These cases are of interest because they are leadership cases in sectors where Brazil has no tradition. Despite not having become world leaders, they keep their leading positions in segments where there is tough competition with multinationals in Brazil. Stimuli provided by Lei de Informática is very important to Positivo and may have been crucial to its decision to enter the PC market, however this incentive is available to all assemblers located in Brazil, including transnational companies.

So, in short, what explains these two cases of leadership? It is argued throughout the chapter that untapped local demand, due to tariff restrictions on imports or lack of interest by global players, led to the development of strong marketing capabilities of both companies over time. These marketing capabilities identified market niches that were not properly explored by any company, and the companies adapted their technological capabilities to explore them. In the case of Totvs, its focus on SMEs has proved to be a promising strategy and there is still great potential for growth. In the case of Positivo, the low-cost/low-end strategy proved to be the most adequate to the 'new middle class' which has emerged in Brazil since the mid 2000s.

Indeed, Totvs and Positivo both successfully followed mass customization strategies.[22] Mass customization is the marketing and production strategy that delivers wide-market goods and services that may be modified to satisfy customer needs, combining flexibility and low unit costs generally associated with mass production strategies. In the case of Totvs, verticals and the modularization of ERP solutions, which may be delivered using the internet, are types of mass-customization strategies. In the case of Positivo, in-depth market surveys indicate how computers are being used within a household, and design and aesthetic improvements are suggested, sometimes introducing some degree of customization for customers. The 'Positivo Faces' project is another example of a mass-customization strategy.

Notwithstanding their leadership positions in Brazil, neither Totvs nor Positivo is capable of changing technological trends on a global level. Both companies have technological capabilities that put them in line with the world's best practices; in other words, they 'caught up.' This is not, however, enough to put these companies among the world's technological leaders. It is interesting to note how technological capabilities are pulled up by marketing strategies. Additionally, neither of the companies have strong relationships with their sectoral systems of innovation as there is little cooperation with other firms or with universities, for example.

Regarding the country-level factors, the most important was the role of government, albeit with different approaches in each case. Although one may question whether or not it's a 'pick-the-winner' kind of government support, the fact is that the BNDES's support of Totvs has been crucial for its growth strategy.

Regarding Positivo, it benefited from trade protectionism provided by the IT law. However, despite the institutional environment stimulating local production, the Brazilian market is highly competitive. All major MNCs in the PC-manufacturing segment are established in Brazil. All of them may have the same access to IT law stimuli but none of them has been able to surpass Positivo's position. Combining delivery, financing, and product design in a singular way, Positivo has been able to provide the (generally) first low-cost/low-end computer to the emerging middle-class citizens of Brazil.

Although both Totvs and Positivo managed to be market leaders in Brazil (as defined in Chapter 1), they did not manage to become technological 'trendsetters' on a world level, and they have not signaled that they aim to do so. Totvs and Positivo have been successful in allying some technological capabilities with marketing capabilities, and have achieved market leadership through development of customized products and solutions for specific market segments that have not been properly addressed by world industry leaders.

For the future, it is expected that Totvs must grow hand-in-hand with the growth of the ERP market itself in Brazil. Despite having some international presence which follows the same strategies as in Brazil, it is not expected that international operations will become an important part of Totvs's revenues.

Despite Positivo's leadership for the last seven consecutive years, its advantages are now being challenged. Positivo's low profit margins are symptomatic of the fierce competition it has been facing.

Positivo's business model is highly dependent on two factors: PC sales, which represent about 98 percent of the company's total revenues, and the current Brazilian institutional framework. In contrast, the world market seems to be changing dramatically. In 2010, notebook sales exceeded desktop sales for the first time; in this niche, Positivo's advantages are smaller. New devices such as tablets and smart phones are also globally affecting the PC market, which has stabilized at around 350 million units per year. Additionally, the institutional framework in Brazil is subject to change in the future, as some tax incentives are supposed to be reduced from 2024 onwards, ending by 2029. Moreover, multinational competitors are encroaching on Positivo's ground. In 2010, Hewlett-Packard's net revenue in Brazil surpassed Positivo's[23] and in 2012, Lenovo acquired Brazilian local brand CCE.[24] Nevertheless, in response, Positivo has made some decisions to adapt to the new competitive scenario. Its recent incursions in tablet and smart phone segments prove that the company is expanding its portfolio. Furthermore, Positivo has been able to maintain its leadership in notebook niches in both the Brazilian and Argentinean markets, despite competitors' attacks.

NOTES

1. BRL 1446 million.
2. From http://en.wikipedia.org/wiki/Enterprise_resource_planning.
3. According to http://www.abc71.com.br/padrao.aspx?texto.aspx?idcontent=7372&idContentSection=2380 (accessed December 31, 2012).
4. http://www.tiinside.com.br/07/06/2011/servicos-de-ti-devem-crescer-46-no-brasil-ate-2014/ti/227121/news.aspx (accessed December 31, 2012).
5. Miguel Abunab, the founder of Datasul, is the founder and CEO of NeoGrid, a

       developer of supply management systems with 3000 clients in 60 countries and annual revenues of USD 65 million. NeoGrid must go public in the next few years (source: http://epocanegocios.globo.com/Informacao/Acao/noticia/2014/06/ele-diz-que-vai-fazer-mais-um-ipo.html, accessed April 22, 2015).

6. According to Wikipedia, http://pt.wikipedia.org/wiki/Software_como_servi per centC3 per centA7o (accessed September 28, 2011).
7. Indeed, Totvs estimates that there is one tax legislation change every three days, if one accounts for three levels of tax authority (city, state and federal levels).
8. It should be noted that the elevenfold revenue growth between 2004 and 2011 in USD is partially explained by appreciation of the Brazilian Real, M&A, and organic growth.
9. Regarding tax incentives to innovation in Brazil, see Araújo (2009).
10. BRL 2.08 billion.
11. Smart phones are mobile phones using operating systems, allowing computing capabilities similar to conventional PCs.
12. Although the products are not very differentiable, PC retailers attempt to acquire competitive advantages through embedded software applications and bundled services.
13. Available at: http://www.gartner.com/.
14. 'Posição do mercado mundial, segundo pesquisa da IDC,' available at: http://br.idclatin.com/releases/news.aspx?id=690.
15. CNAE is an acronym for Classificação Nacional de Atividades Econômicas, the Brazilian version of the International Standard Industrial Classification of All Economic Activities (ISIC), Revision 4.
16. BRL 604.1 million.
17. BRL 319 million.
18. http://ri.positivoinformatica.com.br/positivo/web/conteudo_en.asp?conta=44&id=593 27&tipo=3764&idioma=1.
19. http://ri.positivoinformatica.com.br/positivo/web/conteudo_en.asp?conta=44&id=138 277&tipo=3764&idioma=1.
20. http://ri.positivoinformatica.com.br/positivo/web/conteudo_en.asp?conta=44&id=158 178&tipo=3764&idioma=1.
21. BRL 22.5 million.
22. On mass customization, see Pine II (1992) or Silveira et al. (2001).
23. 'HP ameaça liderança da Positivo no mercado de computadores,' available at: http://economia.estadao.com.br/noticias/neg per centC3 per centB3cios,hp-ameaca-lideranca-da-positivo-no-mercado-de-computadores,45435,0.htm.
24. 'Lenovo Acquires CCE to Build PC+ Leader in Brazil,' available at: http://news.lenovo.com/article_display.cfm?-article_id=1628.

REFERENCES

ABES (Associação Brasileira das Empresas de Software) (2016), 'Mercado Brasileiro de Software: panorama e tendências,' in *Brazilian Software Market: Scenario and Trends*, São Paulo: ABES, available at: http://central.abessoftware.com.br/Content/UploadedFiles/Arquivos/Dados%202011/ABES-Publicacao-Mercado-2016.pdf.

Araújo, B.C. (2009), 'Incentivos fiscais à P&D e o custo de inovar no Brasil,' *Boletim Radar: Produção, Tecnologia e Comércio Exterior*, n. 9, 3–11, Brasília: IPEA.

Carvalho, F., I. Costa, and G. Duysters (2010), 'Global players from Brazil: drivers and challenges in the internationalization process of Brazilian firms,' Working paper #2010–016, United Nations University (UNU) / Maastricht Economic and Social Research and Training Centre on Innovation and Technology (MERIT).

Cavalcante, L.R. and B.C. Araújo (2017), 'Market leadership in the Brazilian automotive industry: the case of Marcopolo,' in F. Malerba, S. Mani, and P. Adams (eds), *The Rise to Market Leadership: New Leading Firms from Emerging Countries*, Cheltenham, UK and Northampton, MA: Edward Elgar, pp. 150–175.

Dedrick, J., K. Kraemer, and G. Linden (2007), 'Capturing value in a global innovation network: a comparison of radical and incremental innovation,' Mimeo, September.

Fomin, V., T. Keil, and K. Lyytinen (2008), 'Theorizing about standardization: integrating fragments of process theory in light of telecommunication standardization wars,' Sprouts: Working Papers on Information Systems, Paper 45, available at: http://aisel.aisnet.org/sprouts_all/45.

Gartner (2000–11), *Dataquest Quarterly Statistics: Personal Computer Quarterly Statistics*.

IBGE (Instituto Brasileiro de Geografia e Estatística) (2010a), 'Pesquisa Industrial Anual,' Rio de Janeiro, v. 29, n. 1, 182 pp, available at: http://biblioteca.ibge.gov.br/visualizacao/periodicos/1719/pia_2008_v27_n1_empresa.pdf.

IBGE (Instituto Brasileiro de Geografia e Estatística) (2010b), 'Pesquisa de Inovação Tecnológica 2008,' Rio de Janeiro, 164 pp, available at: http://www.pintec.ibge.gov.br/downloads/PUBLICACAO/Publicacao%20PINTEC%202008.pdf.

Meireles, F.S. (2011), *Tecnologia de Informação nas Empresas: Panorama e Indicadores*, São Paulo: Fundação Getúlio Vargas (FGV).

Pavitt, K. (1984), 'Sectoral patterns of technical change: towards a taxonomy and a theory,' *Research Policy*, v. 13, 343–373.

Pine II, B.J. (1992), *Mass Customization: The New Frontier in Business Competition*, Cambridge, MA: Harvard Business School Press.

Silveira, G., D. Borenstein, and F.S. Fogliatto (2001), 'Mass customization: literature review and research directions,' *International Journal of Production Economics*, v. 72, n. 1, 1–13.

Sousa, R.A.F. (2011), 'Vinte anos da Lei de Informática: estamos no caminho certo?', *Radar: tecnologia, produção e comércio exterior*, v. 16, 27–36.

Totvs (2006), 'IPO Prospectus,' available at: http://www.itaubba.com.br/arquivos/portugues/pdf/prospectos/-Oferta per cent20de per cent20Ações per cent20da per cent20Totvs per cent20-per cent20Minuta per cent20Prospecto per cent-20Definitivo.pdf.

Totvs (2012), '4T11 Report (Fourth quarter 2011 financial statements),' available at: http://www.totvs.com/ri.

Turlea, G., D. Nepelski, G. De Prato, J.-P. Simon, A. Sabadash, J. Stancik, W. Szewczyk, P. Desruelle, and M. Bogdanowicz (2011), *The 2011 Report on R&D in ICT in the European Union*, Luxembourg: European Commission.

Valor Economico (2010), *Valor Multinacionais Brasileiras 2010*, Sao Paulo: Abril Editor.

9. Conclusions: the rise to market leadership – a dynamic interplay between firms and innovation systems

Pamela Adams, Franco Malerba and Sunil Mani

9.1 INTRODUCTION

This book examines the histories of ten firms that have risen to market leadership in three emerging economies – China, India, and Brazil – and in three key sectors – automobiles, information technology, and pharmaceuticals. We have defined market leadership in terms of three dimensions: a dominant position in the domestic market, global reach, and innovativeness in products/processes. This definition rules out companies that compete by producing components or subproducts within wider global value chains, as is often the case in emerging markets. The companies analysed here have risen to market leadership within their own domestic economies by focusing on particular market segments and by offering innovative products to those segments. In some cases, they have also moved on to compete successfully in international markets. But their success is rooted in their rise to market leadership within their home markets.

The cases examined here therefore show that being local matters, and that being local may provide significant competitive advantages to entrepreneurs that are able to recognize and seize the opportunities that local knowledge offers them to rise to market leadership.

The conclusions of this volume are based on two broad observations. First, the rise to market leadership is a dynamic, evolving process. Second, the success of firms that rise to market leadership cannot be explained by a single factor. Rather, such success is the result of multiple factors at three levels: firm, country, and sector. A summary of the main factors working at each level is presented in Table 9.1. In the following sections we will explore these factors in order to bring together the case studies and

Table 9.1   The sources of market leadership

Firm-level factors	Vibrant entrepreneurship
	Learning, capabilities, and strategies
Country-level factors	Active public policies in support of industrial development
	Contexts favorable to private entrepreneurship
	Strong education systems
	Untapped local markets
Sector-level factors	Mastering the sectoral knowledge base
	Presence of capable actors and links with advanced networks
	Effective sectoral institutions

to show how each factor contributed to the ability of these companies to achieve positions of leadership.

9.2   FIRM-LEVEL FACTORS

At the firm level, the most striking similarities between the market leaders examined in this volume regard the presence of strong entrepreneurs and the processes of learning and capability building that characterize their evolution.

9.2.1   Strong and Vibrant Entrepreneurship

In each of the cases examined in this volume, an entrepreneur, either alone or together with a group of partners, had the ability, courage, and vision to launch a new venture in uncertain and highly dynamic sectors. In most cases, the initiative was taken by private individuals with strong motivation and drive for success. Rarely was their development directly supported by public policy, at least in the earliest stages.

In the automotive sector, Geely was founded by a Chinese entrepreneur, Li Shufu. He transformed the company from a producer of refrigerators and, later, motorcycle parts to become the first privately owned automobile manufacturer in China. Tata Motors in India was founded by a family of dynamic entrepreneurs. The Tata family, in fact, was active in the creation of a number of important scientific organizations in the country such as the Indian Institute of Science and the Tata Institute of Fundamental Research, before deciding to enter into the automobile sector. In Brazil, Marcopolo was founded by the eight partners of the 'Carrocerias Nicola' who used their previous experience in assembly, auto mechanics, and auto-repair to launch a venture focused on the manufacturing of vans.

The same pattern of strong entrepreneurship emerges in information technology. Shiv Nadar was an engineer in India who believed in the potential of microprocessors and decided to set up his own company, Microcomp, to develop microcomputers and software. Following the formation of a joint venture with Uptron, this company was renamed UCL. In Brazil, Ernesto Mario Haberkorn teamed up with Laercio Cosentino to found Totvs. Their drive was to create affordable software systems for small and medium-size enterprises in Brazil. Along the same lines, Positivo was founded by a group of teachers that were set on developing improved courses for the Brazilian higher educational system and improving the quality of textbooks and IT tools used across the school system.

In pharmaceuticals, our entrepreneurs were driven by their personal visions about what was needed and what was achievable in their countries. The Indian firm Cipla was founded by Dr Kwaja Abdul Hamied, who had a vision to develop local technological capabilities in pharmaceuticals. Similarly, Yin WeiDong, the founder of Sinovac in China, was deeply touched by the plight of the sick and poor in China and became determined to find a way to produce high-quality and affordable vaccines for the Chinese market. Finally, both PharmaTech and BGI were set up by scientists who were convinced that China had a role to play in their respective fields and that the country could benefit from their ventures in multiple ways.

It is interesting to note that the path to success was not always straightforward for these entrepreneurs. In some cases (for example, Geely) they started in different industries and had to make several changes before achieving success. In other cases, at crucial points in their histories, either due to changes in technologies and markets or due to the challenges of growth, the original entrepreneurs had to change paths and make sharp adjustments in strategy. HCL, for example, moved from hardware to software, while Tata moved into auto only after they had achieved success in other ventures. These patterns make it all the more evident that their achievements were based firmly on their tenacity to innovate and find winning solutions, their courage to take risks, and their skills at problem solving. These are all characteristics of vibrant entrepreneurship.

9.2.2   Learning, Capabilities, and Strategies

The second firm factor refers to learning, capabilities, and strategies. Consistent with the literature on economic development, our studies suggest that the accumulation of capabilities is a critical element in the rise to market leadership. The companies examined in this volume all developed advanced capabilities in technology, production, and marketing which subsequently allowed them to absorb new knowledge, improve existing products, develop new products or production processes, and identify unexploited market segments.

In each case, capability building has been centered around both R&D and informal learning. All of the firms are among the top R&D spenders in their domestic economies in their respective product groups or sectors. More importantly, their commitment to R&D has been persistent over time. They have also shown an ability to learn broadly about new markets, technologies, and production processes in ways that allowed new knowledge to spread from their R&D departments out to other individuals, teams, and departments within their organizations.

Yet their histories also reveal that capability building through R&D and other learning processes takes time and occurs through different stages. At the risk of oversimplification, it is possible to identify three stages of learning and capability building followed over the life cycle of the firms examined here: a first stage of initial learning and capability building, a second stage characterized by the achievement of advanced technological and marketing capabilities, and a third stage in which the focus moved to the international arena and to global strategies of alliances and acquisitions. These three stages are examined in the following sections.

9.2.2.1 The first stage of initial learning and capability building: access to foreign knowledge, the development of absorptive capabilities, and the identification of market niches

The initial stage in the process of the rise to market leadership is related to the entry of these new ventures in the market. This initial period is characterized by some form of access to foreign knowledge through a variety of different channels: licenses, agreements with foreign firms, and broader learning about foreign products and technologies. In parallel, the investments in R&D that were made by these firms early on provided them with the appropriate absorptive capabilities to build on their initial knowledge base and move into domestic market niches that were relatively protected from the fierce competition of multinational corporations. Geely, for example, accumulated basic capabilities in the automobile industry by disassembling foreign-made vehicles and learning how to finish and assemble final products. The firm's first car model was an assemblage of components produced both in-house and by outside suppliers. In addition, Geely adopted a hybrid production system that combined labor-intensive processes with advanced production facilities imported from abroad (for example, the robot welding system). Similarly, Marcopolo targeted a specific market niche – bus bodyworks – in which the key to success was customization at affordable prices. Such customization, however, needed to be done in the final stages of production. Marcopolo was able to use its knowledge of, and experience in, job shop and batch production to meet this need. Tata Motors was able to move into automobile production due to its long-standing investments in in-house R&D and its access to automotive technologies. Sinovac started by focusing on a vaccine for hepatitis, which had already been developed by multinational corporations, but which was too expensive for developing countries and not widely distributed. Sinovac's founder was able to use the knowledge already available to establish collaboration with the researchers at Tangshan CDC. HCL developed its knowledge of software from its earlier efforts in the hardware industry producing microcomputers. Finally, Positivo drew their start from their knowledge of the education and publishing businesses and of the IT needs of the Brazilian government.

It may be noted that the cases of Pharmatech and BGI deviate slightly from this initial pattern due to the challenges related to research in biotechnology and pharmaceuticals. Pharmatech decided to leverage the abundant supply of low-cost and high-quality researchers in China in order to establish open R&D platforms and provide low-cost pharmaceutical ingredients and R&D services to international customers. The birth of BGI, on the other hand, was based on the founders' experience in research linked to the international Human Genome Project. These companies drew upon their links to international networks much earlier than the firms in other sectors.

9.2.2.2   The second stage involving advanced technological and marketing capabilities: continuous innovation and full-scale R&D

In their second stage, the new firms examined here moved to full-scale R&D and continuous innovation in their respective product markets. Geely developed skills in product assembly and scaled up R&D on key auto components such as engines and automatic transmissions. This effort was then continued and complemented by the creation of several R&D centers, all of which led to the successful development of new car models for the Chinese market. Similarly, as Marcopolo grew in size, the company increased significantly its R&D investments compared to its competitors and adopted lean production and just-in-time processes. It also integrated vertically into new product lines in order to capture greater value from its production. Such efforts in R&D were mirrored in firms such as Cipla, Sinovac, HCL, and Totvs. But beyond their focus on R&D, these firms also invested in marketing capabilities to understand their markets and build relationships with critical customers. Marketing capabilities, in fact, became a major distinguishing feature at the base of the commercial success of these firms and acted as a resource to keep them sheltered from the competition of multinational companies that were active in their domestic markets (this aspect will be examined further in Section 9.3.4). Marcopolo, for example, used its relationships with bus companies to learn their specific needs and customize bodyworks for different routes throughout the country. Similarly, Positivo established close relationships and strong agreements with large retailers across Brazil to get their low-end computer products into the market quickly.

9.2.2.3   The third stage of full internationalization: strategic alliances, key partnerships, and mergers and acquisitions

Finally, the third stage is characterized by full internationalization, including mergers and acquisitions, and the establishment of key strategic alliances with global partners. Having reached a stable point of growth, Geely moved to establish joint ventures with other foreign firms and even acquired Volvo. Marcopolo adopted similar strategies. During the later phases of development, Marcopolo began to move into international markets in Europe (for example, Portugal), Latin America, and Central America. Marcopolo also made several foreign acquisitions and established a joint venture with Tata in India. Similarly, Tata established a joint venture with the Fiat Corporation, acquired a division of Daewoo in South Korea, and began to move directly into international markets by the early 2000s. Such strategies were also followed by Cipla and Totvs with mergers and acquisitions in Africa and Latin America, and by Positivo with acquisitions in Latin America.

Again, for companies active in biotechnology and pharmaceuticals, internationalization was focused mainly on research alliances and partnerships in global research networks. Sinovac was granted membership in the IVSITF (Influenza Vaccine Supply International Task Force) as the only member from a developing country. This allowed the company to expand its cooperation with the international research community. Pharmatech, on the other hand, developed an integrated R&D platform for international customers, was listed on the NYSE (New York Stock Exchange), and expanded its base in the US by acquiring an R&D firm. BGI strengthened its international network of relationships through its cooperation with the Danish Pig Genome Consortium, the Chick genome sequencing program in UK, and the HapMap project that involved five other countries.

What appears from these cases is that most of these firms initially focused their internationalization efforts on foreign markets that were similar to their home markets in terms of customer segments, or that shared similar usage patterns, similar cultures, or similar needs. They did not leverage their success in their domestic markets to jump immediately into advanced markets or into the production of mass, standardized products. This strategy of incremental expansion has proven successful for the firms examined here, and has provided them with a solid base for growth. Many of these new markets, in fact, were large in size and located within fast-growing economies. Their similarities to the domestic market also made them easier targets for our firms to establish and maintain a competitive advantage with respect to multinational corporations that modeled their solutions on the needs of more advanced economies.

9.3   COUNTRY-LEVEL FACTORS

The second group of factors affecting the rise to market leadership operates at the country level. The cases examined in this book suggest that four factors worked to support the growth of market leaders: active public policy in support of industrial development; a national context and policies aimed at unleashing private entrepreneurship; strong educational systems; and untapped local markets. These four factors are examined in succession in the following sections.

9.3.1   Active Public Policies in Support of Industrial Development

Public policies in China, Brazil, and India have been active in supporting industrial development through a host of different mechanisms. The policies adopted in each country are compared and contrasted in Table 9.2 (pp. 212–213). In China, public policy has been characterized by strong government intervention in the economy. This is true not only for the central government in Beijing, but also for various local government agencies that have worked to support the growth of new privately owned companies, such as Geely. The Chinese government has also supported growth in sectors such as pharmaceuticals through the opening of public research institutes. These institutes were instrumental to the success of new ventures such as Sinovac and Pharmatech. In Brazil, the government also worked to establish public research institutes in key scientific and technological areas that were critical in several sectors. Yet support for firms was strongly oriented towards the support of large state-owned enterprises in key sectors. Government policy in Brazil has also been more liberal than in China with respect to foreign direct investments (FDIs). This may explain in part the lower success rate of policies in Brazil to stimulate innovation and foster the competitiveness of domestic firms. By contrast, public policy in India was traditionally more horizontal in nature and less focused on specific sectors. Only in recent decades has the Indian government begun to adopt policies that target the development of specific sectors. Tata, for example, has benefited from various programs aimed at developing an advanced auto industry, including tax incentives to support its R&D activities.

9.3.2   Contexts Favorable to Private Entrepreneurship

Most of the new ventures examined in this book benefited from contexts that favored the emergence of private entrepreneurship. These favorable contexts were characterized by several elements. The first was the existence of large populations, especially in urban areas, with increasing levels of education and experience. As a result, the pool of potential entrants with skills to start new businesses was also large. Local contexts, however, were also increasingly populated with pockets of returnees who had come back to their home country after years of education, training, and experience abroad. These returnees increased the pool of potential new entrants and provided new firms with the advanced human capital that was needed to succeed in their ventures. Finally, many industrial contexts in these domestic economies were characterized by relatively low barriers to entry. Switching costs to move from one supplier to another were low and distribution channels were relatively open to new competitors. By focusing on narrow market niches, at least initially, new ventures also limited the capital requirements they needed to enter production in specific fields. Given the low cost of labor in these countries, they also benefited from cost advantages independent of scale. Finally, government regulations tended to favor, rather than hinder, the entry of new domestic competitors into these industries.

But beyond such favorable contexts, vibrant entrepreneurship was also supported in these countries through public policies. Such policies did not necessarily involve the deliberate picking of sectors or champion firms, as had been the case in many European countries decades earlier. Rather, governments in China and India, and to some degree in Brazil, sought to unleash private entrepreneurship through indirect measures such as tax incentives for new ventures, the removal of bureaucratic regulations, and the development of transportation, ICT, and research infrastructures that would benefit new firms across a wide array of industrial sectors.

9.3.3   Strong Education Systems

A third country factor at the base of the emergence of new enterprises and their rise to market leadership is related to the presence of strong education systems, especially in the fields of science and engineering. As noted in Table 9.2 (overleaf), public policies were used to varying degrees to support education. This factor is most evident in the cases of China and

Table 9.2   Characteristics of China, India, and Brazil that affected the rise
of market leaders

Characteristics	China	India	Brazil
Active public policies to support industrial development	● Articulated policies for becoming an important player in a select set of high and medium-high technology industries ● State very supportive to high and medium technology industries	● Only general industrial and technology policies – sector-specific policies discernible since 2000 ● The Indian Patents Act 1970 very helpful in building up technological capability in the pharmaceutical and agro chemical industries ● Co-evolution of policies for strategic sectors after some initial success shown by the industry	● Specific policies for certain high-technology industries ● Funding of technology development through targeted research grants ● Mainly promotion of production through state-owned undertakings
Unleashed private entrepreneurship	● Short history of private entrepreneurship – not more than 30 years ● Ingenious ways of promoting domestic entrepreneurship ● Engineering positive spillovers from MNCs to local firms and thereby strengthening the technological capability of local firms ● Inviting Chinese diaspora to establish technology-oriented firms in the country ● Assisting the acquisition of foreign firms to serve markets and acquire technology ● Tremendous improvement in physical infrastructure	● Long history of private entrepreneurship ● Fetters on private entrepreneurship removed in 1991 ● Policy on privatization through both divestiture and deregulation increase the space for private sector to operate in areas hitherto reserved exclusively for public sector, thereby increasing market opportunities ● Ease of doing business improved but only by specific states ● Assisting Indian companies to acquire foreign companies for expanding markets, acquiring brands and technology ● Improvements in physical infrastructure ● Encouraging venture capital and incubation centers to spur the growth of new companies	● Private entrepreneurship stultified in the country ● Some efforts at nurturing start-ups initiated recently ● Long history of welcoming FDI ● Important industrial sectors such as the automotive industry dominated entirely by FDI companies

Table 9.2 (continued)

Characteristics	China	India	Brazil
Strong education systems	• Policies for improving the quality of Chinese higher education system in both Science and Engineering • Engineering education actively promoted • Taking advantage of foreign talent, both well-qualified diaspora and well-known foreign scientists to improve quality of higher education	• Adoption of cluster approach • Important tax breaks for the corporate sector • Historically, higher education system biased in favor of science-based education • More scientists than engineers offering a favorable input to science-based industries such as pharmaceuticals • Engineering education received a fillip over the last 25 years • Quantity of engineers has increased but quality and hence employability remains a major challenge • Leading engineering-based companies invest in in-house training programs to make the engineers suitable for shop floor	• Large number of western-type universities • Quantity and quality of science and engineering degree holders a major challenge • Many recent schemes for improving quality

Source: Authors' compilation.

India where such systems were able to produce an abundant supply of well-trained graduates for new firms in many fields. Compared to graduates in more advanced economies, moreover, human capital in these countries came at lower costs, providing these firms with a competitive advantage in both R&D and technical manufacturing with respect to competitors from outside their domestic markets.

In broader terms, the cases examined here also suggest that education systems that favored engineering or technical fields tended to foster the birth of enterprises focused on manufacturing capabilities (for example, Geely in China) while systems that favored pure science education tended to foster stronger science-based industries (for example, Cipla in India). In India, in fact, firms operating in manufacturing often had to find innovative ways to overcome the shortage of high-skilled manufacturing engineers. Tata, for example, developed extensive in-house training facilities for engineers in the Motors Division and even put executives through in-house programs to make sure they kept pace with the rate of technological change in their fields.

9.3.4 Untapped Local Markets

Untapped domestic demand represents a crucial factor in the rise to market leadership. From these studies, it is possible to identify two types of untapped demand, each of which has different effects on firm growth. The first type refers to price-sensitive, low-end markets. For these markets, new ventures sought to provide low-price solutions. During its early years in operation, for example, Geely offered low-priced sedans to Chinese buyers located in small cities and peripheral markets. Similarly in India, Tata Motors focused on the growing demand for low-priced compact cars that were also able to meet the stringent safety standards and fuel-efficiency norms established by the government. In pharmaceuticals, both Cipla in India and Sinovac in China targeted the huge and untapped local demand for affordable drugs and vaccines. Even in information technology, low-end markets provided large niches for home-grown ventures. Positivo, in fact, targeted household demand in Brazil for low-end computers as well as demand coming from the education market for low-end desktop computers, notebooks, and tablets. Because the demand from each of these low-end segments was different, even with respect to low-end segments in more advanced economies, these markets remained relatively sheltered from competition from large multinationals that had little interest in addressing their specific needs. As a result, local entrepreneurs were granted time and market space to build their strategies and develop products to serve these domestic markets. Given the size of the populations, especially in countries such as China and India, these markets also offered entrepreneurs the possibility of benefiting from economies of scale in production and marketing. When successful, therefore, new companies were able to grow quickly by addressing these large and untapped sources of demand.

A second source of untapped demand refers to specific groups of users that require customized products tailored to their specific needs. Marcopolo, for example, addressed the need for customized bus bodies in the Brazilian market. Both HCL in India and Totvs in Brazil also developed customized software solutions for specialized market segments in their respective countries. While these markets were smaller than the undifferentiated markets for low-end products, they were still large enough to provide these firms with the volumes necessary to reach competitive economies of scale in their operations. Given their specificity, moreover, such markets were sheltered from outside competition coming from multinational firms or other foreign competitors than the larger mass markets. They thus provided a rich and stable base from which new entrepreneurial ventures could survive, learn, and grow in size.

What we observe from the cases examined here, therefore, is that domestic demand may set in motion a dynamic process of new firm growth. The specificity of local demand with respect to global demand in terms of income per capita, consumer preferences, local industrial requirements, and public procurement, may provide a test bed for local firms and shelter them from outside competition for long enough to allow them to stick their necks out into the market and grow. When such demand is also large in size, as was the case in China, India, and Brazil, it also provides the economies needed to set off virtuous cycles of learning, capability building, and growth that eventually allow new firms to rise to market leadership positions.

9.4 SECTOR-LEVEL FACTORS

The third set of factors affecting the rise to market leadership work at the sector level. Sectoral systems differ in terms of their knowledge base, as well as in terms of the actors, networks and institutions involved in innovation and production. Successful firms in different sectors must adapt to the specific sectoral environment in which they find themselves in order to benefit from its characteristics. The firms examined in this volume belong to three different sectors: automobiles, pharmaceuticals, and information technology. We will examine each of these sectoral systems in turn, and analyse how their characteristics affected the evolution of the firms in our study.

9.4.1 Automobiles: The Rise to Market Leadership by Building Advanced Engineering Knowledge and Capabilities, Developing an Efficient and Dedicated Local Supplier Network, and Focusing on an Untapped Segment of Local Demand

In the automobile sectoral system, the rise to market leadership by Geely, Tata Motors, and Marcopolo was based on solid engineering knowhow and production capabilities. These resources involved, in turn, the development of tacit skills, work routines, and shop-floor capabilities needed to effectively integrate and assemble complex automobile products. The capabilities developed by these firms allowed them to compete by selling low-cost and efficient cars and bus bodies. In this sense, modularity in auto technology and production allowed learning by latecomers in a rapid and cost-effective way.

Another critical element for market leadership in the auto sector was the development of a network of local upstream suppliers that not only provided firms with low-cost inputs and components, but was able and willing to customize products to meet the specific needs of local produc-ers. In China, for example, Geely was supported by an extensive network of independent, local suppliers that was maintained over time through relationships based on mutual trust and economic benefits. Similarly, Tata relied on both a network of independent suppliers and the sister compa-nies (for example, Tata steel) within Tata's own network of enterprises. Finally, Marcopolo both worked with a complex tier of local suppliers and followed a strategy of vertical integration in critical areas where it needed tighter control over the supply of key components.

Finally, as mentioned above, the rise to market leadership in the automobile industry was also affected by the presence of large pockets of untapped, local demand for low-priced products. These pockets of demand had not yet been addressed by multinational companies and, therefore, provided substantial markets for local producers.

9.4.2   Pharmaceuticals: Rise to Market Leadership by Developing Scientific Knowledge and Highly Trained Scientists, Establishing Networks with Universities and Public Research Organizations, and Using Government Support

In pharmaceuticals, the sectoral conditions that lead to market leadership were different from those in automobiles. First, scientific knowledge was of paramount importance for pharmaceutical firms. Companies therefore invested heavily in scientific research that, in turn, allowed them to absorb the latest scientific and technological advancements and to generate new knowledge. In addition, the companies examined in this book benefited from the supply of low-cost but high-quality scientific researchers who were coming out of the university system in scientific fields related to pharmaceuticals. The availability of advanced and low-cost human capital allowed these companies to build up their scientific capabilities while at the same time produce affordable drugs for their markets.

The pharmaceutical firms in our study (Cipla, Sinovac, Pharmatech, and BGI) are also noteworthy for the networks of relationships that each built with local universities and public research centres. These rel-ationships provided critical support and complementary scientific and technological knowledge for the in-house R&D efforts of each of these companies.

But it is also true that government policy towards the pharmaceutical industry was quite important for innovation and the rise to market leadership for these new companies, especially in China and India. The establishment of national organizations devoted to pharmaceutical research in India and China was critical for the growth of their research. They also received government support through policies directed at the pharmaceutical industry. In some cases, such as Sinovac, government regulations also worked to provide an environment in which these companies could learn and develop capabilities. Finally, given the weaker IPR regime in China, and the Patent Act passed in India in 1970, pharmaceutical companies were allowed to learn and experiment with new drugs without the presence of blocking patents by multinational corporations.

9.4.3 Information Technology: Rise to Market Leadership by Mastering Application Knowledge, Focusing on Key Customer Groups, and Linking with External Research Centers

The characteristics of the sectoral system in information technology highlight yet more sources of competitive advantage for domestic firms. Developments in IT went through two different phases: an early phase centered on hardware and a more recent phase centered on software and IT services. Our discussion here will focus on this second phase of development.

In software and IT services, application knowledge is critical for growth. To be successful, firms must develop a deep understanding and mastery of knowledge about a variety of final applications and user needs. In general, this knowledge differs greatly from application to application. The companies examined in this volume – HCL, Totvs, and Positivo – all focused on specific customer groups and developed products that had distinctive characteristics or were customized for the needs of particular user groups. In fact, HCL and Totvs developed hardware and vertical software solutions targeted to specific business segments, while Positivo offered software products for the education market and low-end computers for the Brazilian middle class.

In addition, close links with local research centers provided HCL, Totvs, and Positivo with access to complementary technologies and knowledge that proved relevant for the development of new products.

Finally, in terms of government policy, during the earlier phases of the IT industry, when hardware technologies were key to competitive advantage, public policy played a role in protecting the few firms that wanted to enter the computer and microelectronics market and that faced intense competition from multinationals. This is the case of HCL, Totvs, and Positivo, all of which benefited from government protection and government promotion. The tools used by governments in the hardware period of the IT industry, however, were different from the policies used by governments in pharmaceuticals. In IT, government policies were geared more towards public procurement, tax incentives, and trade protection. Only in the case of Positivo in Brazil was there a more direct attempt at picking a winner. In the later phases of the IT industry, when all firms had moved to software, these companies benefited from broader policies adopted by the governments that favored software and IT services.

9.5   BEING LOCAL MATTERS

The cases in this volume show that local focus may provide new firms with strong competitive advantages for long-term growth both at home and abroad. Local entrepreneurs with deep knowledge of the local context started each of the companies examined here. This knowledge helped them to identify important pockets of untapped demand. By first addressing the specific needs of these untapped segments, they then remained sheltered from mainstream competitors and had the time and sales volumes necessary to learn, experiment, and develop the distinctive capabilities that would eventually help them to broaden their focus. Moreover, local knowledge allowed them to recognize and exploit cost advantages offered by their local context. Such advantages ranged from low-cost labor to low-cost materials and supplies. The gains from such resources were also magnified by their ability to build close relationships with local networks of suppliers and distribution channels to lower costs even further or to improve their operations and make them more efficient. Finally, their deep knowledge of, and personal connections within, their local contexts allowed them to seize onto the advantages offered by policies and legislation at both the national and local level. Localness may therefore offer a path to market leadership.

This book also provides significant empirical evidence to the statement that the rise to market leadership is the result of a combination of firm factors and system factors. In particular, we identify a series of factors at the firm, country, and sector levels that have proven critical in the successful entry and growth of the companies examined. While firm-level factors were critical for the growth of these companies in terms of internal learning and capability building, both country- and sector-level factors also played key roles in these processes. Country-level factors may provide differential advantage to firms located in a particular country compared to firms located in other countries. Sectoral-system factors identify those dimensions that affect innovation and competitiveness differently across industries. Therefore firms in different industries need to develop capabilities and strategies in tune with the main features of the national and sectoral systems they are a part of.

Finally, vibrant entrepreneurship has been fundamental in the earliest phases of each of these companies. Yet the initial launch phases were, in each case, followed by the full development of technological and marketing capabilities that allowed these firms to move from one stage of capability building to another. While the birth of new market leaders seems to require strong and visionary entrepreneurs, therefore, the continued success of such ventures requires more complex and multidimensional capabilities that change over time as firms develop and grow.

9.6   POLICY IMPLICATIONS

While the rise to market leadership has in all cases emerged from the efforts of private entrepreneurs and from the ability of management teams to build strong resources and capabilities within their organizations, contextual factors have also supported these domestic entrepreneurs in their efforts. The histories collected in this volume thus have important policy implications for other countries in these or other industries.

First, government policy toward entrepreneurship and capability building needs to focus on improving the ease of doing business in order to allow entrepreneurs to launch new ventures and grow them to their full potential. Government policies that are dysfunctional, or that, either directly or indirectly, create strong barriers to entry, stifle both competition and growth. But just as important are policies that involve public procurement and government investment in education programs, R&D, and the development of physical and research infrastructures. These types of policies support firms by providing them with the resources necessary to build and extend their capabilities in new and emerging industries and technologies.

Second, horizontal policies aimed at the economy may need to be complemented by sector-specific policies if countries aim to have new leaders in specific industries. Because sectoral systems differ so extensively, sector-specific policies may work to strengthen particular dimensions or to eliminate imbalances, lock-ins, or weaknesses that are specific to a distinct sectoral system. Even within a single country, policies that have been successful for one sector cannot automatically be copied, without serious reconsideration and adaptation, to a totally different sector (see, for example, the cases in Dodgson et al. (2008) and Malerba and Nelson (2012)). The success of such efforts, moreover, will depend on the ability of governments to identify the specific characteristics of the system they seek to target and to develop policies that match the needs of firms in a specific sector.

Finally, policies need to maintain a dynamic and evolving perspective. Firms invest and grow, countries develop, and sectors evolve. As a result, policy-makers need to keep abreast of what changes are occurring at each level and to formulate measures that are in tune with these changes. This requires policy structures that are flexible and that can be readjusted and modified over time if conditions change.

In sum, in terms of public policy, a system perspective, a dynamic view, and the integration and coordination of various policies acting at different levels are needed to support firms in their quest to rise to market leadership.

REFERENCES

Dodgson M., J. Mathews, T. Kastelle, and M. Hu (2008), 'The evolving nature of Taiwan's national innovation system: the case of biotechnology innovation networks,' *Research Policy*, 37(3), 430–445.
Malerba, F. and R. Nelson (eds) (2012), *Economic Development as a Learning Process: Evidence from Five Sectoral Systems*, Cheltenham, UK and Northampton, MA: Edward Elgar.

Index

Abbreviated New Drug Applications (ANDAs) 72, 99, 101–102, 113, 122
Acer 190
acquisitions *see* mergers and acquisitions
Active Pharmaceutical Ingredients (APIs) 52, 99, 106, 110, 113
Advent International Corporation 181, 187
agrochemical industries 10
Amgen 44–45
Apollo BT Content Centre 136
Apple 130, 137, 195
AppTech 53
Aptech 139
Araújo, B.C. 182
Arcelor Mittal 71
Argentina 162–164, 183, 188, 195, 201
Arora, A. 141–142, 146–147
Ashok Leyland 79
Asus 190
AT&T 137
Aurobindo Pharma 108
Australia 111, 164, 172
automotive and auto parts industries 3, 11–12, 204, 215
   in Brazil 13, 15, 83, 150–159, 163, 171, 205 *see also* Marcopolo
   in China 13–14, 20–21, 25–31, 205 *see also* Geely
   in India 13–15, 68–69, 71–81, 91–94, 121, 151, 163–165, 171, 205 *see also* Tata Motors Limited
Automotive Mission Plan (AMP) 94
Axon 133–134, 145–146

Bajaj Auto 79
Bangladesh 83
barriers to entry *see* entry barriers
Bellini, Paulo 160

BGH 195
BGI 14, 47, 53, 57, 59–61, 65–66, 206, 208, 216
Bharat Forge 71
B-Index 117
biopharmaceutical industries *see* pharmaceutical industries
BMW 20
Bombardier 170
Bovespa 160, 181, 194–195
branding 185, 195–196
Brazil 1, 3, 10–11, 21, 112, 176, 204
   automotive industry 13, 15, 83, 150–159, 163, 171, 205 *see also* Marcopolo
   ICT industry 13, 16, 176–180, 188–194, 197–201, 206, 208 *see also* Positivo Informática; Totvs
Brazilian Development Bank (BNDES) 170–171, 177, 181, 186–188, 200
Brazilian Innovation Agency (FINEP) 170
Burroughs 127
business models 52, 58–59, 64–66, 111, 122, 177–178, 180, 201
Business Process Outsourcing (BPO) services 124, 136–137, 144
Busscar 157–159

Cadila Health Care 108
Cadó, L.C.D. 160
Caio 158–159
call centers 136, 144
Campos Filho, L.A.N. 167–168
Canada 157
Carvalho, F. 168, 182
Castilho, M. 167
catching-up context 21–22, 25–31, 36–37
CCE 201

centers for disease control and
	prevention (CDCs) 45, 49, 58,
	63–64
Central Drugs Research Institute
	(CDRI) 116
Chandra, Pankai 91
Chaudhuri, Sudip 102, 105, 114, 116
Chen Hongwei 59
Chery Automobile Company 27
Chevrolet 154
China 1, 3, 8–9, 21, 69, 164, 176, 191,
	204
	automotive industry 13–14, 20–21,
		25–31, 205 *see also* Geely
	pharmaceutical industry 13–14,
		43–47, 61–66, 206 *see also* BGI;
		Sinovac; WuXiPharmaTech
China Development Bank 61
Chinese Academy of Sciences (CAS)
	54
Ciferal 157–159
Cipla 15, 100, 105–113, 115, 121–122,
	206, 208–209, 213–214, 216
Cipla Medpro 111
Cipla New Ventures (CNV) 111–112
Citibank 128
Citroën 154
clusters 5, 27, 171–172
Colombia 164
Comil 157–159
Compaq 190
competitiveness 1–3, 46, 48, 54, 59,
	61–64, 70, 85, 93, 105, 129–132,
	142, 145, 153–154, 158, 161, 170,
	177–178, 183, 189, 192, 200–202,
	204, 210, 213, 215, 217–219
contract research organizations
	(CROs) 43–45, 47, 52–53, 58–59,
	65
Cosention, Laercio 206
Council of Scientific and Industrial
	Research (CSIR) 108, 115
country-level factors 3, 6–7, 57,
	69, 94–97, 101, 121–122, 151,
	170–171, 186–188, 197–200, 205,
	210–215, 218
Croatia 112
Crounal 195
customer relationship system (CRS)
	184

Daewoo 35, 79, 83, 89–91, 209
DaimlerChrysler 20, 152, 154,
	163–164
Danish Pig Genome Consortium 55,
	209
Datasul 182, 185, 187
DCM 129–130, 139, 141
Dedrick, J. 189
Deiro, T.A. 169
Dell 181, 190
Deluxe Corporation 136
Deutsche Software 136–137
Digital Equipment Corporation 126,
	130
digital television (DTV) 182
Divi's 108
division of labor 13, 26, 43–44, 138
Dodgson, M. 220
Dong Feng Motors (DFM) 33
dot-com boom 144
Dr Reddy's Laboratories 108, 110, 121
Drug Master Files (DMFs) 102, 113
dualism 30
Duomed Produtos Farmaceuticos 112

economies of scale 10, 25, 27, 36
education 5, 7, 85, 211, 213, 217, 219
	see also universities
	in Brazil 11, 193–194, 196, 206, 208
	in China 8–9, 46, 57
	in India 10, 70, 94, 96, 116, 120–121,
		138–139, 143
Egypt 164
Electronics Corporation of India
	Limited (ECIL) 126–127, 130,
	141, 143
Elizário 160
Embraer 10, 170
Embrapa 11
emerging economy, definition of 1
Enterprise Resource Planning (ERP)
	systems 176–180, 182–185,
	187–188, 198, 200–201
entrepreneurship 5–6, 204–206,
	210–214
	in automotive industries 28, 37, 73,
		84–85, 95–96
	in Brazil 10–11
	in China 9, 28, 37, 57, 59, 62–63, 65
	in ICT industries 133–134

in India 9–10, 73, 84–85, 95–96, 105, 107, 109, 121–122, 133–134
in pharmaceutical industries 57, 59, 62–63, 65, 73, 105, 107, 109, 121–122
entry barriers 10, 24, 26, 36, 96, 131, 140, 211
Essel Propack 71
Europe 1, 83–84, 111, 113, 153, 162, 183, 209 *see also individual countries*
European Union 162, 165
EuroTotvs 183
evolutionary theory 3–5
Export Finance Program (Proex) 170

Far East Computers Limited 130
Fiat 27, 68, 154, 209
financial crisis 2008 *see* global financial crisis
firm-level factors 5–6, 57, 85–91, 107–113, 159–170, 183–186, 195–197, 205–210, 218
First Auto Works (FAW) 31, 33
first-mover advantage 53, 141
Fomin, V. 189
Ford 20, 24, 154
foreign direct investments (FDIs) 1–2, 9–10, 73, 93, 162–163, 182, 210–211
Forgia, Gerard La 120
franchises 83, 183
Freeman, C. 169
Fujitsu 190

Gandhi, Rajiv 139
Gartner 179, 190
GDP 1, 9, 27, 70, 73, 92–94, 158
Geely 14, 20–38, 205–209, 213–216
General Motors 20, 33
Germany 135
GlaxoSmithKline 49, 105
Glenmark 108
global financial crisis 69, 74, 128, 133
globalization 45–47, 55, 64, 71, 84, 89, 97, 103, 107, 117, 129–131, 176
Godrej 71
government 5, 7, 12, 210–211, 218
in Brazil 151, 170–171, 177, 186–187, 194, 197–198, 208, 210

in China 9, 20, 23–24, 27–28, 30, 37–38, 54, 56–58, 60–63, 210, 211
in India 9–10, 74, 92–94, 117–119, 126, 128, 130, 132, 139–142, 144, 146–147, 210–211, 211
Green, William 105
Gu, Shulin 9
Gulf Computers Inc. 137

Haberkorn, Ernesto Mario 181, 206
Hamied, Kwaja Abdul 107–108, 206
Hamied, Yusuf 108
HapMap 55, 209
HCL 206, 208, 214, 217–218
Health Canada 117
health insurance 119–120
Hero Group 76, 79
Hetero Drugs 108
Hewlett Packard (HP) 131–132, 135, 138, 190, 201
Hidesign 71
Hindalco 71
Hindustan Computers Limited (HCL) 15, 125, 127–147
Hispano Carrocera 83
Honda 20, 79, 154
Hong Kong 46
Huawei 9
Human Genome Project (HUGO) 45–46, 53–55, 57, 60–61, 66, 208
human resources 9, 44, 53, 57, 59, 115–117, 138, 146, 186
hybrid production systems 32
Hyundai 20, 154

IBM 124–127, 130, 137–138, 141, 143, 181, 190
ICT industries 3, 11, 204, 211, 215, 217–218
in Brazil 13, 16, 176–180, 188–194, 197–201, 206, 208 *see also* Positivo Informática; Totvs
in India 13, 15, 69–70, 95, 124–128, 130–132, 139–147, 206 *see also* Hindustan Computers Limited
ImClone Systems 59
imitation 2, 4, 51
import substitution industrialization (ISI) model 157

India 1, 3, 9–10, 21, 36, 164, 176, 204
  automotive industry 13–15, 68–69,
      71–81, 91–94, 121, 151,
      163–165, 171, 205 *see also* Tata
    Motors Limited
  ICT industry 13, 15, 69–70, 95,
      124–128, 130–132, 139–147, 206
      see also Hindustan Computers
    Limited
  pharmaceutical industry 13, 15, 43,
      70–72, 99–105, 114–122, 206 *see*
      also Cipla
  recent growth performance 69–73
Indian Institute of Chemical
    Technology (IICT) 116
Indian Institute of Management (IIM)
    139
Indian Institute of Technology (IIT)
    138–139
Indian Patents Act (1970) 100, 102,
    114
Induscar 158–159
industrialization 84–85, 107, 150, 157
Influenza Vaccine Supply International
    Task Force (IVSITF) 51, 209
Infosys 71, 125, 128, 132–133, 144
initial public offerings (IPOs) 132, 144,
    172, 181–182, 187, 194
innovation 2–7, 217 *see also* national
    innovation systems; sectoral
    innovation systems
  in automotive industries 12, 37, 76,
      84, 151–153, 168–169
  in Brazil 151–153, 168–169, 176
  in ICT industries 128–129, 140,
      176
  in India 76, 84, 99–100, 103, 118,
      128–129, 140
  in pharmaceutical industries 13, 51,
      60, 99–100, 103, 118
Institute for Industrial Property (INPI)
    196
Intel 140, 181
intellectual property rights (IPR) 12,
    32, 52, 57, 60, 63, 103, 113–114,
    137, 168–169, 217
International Business Machines Corp.
    see IBM
International Computers Limited
    (ICL) 126, 130

International Data Corporation (IDC)
    190–191
International Federation of
    Pharmaceutical Manufacturers &
    Associations (IFPMA) 51
International Organization of Motor
    Vehicle Manufacturers 156–157
internationalization 6, 150–151,
    162–164, 171, 182–183, 209
Iran 127
Ireland 136
Irizar 158
Israel 43
Iveco 154

Jaguar 82–83
James Martin & Co 136
Japan 63
Jensen, M.B. 35
joint ventures 2, 6
  in automotive industries 20, 23,
      25–27, 30–31, 33–35, 68, 83,
      151, 163–165
  in Brazil 83, 151, 163–165, 196
  in China 20, 23, 25–27, 30–31,
      33–35, 46
  in ICT industries 129–130, 132,
      135–137, 145, 196
  in India 68, 83, 129–130, 132,
      135–137, 145, 151, 164
  in pharmaceutical industries 46
Jubilant Lifescience 110
just-in-time (JIT) production 153–154,
    161

kanban 153
Keltron 141
Kenya 83
Kim, L. 6, 31
knowledge transfers 88–91
Kraemer, K. 189

Laercio Cosentino 181
Land Rover 82–83
lean production 153–154, 161
learning, capabilities, and strategies
    4–7, 21, 23, 36, 85–86, 109–112,
    125, 134–135, 145–147, 206–210
Lee, K. 6, 30, 32
Lenovo 190, 201

Lewis, M. 153
Li Shufu 24, 205
licenses 2, 10, 30, 96, 129, 141
LiGe 51–52, 57, 64
Linden, G. 189
Linx 188
loans 9
Logocenter 181, 185, 187
Lundvall, B.-A. 9
Lupin 108, 110

M&M 76
Mabpharm Private Limited 112
Macao 46
Mahindra & Mahindra 71, 79
'Make in India' program 95, 121
Malerba, Franco 36, 38, 56, 91, 168, 220
Manganese Bronze Holdings 35
Mani, S. 36, 125
manufacturing 66
    in automotive industries 21, 23, 26–28, 31–33, 35, 37, 71, 86, 91, 93, 95, 150–154, 157–160, 163, 166–167, 169, 171–172, 213–214
    in Brazil 150–154, 157–160, 163, 166–167, 169, 171, 176, 188–190, 192–193, 200
    in China 21, 23, 26–28, 31–33, 35, 37, 69
    in ICT industries 127, 129, 131, 135, 141, 143, 176, 188–190, 192–193, 200
    in India 69–71, 85–86, 91, 93, 95, 100, 103, 107, 109–110, 118, 121, 127, 129, 131, 135, 141, 143, 213–214
    in pharmaceutical industries 100, 103, 107, 109–110, 118, 121
Marcopolo 15, 83, 150–151, 153–154, 157–173, 205, 207–209, 214–215
Marico 71
market leadership
    conceptual framework 3–8
    dimensions of 2
market size 22–23, 28–30, 36, 128
marketing 1–2, 6, 51, 132, 143, 183–185, 195–197, 200, 206, 208
Marques, R.A. 170

Martins, J. 163
Maruti Udyog 74, 76
Mascarello 158–159
Matrix Laboratories 108
McKinsey & Company 130
Mercedes 152
mergers and acquisitions 6, 13, 100, 146, 165, 178, 181–182, 186–187, 195–196, 209–210
    in automotive industries 35, 89–91
    in China 35
    in India 89–91
Metalbus 158–159
Mexico 163–165, 183
Microcomp 129, 206
Microsiga 181, 183, 185, 187
Microsoft 179, 181, 183
Midbyte 182
Minicomp 131
Mitsubishi 154
modularization 23, 25–26, 37, 138, 153, 189, 200
Motorola 130, 137, 139–140, 148
Mowery, David C. 1–2
MS Dynamics 180
Mu, Q. 30, 32
multinational corporations (MNCs) 10–11, 208, 217
    in automotive industries 20, 25, 36–37, 72, 74, 76, 79–81, 83, 91, 96, 150, 154, 158, 166, 172
    in ICT industries 125, 180, 190–191, 200
    in pharmaceutical industries 43–45, 48, 53, 56, 65, 105–106, 114
MVC Plastics Components 161, 169
Myrdal, Gunnar 157–158

Nadar, Shiv 129, 132–134, 206
Nagpal, Somil 120
Nanjing Automobile Corporation (NAC) 34
Natco Pharma 108
National Association of Software and Services Companies (NASSCOM) 143–144
National Automotive Testing and R&D Infrastructure Project (NATRIP) 92

National Chemical Laboratory (NCL) 108, 116
National Classification of Economic Activities (CNAE) 154–156
National Equipment Financing Authority (Finame) 170
national innovation systems 5–7, 21
National Institute of Pharmaceutical Education and Research (NIPER) 120
National Manufacturing Competitiveness Council (NMCC) 70
Nayar, Vineet 133–135
NEC 190
Nelson, Richard R. 1–2, 38, 168, 220
Neobus 158–159
Nimbus 160
Nissan 20, 33, 154, 170
North American Free Trade Agreement (NAFTA) 165
Novell 181

Oliveira, L.G. 170
Oracle 179–181, 183
Orchid Chemicals 108

patents 10, 34, 43, 63, 72, 84, 99–100, 102–104, 106–108, 113–116, 137, 168–169
Patni Computer Systems (PCS) 128
Pavitt, K. 190
Perot Systems 136
Peru 183
Petrobas 11
Peugeot 20, 27, 33, 154
Pharma Vision 2020 117
pharmaceutical industries 3, 10, 12–13, 204, 215–217
  in China 13–14, 43–47, 61–66, 206 *see also* BGI; Sinovac; WuXiPharmaTech
  in India 13, 15, 43, 70–72, 99–105, 114–122, 206 *see also* Cipla
Pharmaceutical Research and Development Support Fund (PRDSF) 120
Pharmacopeia 52
Pinhão, C.M.A. 154
Piramal Enterprises 108

policies 7–8, 12, 210–213, 217, 220
  in automotive industries 23, 37–38, 93–96, 150–151, 170–173
  in Brazil 10, 150–151, 170–173, 186–187, 197–198
  in China 23, 37–38
  in ICT industries 132, 141–142, 145–147, 186–187, 197–198
  in India 9–10, 93–96, 117–121, 132, 141–142, 145–147
  and pharmaceutical industries 13
  in pharmaceutical industries 117–121
population size 1, 28, 54, 63, 96, 110, 211, 214
Portugal 162–165, 183, 195, 209
Positivo Informática 16, 176–177, 188, 193–201, 206, 208–209, 217–218
privatization 10
product development 34, 65, 76, 79, 86–88, 124, 165
Progress 181
Prosoft 187–188
protectionism 141–142, 177

Quality Chemical Industries Limited 112
Quality Software 182

Ranbaxy 105, 108, 110, 121
Randon 150
Rangarajan Committee 139–140
Renault 154
research and development (R&D) 2, 6, 9, 207–209, 211–213, 217, 219
  in automotive industries 12, 20–21, 23, 28, 30–31, 33–35, 70, 79–81, 84–89, 92–93, 95, 156, 165–166, 168, 171
  in Brazil 156, 165–166, 168, 171, 176–178, 185–186, 188, 192–193, 196–198
  in China 20–21, 23, 28, 30–31, 33–35, 43–45, 47, 49–53, 55, 57–66
  in ICT industries 130, 132, 134–135, 137, 140, 142, 144–145, 176–178, 185–186, 188, 192–193, 196–198

in India 10, 70, 72, 79–81, 84–89,
    92–93, 95, 99–100, 103,
    105–106, 108, 112–113,
    116–120, 130, 132, 134–135,
    137, 140, 142, 144–145
in pharmaceutical industries 43–45,
    47, 49–53, 55, 57–66, 72,
    99–100, 103, 105–106, 108,
    112–113, 116–120
research centers 5, 7, 12, 22–23, 60, 62,
    92, 116, 121, 196, 216
reverse engineering 23, 31–32, 100,
    102
RM Sistemas SA 182, 187
Russia 21, 83, 164

Sagar, Ambui 91
Santos, A.M.M.M. 154
SAP 179–180, 183
Satyam 128, 144
Saudi Arabia 163, 167–168
Scania 152, 154
Schumpeter, Joseph 5–6
sectoral innovation systems 5, 7–8,
    21–24, 44, 56, 91–94, 100
sector-level factors 7–8, 57, 91, 94,
    114–121, 151–159, 178–180,
    188–190
Senegal 83
Serio, L.C. di 161
Setra 152
Shanghai Automotive Industrial
    Corporation (SAIC) 33
SIGA 180–181
Singapore 87, 130, 142
Sinovac 14, 47–51, 56–58, 63–65, 206,
    208, 214, 216
Sipros 183
Slack, N. 153
small and medium-size enterprises
    (SMEs) 180–181, 183, 185, 200,
    206
smart phones 189
Soete, L. 169
software 12, 124–125, 127–128,
    130–132, 136–138, 140, 143,
    145–147, 178–179, 181, 184, 187,
    190, 198, 206
software-as-a-service (SaaS) approach
    184

Sousa, R.A.F. 198
South Africa 83, 111, 136, 164
South Korea 1, 11, 31, 63, 69, 85,
    89–90, 209
Southern African Development
    Community (SADC) 165
Spain 83, 85, 183
Spencer, J.W. 34
Spheros 169
Sri Lanka 112
state-owned enterprises (SOEs) 20,
    26–27, 38, 61
Sterling Computers 131
stock exchange 62
    Indian 132
    New York 52, 83, 209
    São Paulo 160, 181, 194–195
Sun Pharma 105, 108, 110, 121
supplier networks 11, 32–33, 163, 178,
    186
Suven Life Sciences 108
Suzlon 71
Suzuki 74, 76
Syngenta 60

Taiwan 1, 11, 46, 131
Taj Hotels 71
Tangshen CDC 208
Tata Chemicals 71
Tata Consultancy Services 71,
    125–128, 133, 140, 143
Tata Motors Limited (TML) 13–15,
    68–69, 71, 73, 79, 82–92, 94,
    96–97, 121, 151, 164–165, 172,
    205–206, 208–211, 214–216
Tata Steel 71
Tata Tea 71
Tata Technologies (TT) 87–88
taxation 38, 74, 93, 116–119, 179–180,
    184, 189–190, 195, 198, 218
technology 1, 6–7, 9–10, 24–26, 63, 86,
    91–92, 137–138, 144–145 *see also*
    ICT industries
technology gap 31, 147
technology spillovers 96
telecommunications 9, 30, 95, 188
Texas Instruments 128, 143
Thailand 83, 88
Tianjin Auto Works 30
Toshiba 190

Totvs 16, 176–188, 199–201, 206, 208–209, 214, 217–218
Toyota 20, 32–33, 154
Toyota Production System (TPS) 161
Trade-Related Aspects of Intellectual Property Rights (TRIPS) 103, 113–114

UCL 206
Uganda 112
Ukraine 83
United Kingdom (UK) 55, 83, 85, 88, 124, 133, 136, 157, 209
United States Food and Drug Administration (USFDA) 101–102, 117
United States Patent and Trademark Office (USPTO) 72, 99, 104, 113, 137
United States (US) 1, 43, 51–52, 57, 59, 72, 87, 99–100, 108, 111–112, 124, 130–131, 136, 140, 142, 157, 183, 191, 209
universities 5, 7–8, 12, 22, 216 *see also* education
  in Brazil 11, 186, 193, 196–197, 200, 206
  in China 9, 23, 34–35, 46, 60–62
  in India 115, 138–139
Unix Operating System 130–132, 134, 137–143, 145–146, 148
Uruguay 162, 195
Usha Microprocessors Controls 131

utility model 168–169
Uttar Pradesh Electronics Corporation Limited (UPTRON) 129, 135, 141, 206

vaccines 45, 47–51, 56, 58, 64, 66, 206, 208–209, 214
value added tax (VAT) 74
value chains 6, 37, 43–44, 57, 63, 204
Venezuela 162
venture capital 12–13, 62
Verol, M.A. 167–168
VIP 71
Volkswagen 20, 27, 33, 154
Volvo 24, 35, 152, 154, 209

Wang Jian 53–54, 57
Williamson, P.J. 32
Wipro 125, 128, 131–133, 140
Wockhardt 108, 110
World Bank 119–120
World Health Organization (WHO) 113
Wsul 169
WuXiPharmaTech 14, 47, 51–53, 57–60, 64–66, 206, 208–209, 216

Y2K bug 132, 136, 140, 144
Yang Huanming 53–54, 57
Yin WeiDong 49–51, 57–58, 63, 206

Zeng, M. 32
Zignani, C. 169
ZTE 9